ONLY IN
ZURICH

Duncan J. D. Smith

ONLY IN
ZURICH

A Guide to Unique Locations,
Hidden Corners and Unusual Objects

Photographs by
Duncan J. D. Smith

**The
Urban
Explorer**

I dedicate this book with love and thanks to Roswitha,
without whom the following pages
could not have been written

Contents

Northern Suburbs:
District 9 (Albisrieden, Altstetten)
District 10 (Höngg, Wipkingen)
District 11 Zürich Nord (Affoltern, Oerlikon, Seebach)
District 12 Schwamendingen (Hirzenbach, Saatlen,
Schwamendingen Mitte)

Appendices

Introduction

The City of Zurich is the largest and richest in the federal state of Switzerland, and is the capital of one of the country's twenty six sovereign cantons. Nestled amongst wooded hills it is located at the northern end of Lake Zurich (Zürichsee). Novelist James Joyce's comment makes light of the city's reputation for cleanliness. But Zurich today is a more complex place than that, and it shouldn't be forgotten that the Swiss Reformation of the 1520s also brought with it freedom of thought, attracting not only Joyce but also the likes of Lenin, Rosa Luxemburg, and the Dadaists.

Zurich was founded around 15 BC by the Romans as a customs post. In the early ninth century it became the site of a Carolingian-era palace before passing into the hands of the Holy Roman Empire four hundred years later, when it was made a free imperial city. During the eleventh and twelfth centuries Zurich's merchant nobility grew rich from the trade of wool and silk but this came to an abrupt end in 1336, when they were ousted in favour of the town's newly founded guilds *(Zünfte)*. The city reached its zenith of power in the sixteenth century before falling into relative obscurity for two centuries.

As Europe's political laboratory, Switzerland experimented with new forms of direct democracy and self-government, resulting in the formation of a federal state in 1848. Zurich's economic fortunes were subsequently revived during the Industrial Revolution, and as a result of the country's neutrality and relative political stability, it emerged after the Second World War as an international finance centre.

A recent relaxing of Zurich's curfew laws together with the city's easygoing riverine geography prompts many of the more leisurely recommendations in today's mainstream guidebooks. The undemanding visitor thereby gains easy access to a broad array of parks, swimming facilities, galleries, restaurants, cafés, and clubs. However, there is far more to Zurich than meets the eye, and this guidebook has been written for independent travellers wishing to discover something more of the place. It only takes a few minutes of planning, and a glance at a good street map**, to escape the crowds and discover a very different Zurich.

Based on personal experience walking through the city's twelve districts *(Stadtkreise)* the author points his fellow explorer in a new and unusual direction. This is the Zurich of Roman ruins and abandoned medieval walls; curious museums and intriguing places of worship; secret gardens and converted factories; unusual shops and offbeat accommodations; not to mention the world's first 'Dark Restaurant' and an underground hospital preserved from the Second World War.

As might be expected, a good number of these unusual historic locations are to be found within Zurich's formerly walled medieval Old Town (Altstadt), which straddles the banks of the Limmat; it was here that the history of the city really began. Many more, however, lie *outside* these well-trodden areas, especially in the suburbs to the west (Districts 2–5) and to the east (Districts 6–8). Many fascinating places are dotted along on the shores of Lake Zurich, for example. A smaller number of no less interesting locations are contained within the more distant and predominantly residential suburbs to the north (Districts 9–12).

Zurich's transport network of trams (Lines 2–17), buses and trolleybuses (Lines 29–916), and suburban trains *(S-Bahn)* (S2–55) is completely integrated so the city explorer can quickly reach all the locations described. Directions have been kept to a minimum, however, leaving the visitor free to find their own particular path. Whether dining in a former factory, touring the city's waste water treatment plant, attending a Hare Krishna temple ceremony, or playing pinball in a private museum, it is hoped that the explorer will gain a sense of having made the discovery for themself.

Duncan J. D. Smith, Zurich & Vienna

* The dates given after the names of rulers are the actual years they reigned for, whereas those given after important non-ruling personalities relate to their birth and death.

** Most street maps of Zurich cover the city centre; the excellent Falk Stadtplan Extra covers all twelve districts *(Stadtkreise)* and the thirty four quarters *(Stadtquartiere)* they contain, and shows rail, S-Bahn, tram, and bus routes.

(District numbers are given beneath each chapter title (with quarter names in brackets). At the end of each chapter there is a selection of other locations within a short walking distance. An alphabetical list of opening times appears at the back of the book.)

A Roman gravestone on Pfalzgasse

1 What's Left of Roman Turicum?

District 1 (Lindenhof), a Roman gravestone on Pfalzgasse
Tram 6, 7, 11, 13, 17 Rennweg

The earliest evidence for human settlement in the Zurich area is provided by Neolithic and Bronze Age remains found along the shores of Lake Zurich (Zürichsee) (see no. 16). The first settlement on the site of Zurich itself dates from the pre-Roman Celtic period, when Iron Age La Tène settlements appeared on the Lindenhof hill (Lindenhofhügel), and on the slopes of the Uetliberg. The real story of Zurich, however, begins with the arrival of the Romans around 15 BC – although today only a few tantalising remains bear witness to it.

Like the Celts, the Romans identified the Lindenhof hill as a suitable location for their activities. Left behind by the retreat of the Linth Glacier between 24000 and 16000 years ago, it provided an excellent view of the point where Lake Zurich narrows and empties northwards into the Limmat River. The Romans fortified the existing Iron Age settlement making it into an *Oppidum* from which to administer the surrounding area. They built Zurich's first stone buildings, established vineyards, and created an extramural settlement area known as a *Vicus*.

Roman Zurich was known as Turicum (whence the name Zurich may be derived) and served as a customs post at the border of the Roman provinces of Gallia Belgica and Raetia, for goods transferred between the lake and the river. It is tempting to think that the stationing here of the *beneficiarii* (the military units who collected road tolls) was a precursor of the city's later international financial role.

The earliest written record of Turicum is a gravestone from around 200 AD for the son of a customs officer. Unearthed in 1747 on Pfalzgasse, on the southern slope of the Lindenhof, it is displayed in the Landesmuseum Zürich at Museumsstrasse 2 (City), although an exact copy stands close to where the original was found. It reads as follows:

HIC SITUS EST/L. AEL(IUS) URBICUS/QUI VIXIT AN(NO)/UNO M(ENSIBUS) V D(IEBUS) V/UNIO AUG(USTI) LIB(ERTUS)/P(RAE)P(OSITUS) STA(TIONIS) TURICEN(SIS)/(QUADRAGESIMAE) G(ALLIARUM) ET AE(LIA) SECUNDIN(A)/P(ARENTES) DULCISSIM(O) F(ILIO)

And it is translated thus: Here lies Lucius Aelius Urbicus, who lived one year, five months and five days. Sweetest son of parents Unio, a

Part of a Roman hoard in the Landesmuseum Zürich

freedman of the emperor, officer of the Gallic customs post of Turicum, and Aelia Secundina. (The text D(IIS) M(ANIBUS) at the top of the stone, incidentally, translates as "To the spirits of the dead", the *Manes* being the deities thought to represent the souls of deceased loved ones, to whom offerings were made.)

Turicum's fabric has been almost totally obscured by Zurich's later development, although a few fragments have been revealed by archaeologists. Deep beneath the Lindenhof, for example, the walls of a Roman building have been excavated, which can be accessed by means of a hydraulic trap door outside Lindenhof 4 (a key for the excavations can be obtained on production of a passport from the Building History Archive (Baugeschichtliches Archiv) at Neumarkt 4). Although the walls are only modest the visit itself is quite an adventure.

A chance find south of the Lindenhof has revealed another aspect of the Roman settlement. In 1983, during renovation work on a toyshop, the ruins of a thermal bathhouse from the first century AD were revealed, complete with under-floor heating system *(Hypocaustum)*. The building would have been located alongside a dock, where goods were transferred from lake to river vessels, and would have been a popular meeting place for Turicum's two hundred and fifty inhabitants. A catwalk has been constructed directly over the remains providing a year-round overview, and the narrow passageway (renamed Thermengasse) now contains a display of associated artefacts.

North of the Lindenhof, on the natural plateau called the Sihlbühl, another Roman inscription was found suggesting the former presence of a temple from the second and third centuries AD. Roman gold bracelets and rings were also recovered, and although the site has now been obliterated by the Urania underground garage, there are information boards to recall what was once here.

Turicum was of strategic importance, too. After AD 318 the border between Gaul and Italy (two of the four praetorian prefectures of the Roman Empire) was located east of Turicum, and during the 370s the Emperor Valentinian I constructed a new fort at Turicum as part of the *Limes Romanus*, the defensive line marking the boundary of the Roman Empire. The fort was abandoned in the early 400s when the Romans eventually withdrew from Zurich, and nothing remains of it (although a well-preserved Roman fort lies some thirty minutes by train to the south-east of Zurich at Pfäffikon).

With the Roman departure, an alliance of Germanic tribes from the Rhine called the Alamanni settled the Swiss Plateau, bringing with them the language that became today's Swiss German dialect *(Schwyzerdüütsch)*. In 835 Turicum's Roman fort was replaced by a Carolingian-era palace erected by Louis the German (817–876), grandson of Charlemagne, and its remains can also be viewed beneath the trap door at Lindenhof 4. It was Louis the German, incidentally, who founded the Fraumünster, thereby opening up an entirely new chapter in the history of Zurich (see no. 2).

Beneath the Lindenhof are the walls of Roman Zurich

Other places of interest nearby: 2, 3, 5, 6, 10, 11, 12

2 Stunning Stained Glass

District 1 (Lindenhof), the Fraumünster on Münsterhofplatz
and the Grossmünster on Grossmünsterplatz (Rathaus)
Tram 2, 6, 7, 8, 9, 11, 13, 17 Paradeplatz

It is unclear exactly when the Fraumünster on Münsterhofplatz (Lindenhof) was founded but in 853 King Louis the German (817–876), grandson of Charlemagne, signed over to his daughters Hildegard and Berta a monastery that already occupied the site. The daughters became the first abbesses of the new Benedictine convent, which was occupied by noble women, and received protection and estates from Louis. According to legend the site was made known to Louis by a stag with glowing antlers. Both stag and daughters are depicted in an atmospheric series of murals by Paul Bodmer (1886–1883) inside the church's shadowy neo-Romanesque cloister, itself the work of city architect Gustav Gull (1858–1942).

The ruins of the first convent church have been revealed beneath the choir of the present Fraumünster, and can be visited by appointment (tel. 0041 (0)44 201 3031). In 1045, King Henry III of Germany (1028–1053) granted the convent the right to hold markets, collect tolls, and mint coins, effectively making the abbess the ruler of the city. Furthermore, in 1234 Holy Roman Emperor Frederick II (1220–1250) promoted the abbess to the rank of duchess, giving her the right to appoint Zurich's mayors.

Everything changed in 1336, however, with the establishment by Rudolf Brun of Zurich's guild laws *(Zunftordnung)*. Brun became the city's first independent mayor not assigned by the abbess, and as power devolved to the guilds so the influence of the convent waned. With the Swiss Reformation in the 1520s the convent was dissolved and ownership passed to the City of Zurich, eventually to be replaced by today's neo-Gothic Stadthaus.

Despite the dissolution of the convent, its church the Fraumünster survived. People now come here to marvel at the canton's largest organ (with its 5793 pipes) and the beautiful stained glass windows. The rose window depicting Paradise in the north transept by Augusto Giacometti (1877–1943) (uncle of the more famous Alberto Giacometti) was installed in 1945 (see no. 14). Impressive as it is, however, it is the five explosively colourful windows in the thirteenth century choir, the oldest part of the present structure, that get most attention. Created in 1967 by the Russian-French modernist Marc Chagall (1887–1985),

each window is almost ten metres tall, and has its own colour theme: the blue Jacob window, the green Christ window, and the yellow Zion window, flanked by the red Prophets window, and the blue Law window. It is interesting to note how many New Testament symbols (for example Jesus' crucifixion) appear in the work of an artist hailing from a strictly Orthodox Jewish background. Commentators have suggested this is explained by Chagall's early exposure to Russian Orthodox ico-

The peaceful garden cloister of the Grossmünster

nography. Chagall is also responsible for the rose window in the south transept depicting the Creation.

After leaving the church notice the pair of iron knobs on the north wall once used for measuring fabric, also the narrow archway on Poststrasse said to have been used to restrict the decadence of women's hooped dresses during the Reformation, and in the Münsterhof (a former pig market) a tablet in the pavement recalling Winston Churchill's 1946 address at Zurich University, in which he invited European countries to form a United States of Europe. Notice, too, high up on the spire a series of gargoyles in the form of dolphins. Dating from the 1780s one of them is said to contain a hidden mechanism that enables the creature's tongue to poke out in the direction of the Rathaus. It is a reminder of times when relations between church and state were not always harmonious.

On the opposite side of the Limmat construction of the Grossmünster began in 1090, possibly on the site of a Roman cemetery. Most of the original construction was completed by 1230. The site is said to have been selected by Charlemagne (768–814) whilst out hunting, his horse falling to its knees on the spot where Zurich's patron saints, Felix and Regula, were buried. They were martyred for their Christianity in Roman times, and buried on what is now Grossmünsterplatz (see no. 6). A column capital in the north aisle of the church depicts Charlemagne and his horse, and his gold-crowned statue is located high on one of the church towers.

Over the following centuries the Grossmünster was modified until Huldrych Zwingli (1484–1531), a contemporary of Martin Luther, initiated the Swiss Reformation here in 1519. In 1524 he ordered the removal of the organ, wall decorations, and religious statuary from the church, and in keeping with his views on Catholic idolatry he left instructions that his own body be burnt after his death and no relics left. The leadership of the Reformation in Switzerland then passed to John Calvin in Geneva.

The Grossmünster is still shorn of its once rich interior decorations but this is more than made up for by its modern stained glass. As with the Fraumünster the work of Augusto Giacometti is represented (a window in the choir installed in 1932 depicts the story of Christmas) but again it has been upstaged by a non-traditional stained glass practitioner. Between 2006 and 2009 the German painter and photographer Sigmar Polke (1941–2010) was commissioned to provide a counterpoint to Giaciometti's efforts. Polke, who as a young man worked in a stained glass factory, has created something highly original without departing too much from traditional forms. Along one side of the church he has filled the window spaces with thin slices of multicoloured stone, bringing vivid, mosaic-like colour to a largely dark and colourless space. Elsewhere he has opted for figurative images inspired by Biblical medieval manuscripts. Both are mesmerising.

Beneath the Fraumünster is a crypt built by Abbess Berta as a repository for the relics of Felix and Regula. The church vied with the Grossmünster for possession of the relics, and they were carried in procession between the two on the saints' day of September 11th. Today the relics are split between the new Church of St. Felix and Regula in Zurich and a church in Andermatt. A triple-aisled crypt beneath the Grossmünster is the largest of its type in Switzerland, and contains the much weathered fifteenth century original of the Charlemagne statue on the tower. Vestiges of Gothic wall paintings that survived the Reformation can be found in the adjacent undercroft chapel. After leaving the Grossmünster visit the delightful cloister in the building attached to the church. With its herb garden and twelfth century Romanesque capitals it is now home to the theological faculty of the University of Zurich (Universität Zürich).

Other places of interest nearby: 1, 3, 5, 6, 7, 10

3 The Curiosities of St. Peter's

District 1 (Lindenhof), the Church of St. Peter (St.-Peters-Kirche)
at St.-Peter-Hofstatt 1
Tram 2, 6, 7, 8, 9, 11, 13, 17 Paradeplatz

The Church of St. Peter (St.-Peters-Kirche) is one of the most distinctive landmarks on Zurich's west bank: its sturdy foursquare clock tower pierces the skyline like no other. All the mainstream guidebooks are quick to point out that the clock face is the largest in Europe, with a diameter of 8.7 metres (fewer note that the four-metre-long minute hand falls back 45 centimetres every time it moves forwards). But the church has other curiosities besides its clock, and together they reveal much about the history of Zurich.

Firstly, there is the church building itself, which stands not far from the Lindenhof hill (Lindenhofhügel), where Zurich was founded as the Roman trading post of Turicum (see no. 1). Archaeologists surmise that a Roman Temple of Jupiter originally stood on the site of the church; certainly excavations have demonstrated that the church choir occupies the site of a pre-Romanesque structure dating back to the eighth or ninth century (these subterranean remains can be viewed by appointment only, tel. 0041 (0)44 211 1441).

Around 1000 the structure was replaced by an early Romanesque Catholic church, which in turn was replaced by a late Romanesque one in 1230. Of this building vestiges are still visible, including the simple rectangular choir (with some faded wall paintings illuminated by an arched Romanesque window), and the lower part of the tower (the upper section is Gothic and dates from the mid-fifteenth century). Rudolf Brun (c. 1290–1360), Zurich's first independent mayor, was buried beneath the choir in 1360, although his remains were subsequently relocated to a new grave at the foot of the tower (see no. 6).

The nave of St. Peter's was rebuilt around 1450 in Late Gothic style. By the time of the Reformation in Switzerland during the early 1520s it was still the only parish church in Zurich (all other churches at the time belonging to monasteries). During the Reformation, however, the church's power was reduced and its altars smashed as being too opulent. The monastery churches were secularized at the same time: the Augustinerkirche on Münzplatz (Lindenhof) became a mint (now used by the Christ Catholic church), the Predigerkirche on Zähringerplatz (Rathaus) housed a wine press (the choir is now the music department of Zurich Central Library (Zentralbibliothek Zürich)), and the

The Church of St. Peter (St.-Peters-Kirche) boasts the largest clock face in Europe

Barfüsserkloster a few roads away on Hirschengraben served as a grain depot (now the cantonal high court) (see no. 28)). Thereafter the first Reformed minister at St. Peter's was Leo Jud (1482–1542), known to his friends as Meister Leu, who assisted the Swiss reformer Huldrych Zwingli (1484–1531) on the translation of his Zurich Bible (Zürcher Bibel).

The main body of the present St. Peter's was consecrated in 1706,

MATTH. IV. IO.
Du soll anbätten
Den Herren deinen Gott
Und Ihm allein
dienen.

God's name in Hebrew can be seen above the pulpit

as the first Presbyterian church erected under Protestant rule. It takes the form of a galleried, three-aisled Baroque nave, its wooden panelling complementing two rows of red Tuscan-style columns. Above the pulpit is a white stucco *bas-relief* inscribed with a quotation from the Bible, above which is the unusual sight of the name of God in Hebrew, a legacy of the Reformers' desire to reclaim the original Biblical sources of Christianity (the same device appears in the Predigerkirche on Zähringerplatz (Rathaus) on the opposite side of the river).

Outside the church door is the gravestone of the poet and physiognomist Johann Kaspar Lavater (1741–1801), a preacher so popular that parishioners reserved seats in St. Peter's to listen to him. Lavater was a friend of Goethe (1749–1832), and the two had long conversations over wine in the nearby Restaurant Kaiser's Reblaube at Glockengasse 7, where there is still a room called the *Goethestube*. Lavater lived just across the St.-Peter-Hofstatt, one of Altstadt's loveliest squares, and it is from here that another of the curiosities of St. Peter's can be reflected upon. From medieval times until 1911 the church tower was used for fire watching, the angled windows on the four sides providing a 360 degree view of the surrounding buildings. The duty of the watchman was to look out of each window every fifteen minutes. If he saw a fire he would sound an alarm, and hang a flag from the window nearest the conflagration. It is for this reason that the tower of St. Peter's is owned by the City of Zurich, while the nave of the church is owned by the Swiss Reformed Church.

Other places of interest nearby: 1, 2, 5, 6, 7, 10, 11

4   Across the Lake to Ufenau

District 1 (Lindenhof), a boat trip to the island of Ufenau
ZSG (Zürichsee Schifffahrtsgesellschaft) ferry
from Bürkliplatz to Ufenau (Note: sailing times available
at www.zsg.ch)

Lake Zurich (Zürichsee) stretches from the City of Zurich and the Limmat River as far south as the Seedamm at Rapperswil, beyond which point it is known as the Obersee (Upper Lake). Within Zurich's city boundaries the shores of the glacial lake contain many popular attractions, most notably Zürichhorn Park in Seefeld (see nos. 69–72). Budding Robinson Crusoes, however, might prefer to escape the crowds – and indeed the city – by boarding a ferry at Bürkliplatz, and sailing down into the Canton of Schwyz to visit the historic island of Ufenau.

An hour and a half sailing time brings ferries to the south side of the island and it quickly becomes apparent that Ufenau offers an intimate experience, since it measures only 470 by 220 metres (despite this it is the largest island in Switzerland!). A designated *Insel der Stille* (Island

The island of Ufenau emerges from the mist

of Tranquillity) Ufenau has been a protected nature reserve since 1927, where swimming and camping are strictly forbidden.

At the end of the jetty a wheelchair-friendly track signposted 'Inselweg' makes an anticlockwise circuit of the island. The most prominent structure other than the popular restaurant Zu den Zwei Raben is the Church of Sts. Peter and Paul, which was erected in the 1140s. Documentary evidence points to an earlier church on the same site around 970 although worship here dates back farther than that. Archaeologists have uncovered walls beneath the church that belonged to a Gallo-Roman temple from the first or second century AD. The temple was connected with the Roman trading centre of Centum Prata (today the modern village of Kempraten), which acted as a commercial centre on the alpine trade route out of Rome. The route also included the Roman trading post of Turicum where modern Zurich now stands (see no. 1). Even older Stone Age remains on the island from around 4000 BC may also have had some religious significance.

The temple was destroyed sometime after the Roman withdrawal from the area in the early 400s. Thereafter the first Christian church was probably erected on the former site of the temple during the fifth century, and the island is first mentioned by name in 741, when it is referred to as the Island of Huphan.

After the first church was destroyed by the Huns around 900, Burchard II Duke of Swabia (917–926) appears on the scene. In 919 he defeated King Rudolph II of Upper Burgundy (912–937) and seized the area around Zurich. Burchard's son Adalrich died on Ufenau in 973 (he was canonized in 1659) and his wife was buried at Einsiedeln Abbey, to whom Ufenau was given in 965 by the Holy Roman Emperor Otto I (962–973). The island is still in the hands of the abbey's Benedictine monks and the wooden bridge straddling the lake between nearby Rapperswil and Hurden is used by the abbey's pilgrims walking the Way of St. James (Jakobsweg).

The Church of Sts. Peter and Paul served for many years as parish church for the villagers of Lake Zurich's upper shores, a task it shared with the more modest Chapel of St. Martin a few metres away from it. In 1523 the pastor of Ufenau advised the leader of the Swiss Reformation Huldrych Zwingli (1484–1531) to offer sanctuary on Ufenau to the outspoken Lutheran reformer Ulrich von Hutten (1488–1523). Hutten died there two years later and is buried alongside the church, which since the 1980s has been flanked by a vineyard.

Both church and chapel were damaged during the Second Villmergen War, waged between Reformed and Catholic Swiss cantons in 1712.

The Chapel of St. Martin with the Church of Sts. Peter and Paul in the background

The Protestant side was successful, bringing to an end Catholic hegemony in the Old Swiss Confederacy, and staving off further conflict until civil war broke out again in 1847, the so-called *Sonderbundskrieg* that led to the formation of Switzerland as a federal state in 1848. Since then peace and tranquillity has returned to the island of Ufenau.

Other places of interest nearby: 2, 5, 6, 32

5 A Mechanical Universe

District 1 (Lindenhof), the Türler Clock in Türler Uhren & Juwelen
at Bahnhofstrasse 28/Paradeplatz
Tram 2, 6, 7, 8, 9, 11, 13, 17 Paradeplatz

The Türler Clock in Türler Uhren & Juwelen
on Bahnhofstrasse

On 21st June 1995 a unique clock was set in motion in the shop of Türler Uhren & Juwelen at Bahnhofstrasse 28/Paradeplatz (Lindenhof). Built from 1.2 tons of brass over a period of nine years, and with a movement comprising 251 wheels and 155 pinions, the Türler Clock is one of the most complex time pieces ever created. Designed to mark the time from its location in Zurich in relation to the movement of the entire surrounding cosmos it is perhaps better described as a mechanical universe.

The idea for the clock came from shop owner Franz Türler, who in 1986 decided to realise his dream of creating a mechanism that would provide a real-time model of the known cosmos. Standing 2.2 metres high including its granite pedestal, the clock was created by master watchmakers Ludwig Oechslin and Jörg Spöring. It is powered by solar panels mounted on the shop roof and is synchronised to UTC (Universal Coordinated Time) by means of a signal transmitter. An electromagnet in the base of the clock advances and retards the pendulum accordingly so that perfect timekeeping is maintained.

The Türler Clock is on permanent display at the shop, where the friendly staff will gladly provide access and explain its workings. The clock has five main features, namely a globe on top and four faces below. The globe represents the Earth and is surrounded by four crystal spheres on which the moon, sun, firmament (or visible sky), and Zodiac are represented (a fifth sphere is marked with orientation lines). It is humbling to learn that the crystal sphere depicting the firmament will take 25 794 years to make a single revolution!

One of the four faces of the Türler Clock

The first of the clock's four faces is a 360 degree representation of Zurich as seen from the roof of the shop's location on Bahnhofstrasse, against which the rising and setting of the sun and moon are shown (in other words it depicts the exact relation of Zurich to the horizon at any given moment).

The second face is a traditional perpetual calendar clock, with subsidiary dials indicating seconds, minutes, hours, the day of the week, the month, the year, the decade, the century and the millennium, with all Gregorian leap days taken into account.

The third face is a so-called *tellurion* being a mechanism by which the relative movements of the earth, moon, and sun are depicted three dimensionally. The mechanism explains how day, night, and the seasons are caused by the movement of the Earth on its axis and its orbit around the sun.

The fourth and final face is a planetarium, which depicts the nine planets of the solar system in their heliocentric orbits around the sun. It is interesting to note that whilst the nearest planet to the sun, Mercury, takes only eighty seven days to make one revolution, the most distant, Pluto, requires a more leisurely two hundred and forty seven years!

Other places of interest nearby: 1, 2, 3, 6, 7, 10

6 Walking with Ghosts

District 1 (City), the Ghost Walk of Zurich beginning on Paradeplatz
Tram 2, 6, 7, 8, 9, 11, 13, 17 Paradeplatz

Few people today recall Lewes Lavater (1527–1586), onetime chief pastor of Zurich's Calvinist Church. In 1572 he wrote a book called *Of Ghostes and Spirites walking by nyght*, in which he concluded that "after making the fullest allowance for ocular illusion, hallucination, and jugglers' tricks, there can be no doubt that genuine ghosts do really appear." As evidence for this he states that "all literature, sacred and profane, as well as an abundance of experiences among men now living, put this beyond all possible doubt." It was Lavater's belief that ghosts were not the dead reincarnated but in fact devils, and that the power of the Devil was proved by the existence of witchcraft.

That was all a very long time ago, and Zurich today might seem one of the last places to go looking for ghosts. But not according to the people who gather on Paradeplatz on Thursday and Friday evenings at 8pm (February-May and August-November). They do so to take part in a 70-minute ghost walk led by Englishman Dan Dent, whose tales of headless saints, poisoned mayors, and drowned pilgrims paint a rather different picture of Zurich (www.ghostwalk.ch).

Zurich's Old Town (Altstadt) has many dark corners and narrow alleyways, providing the perfect backdrop for a ghost walk. First stop is the Stadthausquai (Lindenhof) from where there is a clear view of the Wasserkirche, a Late Gothic chapel completed in 1484 on what was once an island in the Limmat. According to the legend of Zurich's foundation it was to this location that the city's patron saints Felix and Regula, together with their servant Exuperantius, came in 286 AD, after deserting a Roman legion based in Valais. When their presence was revealed they were beheaded for their Christian faith, and an ancient stone purporting to mark the site lies in the chapel's crypt. Not yet ready to rest it is said the trio rose to their feet, picked up their severed heads, and walked away leaving a trail of blood behind them. Reaching a clearing on a nearby hill the ghostly martyrs dug their own graves and buried themselves! According to local legend when the graves were re-discovered by Charlemagne (768–814) whilst out hunting he earmarked the site for a church, on the spot where today the Grossmünster stands (see no. 2). The headless saints figure on the bronze south door of the church by German artist Otto Münch (1885–1965), as well as on the Seal of the City of Zurich.

Next stop is the Church of St. Peter (St.-Peters-Kirche) on St.-Peter-Hofstatt (Lindenhof), where the grave of Rudolf Brun (c. 1290–1360) can be found beneath the clock tower (see no. 3). Brun is remembered as the first independent mayor of Zurich – mayors had previously been appointed by the abbess of the Fraumünster – and as founder in 1336 of Zurich's guild laws *(Zunftordnung)*. He diluted the power of the hitherto aristocratic city council by including in its ranks an equal number of members from the city's thirteen newly-founded guilds *(Zünfte)*. In 1360 Brun endured a painful and mysterious death, some say the result of poisoning. So tenacious was the tale that during the 1970s Brun's remains were exhumed for an autopsy. Traces of arsenic were discovered but since the chemical was once used medicinally it has never been

Zurich's old streets provide the perfect backdrop for a ghost walk

proven that the mayor was deliberately poisoned. But the story does not end there. When Brun's bones were reburied his skull was found to be missing. A few weeks later two boys playing football near the site claim to have seen a dark figure pass effortlessly through the wall of the tower without using the door. Was it the ghost of poor Brun looking for his missing skull?

A third ghostly location is the Rathausbrücke, known to locals as the Gemüsebrücke on account of the longstanding Saturday vegetable market held here. On Whit Wednesday 1375 a group of worshippers from the Fraumünster were on their way to the Lindenhof. As they approached the narrow bridge they saw another group on the other side coming from the

Three headless saints adorn a door of the Grossmünster

direction of the Grossmünster. Neither group was prepared to give way and as they surged onto the old bridge it collapsed causing the drowning of eight people in the Limmat. Their ghosts are still at large in the area.

Dan Dent certainly knows how to tell a good ghost story since he's been leading his walk for almost a decade now. Locals and visitors alike are shocked by his tales of haunted Zurich, and surprised that there are so many of them given that Reformist cantons such as Zurich are traditionally home to far fewer ghost stories than Catholic ones.

Other places of interest nearby: 2, 3, 5, 7, 8, 10

7 A Clockmakers' Paradise

District 1 (City), the Beyer Clock and Watch Museum
(Uhrenmuseum Beyer) at Bahnhofstrasse 31
Tram 2, 6, 7, 8, 9, 11, 13, 17 Paradeplatz

Switzerland has been regarded as a watchmaking centre since the mid-sixteenth century, when the Protestant reformer John Calvin (1509–1564) forbade the wearing of jewels. Jewellers and goldsmiths were forced to turn to watchmaking instead, and by the end of the century Geneva-made watches were renowned for their precision and appearance. Watchmakers soon spread out across the Jura region and beyond, where they have remained ever since, notching up many horological firsts including the first wristwatch, the first quartz and water-resistant watches, and the invention of the self winder and perpetual calendar.

The Griffin table clock is a highlight of the Beyer Clock and Watch Museum (Uhrenmuseum Beyer)

It is little wonder that one of Zurich's most fascinating specialist museums is the Beyer Clock and Watch Museum (Uhrenmuseum Beyer). Opened in 1970 the museum represents the private collection of Theodor Beyer (1926–2002), and is located in the basement of the Beyer Chronometrie shop at Bahnhofstrasse 31 (City). Founded in 1760 it is Switzerland's oldest watch and clock retailer. The museum contains more than five hundred chronological instruments used to illustrate the long history of timekeeping from before the time of Christ right up to the present day, and is of interest to visitors young and old.

Mankind's first attempt at timekeeping occurred around 4000 BC and took the form of elemental clocks: sundials by day and water clocks by night. The museum's oldest exhibit is a copy of an ancient Egyptian water clock dating from 1400 BC, which was provided by the British Museum. By 800 AD the time in Northern Europe was still being measured using marked candles, and it was not until the twelfth century that the first mechanical clocks were installed in church towers in England and Italy. They were constructed by blacksmiths from wrought iron and wood.

The trade of clockmaker does not appear in historical records until 1583, when the blacksmiths of northern Italy and southern Germany embarked on the earliest stages of clock miniaturisation, resulting in the first living room clocks in around 1450. The first portable watches appeared in 1550 and only featured an hour hand. One of them was the so-called Nuremberg Egg, an example of which is displayed in the museum. With both Arabic and Roman numerals the watch had an inherent accuracy of thirty minutes a day.

The Renaissance period heralded a golden age in clock making in southern Germany. Surrounding countries used the same technology but the high prosperity of southern Germany meant that precious metals could be incorporated into some highly ornate table clocks. A magnificent example is the museum's unique gold-plated Griffin table clock (1640), which has been declared a national cultural treasure. The creature's eyes move in time with the clockwork mechanism, the beak in time with the chiming mechanism, and the wings flap, too!

Meanwhile in France the Duke of Burgundy and King Henry IV became enamoured with clockmaking and during the seventeenth century French craftsmen turned out many fine enamelled, inlaid *(Boulle)*, and longcase clocks, as well as marine chronometers. After 1685, however, religious persecution saw Huguenot craftsmen fleeing to Calvinist Geneva, bringing their clockmaking and enamelling skills with them. France's loss was Switzerland's gain – although Switzerland's status as a worldwide centre for the manufacture of clocks and watches was not fully established until the arrival of the Industrial Revolution in the mid-nineteenth century. The museum contains many examples of matchless Swiss watchmaking from this later period, including a Patek Phillipe pocket watch (1898) with representations of sunrise and sunset. There is also a display of gold and silver pocket watches made by the Swiss watchmaker Breguet in Paris.

Novelties in the museum include the smallest watch in the world made by Jaeger LeCoultre (1930), and several late nineteenth century clocks incorporated into oil paintings, with automata that bring the various mountain and maritime scenes alive. Also displayed is the

Rolex Oyster Perpetual watch worn by Sir Edmund Hillary (1919–2008) during his conquest of Mount Everest, and another watch designed to withstand a descent into the Marianas Trench, the deepest part of the world's oceans. The collection concludes with a Patek Phillipe quartz watch that checks the time every second via a wireless connection to the atomic clock in Neuchâtel: it is accurate to within a millionth of a second.

The items for sale in the shop on the ground floor are almost as extraordinary as those in the museum, and include not only Swiss watch brands such as Rolex, Chopard, Breitling, Girard-Perregaux, and the shop's own brand Chronometrie Beyer, but also state-of-the-art navigational aids and many valuable antique clocks.

The museum also contains the watch worn by Sir Edmund Hillary when he conquered Everest

Between 1964 and 1988 the Beyer shop included a department for electronic clocks, examples of which can still be seen on the streets of Zurich (the best known are the Meeting Point clock at the Zurich Main Station (Zürich Hauptbahnhof) and the Flower Clock on Bürkliplatz). Since 2006 the museum's electronic clock collection has been located at Sihlfeldstrasse 10 (Sihlfeld), and is open by appointment only on the first Wednesday of the month from 2–5pm, tel. 0041 (0)43 344 63 63.

Other places of interest nearby: 1, 3, 5, 6, 8, 9, 10, 11

8 A Unique Ethnographic Experience

District 1 (City), the Ethnographic Museum of the University of Zurich
(Völkerkundemuseum der Universität Zürich) at Pelikanstrasse 40
Tram 2, 9 Sihlstrasse, 8 Bahnhof Selnau; Bus 66 Sihlstrasse

Tucked into a leafy corner of an old botanical garden at Pelikanstrasse 40 is the Ethnographic Museum of the University of Zurich
(Völkerkundemuseum der Universität Zürich) (City). This small but
highly-acclaimed museum is dedicated to non-European cultures – and
it leaves a powerful impression on the visitor. History, a lack of space,
and visionary management account for its success.

First the history. The idea for the museum was initially proposed
in 1887, as a research and teaching institute by a group of likeminded
scientists, industrialists, and politicians. The response was enthusiastic
and the museum opened in 1889 beneath the dome of the old stock
exchange at Börsenstrasse 21. At its heart were the private collections
of several prominent Zurich citizens. One of them, for example, had
travelled around the world as a Russian court astronomer, whilst another had served as a minister at the court of Emperor Menelik II in
Ethiopia. Other artefacts were donated by the French consul to Zurich,
bolstered by various gifts made by foreign nations to the Old Swiss
Confederacy. This meant that upon opening the museum was able to
display representative exhibits from Africa, East Asia, Central America,
Oceania, Madagascar, and the polar regions.

During the 1890s the collection was increased through personal be-
quests, bringing in further artefacts from North America, Central and
South Asia, and Japan. In the same decade the museum relocated to
Seilergraben (Rathaus), and in 1899 the founding association merged
with the local geographical association, enabling the collection to grow
further by the addition of objects from Indonesia, Australia, and the
Amazon. Then in 1913 the entire collection was handed over to the university, and relocated to their premises on Rämistrasse (Hochschulen).
During this period a Thai prince donated the valuable northeast Indian, Nepalese and Tibetan holdings, and a private collection of West
and Central African art was acquired through public and private do-
nations. In time the museum also acquired a collection of papers and
other items of Peter Aufschnaiter (1899–1973) and Heinrich Harrer
(1912–2006), two Austrian mountaineers who escaped a British pris-

Traditional Chinese porcelain manufacture celebrated in the Ethnographic Museum of the University of Zurich (Völkerkundemuseum der Universität Zürich)

oner of war camp in North India and travelled to Lhasa in 1944, where the two created the first accurate map of the holy city.

In 1972 the university collection changed to a public university museum. Later on in 1979 the museum moved to the sylvan setting of the Park zur Katz, atop the old city walls on Schanzengraben; at the time the park was home to the university's botanical gardens, which were relocated in 1976. (see no. 9). A lack of space dictated that the museum's holdings of around thirty thousand objects – from Benin bronzes to Inuit sculptures – were stored in three separate depots across the city. The artefacts are complemented by an important and extensive visual archive, containing approximately forty thousand historical photos and almost two thousand films and videos, with a library containing almost as many books and periodicals.

No attempt is made to display these objects in the permanent manner seen in ethnographic collections elsewhere. Instead the museum mounts fascinating temporary exhibitions running for six to twelve months. The current management has placed the focus of these exhibitions squarely on revealing non-European human skills, religious rites, and cultural traditions, and in the process exploding long held examples of Eurocentric ethnographic stereotyping. Being a university research museum, with a permanent staff of experts and a supply of students eager to learn, means that the museum is not tied to the whims of a fee paying public.

The exhibitions are both experimental and daring. Recent topics include the art of the forger, rarely seen modern prints from Ethiopia and the Inuit of Canada, and a private collection of photos, objects and personal effects donated by the family of a Swiss geologist from his time in 1920s Borneo. The latter challenged the popular opinion that only savage headhunters lived in Borneo at this time. Another particularly effective exhibition illustrated the complete porcelain manufacturing process as witnessed by a research team in a village in China. The aim this time was to remind Westerners that mass production is still possible without recourse to industrialisation. The exhibition acts as a timely reminder that in some parts of the world man's entire body remains a tool, and not just his hand.

Other places of interest nearby: 2, 3, 5, 6, 7, 9, 10

9 In an Old Apothecary Garden

District 1 (City), the Old Botanical Garden (Alter Botanischer Garten)
in the Park zur Katz on Schanzengraben
Tram 2, 9 Sihlstrasse, 8 Bahnhof Selnau; Bus 66 Sihlstrasse

In 1976 the University of Zurich opened its New Botanical Garden (Neuer Botanischer Garten der Universität Zürich) in the suburban quarter of Weinegg (District 8). With ten distinct planting zones and state-of-the-art glasshouses the new location reflects the demands of a modern garden used by students and visitors alike (see no. 66). By contrast the city's Old Botanical Garden (Alter Botanischer Garten), atop a former medieval bastion on Schanzengraben, seems cramped and outmoded. But what it lacks in space and modernity it more than makes up for in charm and atmosphere.

The Gessner-Garten is part of the Old Botanical Garden (Alter Botanischer Garten) on Schanzengraben

The Old Botanical Garden finds its origins in the private herb garden of the doctor, natural scientist, and apothecary Conrad Gessner (1516–1565). One of Gessner's descendants, the physician and naturalist Johannes Gessner (1709–1790), founded Zurich's first botanical garden in 1746 in conjunction with the Zurich Botanical Society (Naturforschende Gesellschaft Zürich). In 1834 the garden moved to the newly obsolete Zur Katz bastion on Schanzengraben, a part of Zurich's third and final city wall, where it remained until 1976 (see no. 22).

The garden was initially designed by university gardener Leopold Karl Theodor Fröbel (1810–1907), and in 1851 a distinctive octagonal pavilion was added, which was later rebuilt in iron. By the end of the nineteenth century the garden had become increasingly popular with the public. Unfortunately, however, it could not be expanded beyond the confines of the old bastion, which was hemmed in by a former defensive moat called the Schanzengraben on one side and by build-

This nineteenth century garden pavilion is used to over winter citrus trees

ings on the other. This situation pertained right up until the 1960s, when some of Zurich's new taller buildings began throwing their unwelcome shadows across the garden, impeding plant growth in the process. So it was that in 1971 a former private park in Weinegg was secured, and the university made plans to re-locate their new garden there.

Far from being abandoned, or worse still built over, the Old Botanical Garden has been retained in its old-fashioned form. Since 1976 it has served purely recreational purposes with the pavilion, for example, being used for concerts, theatrical presentations, and exhibitions. The garden also provides a leafy backdrop for Zurich's Ethnographic Museum (Völkerkundemuseum), too (see no. 8). In 1997 the garden was restored to its original appearance so that today it provides a peaceful and very welcome oasis in the city.

An important part of the restoration is a well-stocked herb garden – the so-called Gessner-Garten – established in honour of Conrad Gessner, to whom a memorial bust has also been dedicated. It lies at the highest point of the garden and contains over fifty medicinal plants, each of which would have been familiar to Gessner and his fellow natural scientists in the sixteenth century. They include *Potentilla erecta* (an astringent and blood coagulant), *Silybum marianum* (to protect the liver and gall bladder), *Juniperus communis* (for urinary infections), and *Artemisia absinthium* (for pain relief and a stomach tonic).

Other places of interest nearby: 1, 3, 5, 6, 7, 8, 10, 11

10 Butchers, Bakers, Blacksmiths

District 1 (Lindenhof), a tour of Zurich's guildhalls
finishing at the Metzgermuseum beneath the Hotel Widder
at Rennweg 7
Tram 6, 7, 11, 13, 17 Rennweg

One of the most important dates in Zurich's history is 1336. It was in this year that Rudolf Brun (c. 1290–1360), the city's first independent mayor, established Zurich's guild laws (Zunftordnung). During the eleventh and twelfth centuries the merchant nobility had amassed great wealth, mainly from textiles such as wool, silk, and linen, as well as leather, and they controlled the city council. Brun diluted their power by in-

A belt buckle in the Metzgermuseum
(Butchers' Museum) on Rennweg

cluding within the council's ranks an equal number of members from the city's thirteen trade guilds (Zünfte) (see no. 2). This way the workers took control of the city until the nineteenth century, by which time the guilds had ceased to be tied to specific trades. Instead they acquired a mostly symbolic and societal function best represented today by the city's annual Sechseläuten festival (see no. 32).

Each of Zurich's original guilds had its own guildhall (Zunfthaus), the majority of which have since been converted into hotels and restaurants, where many of them still meet. Several are strung out along the Limmatquai, in the vicinity of the Rathaus, which was Zurich's administrative centre during the period of the Old Swiss Confederacy. They include the Zunfthaus zur Zimmerleuten at number 40 (used by the guild of carpenters, builders, wainwrights, and coopers), the Zunfthaus zur Haue at number 52 (used by the Zunft zum Kämbel, the guild of food dealers and wine merchants), and the Zunfthaus zur Saffran at number 54 (textiles workers and spice merchants). The splendid Late Gothic Haus zum Rüden at Limmatquai 2 was originally home to the aristocratic Gesellschaft zur Constaffel but from 1490 until 1798 it was used by adults not belonging to another guild (the restaurant there today specialises in the local veal and mushroom ragout known as Züri Gschnätzlets).

The Rathaus quarter includes three other guildhalls, namely the Zunfthaus zur Schmiden at Marktgasse 20 (blacksmiths, silver- and

A detail of the Zunfthaus zur Haue on Limmatquai

goldsmiths, clockmakers, and physicians), the Zunfthaus zur Schneidern at Stüssihofstatt 3 (tailors), and the Zunfthaus zum Weggen at Oberdorfstrasse 20 (bakers and millers). The remaining guildhalls are all located on the west bank of the Limmat (Lindenhof), including the Zunfthaus zur Waag at Münsterhof 8 (weavers, hatters, and linen merchants) and the Zunfthaus zur Meisen at Münsterhof 20 (wine merchants, saddle makers, and painters). The latter now serves as a showcase for the eighteenth century porcelain collection of the Landesmuseum Zürich at Museumstrasse 2 (City). The Zunft zur Schiffleuten (fishermen and boatmen) meet at the Hotel zum Storchen at Weinplatz 2, and the Vereinigte Zünfte zur Gerwe und zur Schuhmachern (formerly two guilds, tanners and shoemakers) meet at the Hotel Savoy on Paradeplatz.

That just leaves the guild of butchers and cattle merchants (Zunft zum Widder), whose drinking hall dating back to 1401 is today a part of the Hotel Widder at Rennweg 7 (Lindenhof) (see no. 46). The guild still meets here, and when the hotel was opened in 1995 the opportunity was taken to memorialise its activities with a specialist museum in the basement. Called the Metzgermuseum (Butchers' Museum) it is open to visitors by appointment only (tel. 0041 (0)44 224 25 26, www.zunftwidder.ch). The walls of the museum are lined with all the tools of the butcher's trade, including knives, cleavers, and sausage machines, as well as the skulls of a pig, cow, and sheep, since these were the animals that provided the raw material for the butcher's trade.

Other places of interest nearby: 1, 2, 3, 5, 7, 10, 11, 12, 13

11 Toys for Young and Old

District 1 (Lindenhof), the Zurich Toy Museum (Zürcher
Spielzeugmuseum) at Fortunagasse 15
Tram 6, 7, 11, 13, 17 Rennweg

The toy shop of Franz Carl Weber at Bahnhofstrasse 62 (Lindenhof)
is one of the largest of its kind in Europe. With its impressive window
displays and extensive range of toys for all ages the shop represents
every child's dream. Around the corner the experience continues – but
not only for children. At Fortunagasse 15 on the fifth floor is Weber's
collection of historic toys, open to the public as the Zurich Toy Museum (Zürcher Spielzeugmuseum). For many adults a visit will be a
nostalgia-filled trip down memory lane.

The shop's founder, Franz Philipp Karl Friedrich Weber (1855–
1948), was born in Bavaria in 1855. Exposure to the toy industry came
early, when as a young man he worked for the toy firm Ullmann &
Engelmann. Aged twenty four Weber headed to Zurich, where his
brother Conrad was based. After working for a year in a chemist's
shop he decided in 1881 to establish his own toy business. He named

Tin toys in the Zurich Toy Museum (Zürcher Spielzeugmuseum) on Fortunagasse

the company after a contracted version of his own name – Franz Carl Weber – and set up shop with Conrad at Bahnhofstrasse 48.

Weber was not discouraged by the fact that there were two other toy shops in Zurich. Relying on his previous experience he ensured that the latest toys from Nuremberg were prominently displayed in his shop windows. The gamble paid off, the business grew, and nine years later Weber relocated his shop to the company's present address.

Weber died in 1948 at the grand old age of ninety three, bequeathing the business to his son and grandson. In 1956 the museum was established on the initiative of Margrit Weber-Beck, as a way of celebrating the seventy fifth anniversary of the company's founding. Both shop and museum continue to use the company's logo of a rocking horse *(Schaukelpferd)*, one of the first toys sold by Weber back in the 1880s.

There are more than twelve hundred different types of toy represented in the Zurich Toy Museum, dating from between the late eighteenth and early twentieth centuries. Each type mirrors in miniature the historical backdrop against which it was manufactured. The stationary steam engines, Märklin-brand clockwork locomotives, and tin racing cars, for example, reflect the technological advances made possible by the Industrial Revolution. Similarly with the colourful clockwork fairground rides, such as the Ferris wheel and the carousel. Nineteenth century domestic life is reflected in the dolls' houses and model shops on display, notably in their intricate room furnishings. The dolls themselves provide a useful record of bygone fashions. The importance of the countryside, as well as religious beliefs, is demonstrated by the popularity of wooden farm animals, horses and carriages, and Noah's Arks.

The museum also highlights the dramatic difference between the way today's children and those of yesteryear entertain themselves. In the pre-television age, evenings would be spent reading, playing with cardboard cut-out theatres, and on special occasions watching slides projected from a magic lantern, examples of which are displayed in the museum. New technology has now changed everything, and the shift is well illustrated by visiting the company's website (www.fcw.ch), which contains an illustration of every toy catalogue issued by Weber from 1892 until the present day.

With so many delightful toys on show it's all too easy to miss the museum's oldest exhibit. Tucked away in the corner of one of the cabinets it is a tiny rough hewn wooden chicken hutch. Designed to be held in the hand when a handle is turned six little chicken heads

A fully equipped dolls' house kitchen

appear and start pecking at grain in a trough. This delightful object dates to around 1800 and was carved on a farm in the alpine Canton of Graubünden.

The Landesmuseum Zürich at Museumstrasse 2 (City) contains a small collection of antique children's toys and dolls' houses from different periods. Other well-stocked toy shops include Pastorini Spielzeug at Weinplatz 3 (Lindenhof) and Nepomuk-Kinderladen at Klingenstrasse 23 (Gewerbeschule).

Other places of interest nearby: 1, 3, 7, 10, 12, 13, 14

12 A Martyr to the Reformation

District 1 (Lindenhof), the memorial to Felix Manz opposite
Schipfe 43
Tram 6, 7, 11, 13, 17 Rennweg

Between the Lindenhof hill (Lindenhofhügel) and the left bank of the
Limmat stands a charming huddle of old houses known as Schipfe. The
name is first documented in 1292 as *Schüpfi*, which is Swiss German for
the verb to push or shove (from the German *Schubsen*), since it is here
that fishing boats were once launched into the river. There is, however,
more to the history of this area than initially meets the eye. Attached
to a wall on the riverbank opposite Schipfe 43 is an inscribed stone
all too easy to miss. It is a memorial to Felix Manz (c. 1498–1527), the
first martyr of the so-called Radical Reformation, who was executed by
drowning in the early sixteenth century.

It is an oft-told story how Huldrych Zwingli (1484–1531) arrived in
Zurich in 1519 to take up a position as priest in the Grossmünster. From
here he initiated the Swiss Protestant Reformation across German-
speaking Switzerland, furthering Martin Luther's crusade against corruption in the Catholic Church (see no. 2). Manz, the illegitimate son
of a canon in the Grossmünster, quickly became a follower of Zwingli,
and also befriended Conrad Grebel, after he too joined the movement
in 1521. The friendship proved divisive, however, as Manz and Grebel
began independently questioning the mass and the nature of the relationship between church and state, and most controversially suggested
the replacement of infant baptism with adult baptism.

During the Second Disputation of Zurich in 1523, the subject of
which was the removal of religious statues and icons, Manz and Grebel
grew impatient with the slowness at which the Swiss Reformation was
unfolding, believing that Zwingli was making too many concessions to
Zurich's city council. A further disputation was held in 1525 at which
Zwingli and the council decided that anyone refusing to have their
children baptised would be forced to leave Zurich, and that the radicals
should submit to the decision.

The radicals ignored Zwingli and on 21st January 1525 they met at
the home of the mother of Felix Manz, where Grebel baptised a third
radical, George Blaurock, who in turn baptised the others. Following
this earliest case of adult re-baptism the first Anabaptist church of the
Radical Reformation was born, and the break with Zwingli was complete.

The Radical Reformation gained ground quickly and Felix Manz played an important part in it, using his talents for evangelising and translating texts into the language of the people. It was not long before Manz was arrested, whilst preaching with Blaurock in the Grünningen region. The two were taken to Zurich and imprisoned in the Wellenbergturm, a sturdy, fifteen-metre high tower in the middle of the Limmat between Mün-

A memorial to the reformer Felix Manz on Schipfe

sterbrücke and Quaibrücke, opposite Schiffländeplatz. Accessible only by boat, the tower formed part of Zurich's city wall from the second half of the thirteenth century, and is where the mayor Hans Waldmann (1435–1489) had been imprisoned in 1489 (see nos. 22 & 30). (The redundant tower was demolished in 1837 to increase the flow of water to mills downstream, and the stones used to build the Münsterbrücke.)

On 5th January 1527 Felix Manz became the first victim of an edict passed by the city council in 1526 making adult re-baptism punishable by drowning. Zwingli accused Manz of obstinately refusing to recant, as a result of which he was taken out into the river by boat, where his hands were bound and pulled behind his knees and a pole placed between them. Ignoring a last opportunity to recant, and egged on by his mother and brother, Manz met his watery end with the words "Into thy hands, O God, I commend my spirit". He was the first Swiss Anabaptist to be martyred at the hands of other Protestants. As for Huldrych Zwingli, he later died defending Zurich against the Catholics at the Battle of Kappel.

The fate of Felix Manz can be considered at leisure at the Restaurant Schipfe 16, which is run by the local council as a way of helping the unemployed back into work. It's a good base from which to explore the area's craft shops, which include a leather worker and ceramic artist in the nearby riverside arcade, as well as a traditional bookbinder at Wohllebgasse 9.

Other places of interest nearby: 1, 3, 10, 11, 13, 14

13 Homage to Urania

District 1 (Lindenhof), the Urania Observatory (Urania-Sternwarte)
at Uraniastrasse 9
Tram 6, 7, 11, 13, 17 Rennweg (Note: the observatory is only open
when the sky is clear)

The Urania Observatory (Urania-Sternwarte)
towers above Uraniastrasse

The name Urania stems from the Greek word for 'heavenly' and in mythology it was applied to the muse of astronomy. This explains why astronomical observatories in Vienna, Budapest, Berlin, and Antwerp are all named Urania. Zurich boasts an Urania Observatory (Urania-Sternwarte), too, located in the city's Lindenhof quarter. A visit when the skies are clear can be quite exciting.

Zurich's first astronomical observatory was located on the roof of the Zunfthaus zur Meisen, a Baroque guild hall at Münsterhof 20 (Lindenhof) on the banks of the Limmat (see no. 10). It was here in 1759 that the local astronomical commission succeeded in defining the *Culminatio solis* – the altitude (or elevation angle) reached when the sun transits over the observer's meridian – thereby calculating for the first time the exact global position of the City of Zurich. Observations were later taken from the southern tower of the Grossmünster until in the early 1860s the Swiss Federal Observatory was established at Schmelzbergstrasse 25 (Fluntern), for use by the Swiss Federal Institute of Technology (Eidgenössische Technische Hochschule) (ETH). Built to a design by the German architect Gottfried Semper (1803–1879) this observatory remained in use until 1980, when increasing light pollution and encroaching buildings saw its closure (it is today used by the Collegium Helveticum interdisciplinary research institute).

Meanwhile, in 1899 the wealthy Zurich merchant Abraham Weill Einstein initiated the construction of the Urania Observatory, Switzerland's first public astronomical observatory, on what subsequently became Uraniastrasse. Inaugurated on 15th June 1907 the observatory is perched at the top of a tower fifty one metres in height, which still dominates the west end of Zurich's Altstadt. Tower and observatory were originally slated to be just one element in an architectural masterplan of offices and residences by city architect Gustav Gull (1858–1942) but which was never realised. Gull was the

Lake Zurich (Zürichsee) seen from the Urania Observatory (Urania-Sternwarte)

leading Historicist architect of his day and was responsible for designing the Landesmuseum Zürich at Museumstrasse 2 (City) (see no. 16). By comparison, Gull's Urania tower, with its octagonal footprint and oxidised green copper roof, is reminiscent of Art Nouveau.

The Urania Observatory is open to visitors on Thursday, Friday and Saturday evenings when stargazing conditions are right. The original optical telescope is still in use and was built by the celebrated Carl Zeiss in Jena. Weighing twelve tons it consists of two instruments on a common mount, namely a 15cm refractor and a 30cm reflector. To avoid unwanted vibration the telescope stands on top of a freestanding pillar, which runs down through the centre of the tower to the foundations of the building below. In 2006 the telescope was returned to Jena for a complete overhaul and then hoisted back into the observatory in time for its centenary in 2007.

Directly below the observatory, on the tenth floor of the tower, is the Jules Verne Panorama Bar. Accessible by lift from the ground-floor Brasserie Lipp at Uraniastrasse 9 it offers magnificent vistas across the surrounding rooftops and steeples. Some tables offer twilight views of the Alps.

Other places of interest nearby: 1, 3, 10, 11, 12, 14

14 Giacometti's Glorious Entrance Hall

District 1 (Lindenhof), the Giacometti-Halle in Amtshaus 1
at Bahnhofquai 3
Tram 4, 15 Rudolf-Brun-Brücke, 6, 7, 11, 13, 17 Bahnhofstrasse
(Note: identification is required on entry)

The Surrealist Swiss sculptor Alberto Giacometti (1901–1966) is today considered one of Switzerland's most important artists. Accordingly his work adorns the Kunsthaus Zürich at Heimplatz 1 (Hochschule). He was born amongst the mountains in the Canton of Graubünden (Italian: Grigioni; Romansh: Grischun), where his father Giovanni was a post-Impressionist painter. But the family involvement in art didn't end there: Alberto's brother Diego was also a sculptor, and his brother Bruno was an architect. All left an artistic legacy but in Zurich none is greater than Alberto's uncle, the artist Augusto Giacometti (1877–1947).

Augusto Giacometti was also born in Graubünden, and between 1894 and 1897 he lived in Zurich, where he gained a teaching diploma in drawing at the School of Arts and Crafts. He thereafter enrolled at an art college in Paris, where he was taught by the Swiss pioneer of Art Nouveau, Eugène Grasset. In 1902 he relocated to Florence and studied Renaissance art. Suitably inspired, Augusto began lifting motifs from both fifteenth century Italian art favoured by the Pre-Raphaelites as well as the floral style of William Morris, and using them in his own artisanal designs for mosaics, clocks, posters, and painted glass.

Giacometti received his first public commissions back in Switzerland in 1914, including mosaics for the University of Zurich (Universität Zürich). Around the same time he began distancing himself from purely ornamental art. This process was hastened from 1917 onwards through his association with the Dadaist movement in Zurich (see no. 25). Admiring the movement's freedom of expression he became more experimental in his approach to the decorative treatment of surfaces, developing a technique of applying colours with a spatula in order to create a range of different textures and effects.

The best place to experience Giacometti's gift as a colourist is the sprawling building at Bahnhofquai 3 (Lindenhof) – and it is one of Zurich's best kept secrets. A former orphanage the building was con-

The Giacometti-Halle on Bahnhofquai

verted into an administrative building *(Amtshaus)* between 1911 and 1914 by city architect Gustav Gull (1858–1942). The original vaulted cellar became the new entrance hall, and between 1923 and 1925 Augusto Giacometti was commissioned to decorate it. At the behest of local councillor Emil Klöti, the artist and three assistants created a series of scenes reflecting aspects of Swiss society between the wars.

Known as the Giacometti-Halle the entrance hall is today part of a police station. When visiting one will be asked to provide a passport, which will be retained for the duration of a ten minute visit. But it's worth the inconvenience. Using a rich palette of reds and golds, together with splashes of vivid blue and green, the paintings of Giacometti are both heady and eclectic, featuring scenes of stone masons and carpenters on one wall, and a magician and an astronomer on another. Recently restored the paintings certainly provide the grandest entrance to a police station anywhere!

The success of the Giacometti-Halle led to commissions across Europe, including two further colourful works in Zurich. In 1933 he created the windows for the choir of the Grossmünster, and in 1945 a rose window for the Fraumünster (see no. 2). It is fitting that after

Giacometti died in Zurich in 1966 his gravestone in Graubünden was inscribed with the words "Il Maestro dei Colori" (The Master of Colour).

Zurich boasts several other stunning painted interiors. One is the Restaurant zum Kropf at In Gassen 16 (Lindenhof), which features a marvellous late nineteenth century interior in the style known as Bavarian Beer Hall Baroque. Less flamboyant but no less impressive is the Roman Catholic Liebfrauenkirche at Zehnderweg 9 (Unterstrass). Zurich's Catholic community was established around 1800 and given a small chapel on the banks of the Limmat. With rapid industrialisation Zurich witnessed an influx of workers from rural Catholic areas, and the Liebfrauenkirche was constructed in the 1890s. As the city's first Catholic church it followed the style of early medieval Italian churches replete with a campanile tower. The originally bare walls were covered in frescoes between 1910 and the 1920s, and depict scenes from the life of Christ.

Other places of interest nearby: 1, 10, 11, 12, 13, 15

15 The Spanish Bun Railway

District 1 (City), Zurich Main Station (Zürich Hauptbahnhof)
on Bahnhofplatz
Tram 3, 10, 14 Bahnhofplatz; Bus 31 Bahnhofplatz

Zurich Main Station (Zürich Hauptbahnhof), known by locals as the HB *(haa-bay)*, is the largest railway station in Switzerland. Three thousand trains, carrying around 350 000 passengers, arrive and depart daily on thirty tracks. The station is one of the country's oldest, and it contains enough history and modern facilities to warrant a special trip to see it, whether one is leaving Zurich or not.

The Alfred-Escher-Brunnen and Zurich Main Station (Zürich Hauptbahnhof)

Whereas the station building seen today was completed in 1871, the line itself had already been in Zurich for over two decades. The first station on the site was opened in 1847 by the Swiss Northern Railway (Schweizerische Nordbahn), as the terminus for a railway connecting Zurich and Baden. As such it was the first railway constructed entirely within Switzerland (the first line to enter Switzerland was an extension of a French railway to Basel in 1844). The first train departed Zurich at 1pm on 7th August carrying one hundred and forty invited passengers. The twenty kilometre-long journey followed the south bank of the Limmat and took forty five minutes. A scheduled service commenced two days later with four trips daily in each direction.

Shortly afterwards the line was dubbed the Spanisch-Brötli-Bahn (Spanish Bun Railway). This curious name recalls how the servants of Zurich's gentry used the new railway to purchase special buns that under canton law could only be made in Baden (they are said to have originated in Milan during the seventeenth century, when that city was under Spanish control). Once safely back in Zurich the buns were used by the gentry to impress their guests at high society tea parties. Before the arrival of the railway the servants had to set out from Baden the night before on foot!

The relatively late arrival of the railway in Switzerland was in part because the country's cantons had a say over the route chosen – and they didn't always agree (the celebrated railway engineer Alois Negrelli (1799–1858) had been commissioned to pioneer a route as early as 1837). Internal politics also explains why plans to extend the line were temporarily scuppered, when usage fell away during the civil war *(Sonderbundskrieg)* of 1847. Only after the enactment of the Federal Railways Act of 1852 (made possible by the new constitution of 1848) could plans resume, and in 1858 the line was extended from Baden to Brugg.

From the outside the neo-Renaissance style station looks much as it did in the 1870s, albeit with the addition in 1889 of a monumental fountain to the memory of Swiss politician and railway entrepreneur Alfred Escher (1819–1882), who initiated the construction of the Gotthard Railway and was a founder of what is today Credit Suisse. Designed by architect Alfred Friedrich Bluntschli (1842–1930), with bronze figures by Richard Kissling (1848–1919), the Alfred-Escher-Brunnen recalls the railway on an inscribed shield, whilst attendant dragons restrained by cherubs symbolise the taming of the River Linth by Escher's namesake Hans Conrad Escher (1767–1823). Although unrelated, both men helped shape modern Switzerland.

Inside the station is a different story. Whilst the main concourse is still unchanged in its sobriety, it has been enlivened with various works of modern art. These include a sculpture suspended from the ceiling called *L'Ange Protecteur* (Guardian Angel) by the French sculptress Niki de Saint Phalle (1930–2002). Saint Phalle was married to Swiss installation artist Jean Tinguely (1925–1991), whose own kinetic sculpture *Heureka* can be found at the southern end of Zürichhorn Park (Seefeld). The concourse is used regularly for themed markets including Europe's largest indoor Christmas market (Christkindlimarkt).

A sculpture by Niki de Saint Phalle hangs in the station concourse

Well concealed beneath the main concourse is a modern shopping centre called Shop-Ville RailCity. The two hundred or more shops benefit from the Swiss law exempting public transport hubs from Sunday closing. Those wishing to mark the day of rest, however, can do so here in a tiny chapel (Bahnhofkirche) in which members from all five world religions (Buddhism, Christianity, Hinduism, Islam, and Judaism) are welcome to worship in peace.

Other places of interest nearby: 14, 16, 17

16 A Lost Prehistoric World

District 1 (City), the Landesmuseum Zürich at Museumstrasse 2
Tram 4, 11, 13, 14, 17 Bahnhofquai; Bus 46 Bahnhofquai

It comes as no surprise to learn that the Landesmuseum Zürich at Museumstrasse 2 (City) contains the world's largest collection of objects relating to the cultural history of Switzerland. Opened in 1897 it is housed inside a purpose-built structure designed by leading Historicist architect Gustav Gull (1858–1942). From the outside the museum appears like a sprawling fairytale castle: inside over a hundred rooms tell the story of Switzerland from earliest times down to the present day. Everything is here from medieval weapons, renaissance globes, and antique wristwatches to musical instruments, antique dolls' houses, and farming implements. There are also entire rooms taken from long-demolished medieval and renaissance buildings that have been reconstructed inside the museum.

Some of the most intriguing exhibits are to be found amongst the museum's archaeological holdings on the first floor. There is a Roman hoard, for example, that was unearthed in 1741 at Lunnern/Altstetten in the Reuss Valley. Buried around 260 AD to protect it from Germanic tribal raiders and never recovered the hoard includes a superb embossed gold bowl dating from the Bronze Age, decorated with images of deer and the sun and moon. Even older are the prehistoric artefacts on display, which date as far back as the fourth millennium BC. They remind the onlooker that man was living on the shores of Lake Zurich (Zürichsee) long before even the Romans arrived.

A tantalising glimpse of this lost prehistoric world was gained during the construction of the Bernhard Theatre (Bernhardheater) at Falkenstrasse 1 (Hochschulen) in the 1980s. Four metres beneath the ground archaeologists unearthed the remains of a Neolithic settlement of wooden lakeside stilt houses (Pfahlbaudorf). Such settlements, a model of which is displayed in the museum, were widespread in the Alpine foothills after agriculture and animal husbandry had been introduced to the region. Although the site is now high and dry, in prehistoric times this would have been a marshy but strategic location, overlooking the point where Lake Zurich empties into the River Limmat. A handful of other similar settlements have since been identified around the mouth of the Limmat, which were variously occupied between 4300 and 1000 BC. When the Limmat is especially clear the remains of the settlements can be glimpsed at from the Quaibrücke.

Divers revealing prehistoric Zurich

In 2010 during the construction of an underground garage facility for the Zurich Opera House (Opernhaus Zürich), archaeologists were again called in to investigate. This time they found traces of several clusters of Neolithic stilt houses, which evidence suggests were inhabited between 3700 and 2500 BC. Amongst the artefacts retrieved was a fine flint dagger from what is now Italy, an elaborate hunting bow, bone tools, ceramics, and animal remains. Of the houses themselves usually only the wooden stilts remain, submerged deep in the wet ground where potentially destructive bacteria cannot thrive. It came as a great surprise, therefore, when an intact wooden door was uncovered. Made of sturdy poplar planks and with well-preserved hinges the door is one of the oldest ever found in Europe. Using dendrochronology (the science of counting tree rings) it has been suggested that the door was constructed in 3063 BC, around the same time as Stonehenge was being erected in Britain.

The Zurich door measures 153 by 88 centimetres, and archaeologists suggest that such doors would have been commonplace in prehis-

Europe's oldest wooden door was uncovered near the Zurich Opera House (Opernhaus Zürich)

toric Zurich (a similar example has been retrieved from another former lakeside settlement at Pfäffikon to the southeast of the city). They were used not only for reasons of security but also to keep out the cold wind blowing across the lake; it is thought that climatic conditions in the area were harsher than at present. Once the Zurich door has been adequately preserved it is hoped it will be placed on permanent public display.

Other places of interest nearby: 14, 15, 17

17 Where the Limmat Meets the Sihl

District 1 (City), Platzspitz-Park behind the Landesmuseum Zürich at Museumstrasse 2
Tram 4, 11, 13, 14, 17 Bahnhofquai; Bus 46 Bahnhofquai

Zurich's two main rivers are the sea-green Limmat and the coffee-coloured Sihl, and at the point where they converge is the peaceful Platzspitz-Park. As its name suggests the park occupies a spit of land formed by the rivers as they flow away from the city centre. Located behind the Landesmuseum Zürich on Museumstrasse (City), the park is today rather nondescript – but don't be fooled. For the uninitiated Platzspitz-Park holds some unexpected history.

In medieval times the area occupied by Platzspitz-Park lay outside the city walls, and was used for grazing animals and for military drills. Then, in the early fifteenth century the land was made into a shooting range *(Schiessplatz)*, and during the sixteenth century target shooting competitions *(Schützenfeste)* were staged here. An echo of these can be found in Zurich's *Knabenschiessen*, a shooting competition for teenagers established in the seventeenth century. It still takes, albeit now at a shooting range in the suburb of Albisgütli, on the second weekend in September. Although the competition was originally reserved for boys – the word *Knaben* meaning boys – it has been open to girls since 1991, and is today accompanied by Switzerland's largest fun fair.

From the early eighteenth century onwards Platzspitz-Park was used for quieter, more leisurely pursuits, accounting for its older name of Platzpromenade. In 1780 it was transformed into a French-style pleasure park *(Lusthain)* with riverside avenues and imposing Plane trees (some of these original trees are still standing). Here and there were installed memorials to the city's great and the good, such as Salomon Gessner (1730–1788), who founded the *Zürcher Zeitung* newspaper in 1780, and choir director, pianist, and composer Wilhelm Baumgartner (1820–1867) (see no. 48).

The construction of Zurich Main Station (Zürich Hauptbahnhof) in 1846 brought about the end of the old park, and in 1883 it was transformed into an English-style landscape garden in which a bandstand and eventually the Swiss National Museum were erected. By the early years of the twentieth century the meeting of the waters in Platzspitz-

Platzspitz-Park is where the waters of the Limmat meet the Sihl

Park had become Irish novelist James Joyce's favourite spot in all Zurich (see no. 56).

With this in mind it is difficult to imagine the calamity that befell Platzspitz-Park during the late 1980s. Hidden from the street by the museum, the park was designated by officials as an area where drug dealing (and consequently drug usage) was deemed legal. It was an attempt not only to bring the problem out into the open and address it head on but also through the provision of pure drugs and clean syringes to contain the spread of disease. As a result the area earned the moniker of Needle Park.

An article from 1990 in the New York Times paints a picture unimaginable to today's park visitor: "about 300 to 400 heavy drug users live in the park without shelter, toilets or showers, and...as many as 3000 others pass through daily to buy and use drugs...the midway of the grotesque carnival is a concrete path along the edge of the Limmat River, lined with makeshift counters covered with neatly arranged spoons, bottles of water and paper cups bristling with slender, disposable syringes ... drug hustlers work their way through the sea of bodies clogging the path ... a woman in leather pants and stained blouse wobbled past, a bloody syringe dangling from her neck".

Needle Park was officially closed on 4th February 1992, after which the park was cleaned up ready for its reopening to the public in 1993. Since then there has been much discussion about whether the initiative was a consciously planned initiative to deal with Zurich's drug problem or else a kneejerk reaction to an overwhelming humanitarian crisis. At the time many people were reluctant to even acknowledge the problem, especially since a quarter of the addicts (and a lot more of the dealers) were foreigners. Whatever one thinks it should be borne in mind that Switzerland currently has one of the most progressive drug prevention policies in Europe, with needle exchanges and injection rooms supervised by trained staff. It is also the only country in the world to operate a widespread, government-funded programme of managed heroin prescription.

When leaving the park look out for the row of unusually monumental gardeners' sheds built in 1914 on the riverbank near the Walchebrücke. They are adorned with marine motifs and now also contain public conveniences and an Asian restaurant. A lovely fountain in the form of a maiden in diaphanous clothing is placed under a nearby plane tree.

Other places of interest nearby: 14, 15, 16

18 The Thylacine and Other Oddities

District 1 (Hochschulen), the Zoological Museum
of the University of Zurich (Zoologisches Museum
der Universität Zürich) at Karl-Schmid-Strasse 4
Tram 6, 9, 10 ETH-Universitätsspital

The University of Zurich (Universität Zürich) at Rämistrasse 71 (Hochschulen) was established in 1833. Unlike the neighbouring Swiss Federal Institute of Technology (Eidgenössische Technische Hochschule) (ETH), which is administered by the Swiss federal government, the university is a cantonal institution, with its academic focus set on applied sciences. Several of the university's departments have their own museums, and they rank as some of the most fascinating specialist museums in the city.

The Archaeological Collection of the University of Zurich (Archäologische Sammlung der Universität Zürich) at Rämistrasse 73, for example, contains non-Swiss artefacts from as far afield as Mesopotamia, Assyria, and Persia. The highlight is a collection of Roman mummy portraits from the ancient Egyptian city of Fayoum. Far more ancient are the exhibits displayed in the Palaeontology Museum of the University of Zurich (Paläontologisches Museum der Universität Zürich) at Karl-Schmid-Strasse 4. Worth seeing here is the collection of 230 million year-old fossilised marine reptiles and fish from Monte San Giorgio in Ticino, Switzerland's southernmost canton. Recalling more re-

A stuffed Thylacine
in the Zoological
Museum of the
University of Zurich
(Zoologisches Museum
der Universität Zürich)

The Barbary Lion is now extinct in the wild

cent times is the fascinating Medical History Museum of the University of Zurich (Medizinhistorisches Museum der Universität Zürich) at Rämistrasse 69. This museum illustrates the historical development of traditional and Western medicine since prehistoric times and includes everything from the accoutrements of an African witch doctor to a reuseable coffin with a hinged bottom used during the time of the Black Death.

Equally curious are some of the fifteen hundred exhibits to be found in the Zoological Museum of the University of Zurich (Zoologisches Museum der Universität Zürich) at Karl-Schmid-Strasse 4. They include the skeleton of an Ice Age mammoth (Mammuthius primigenius) reconstructed from bones recovered in Niederweningen in the Canton of Zurich. Stuffed curiosities include a rather ragged example of a Barbary Lion (Panthera leo leo), now extinct in the wild, and in front of it a Striped Polecat or Zorilla (Ictonyx striatus), which is a type of skunk from sub-Saharan Africa.

Of particular interest is a stuffed specimen of a Thylacine (Thylacinus cynocephalus), which was acquired for the museum in 1869. Thylacines once roamed mainland Australia but their numbers declined as humans settled the continent around forty thousand years ago; they declined further after the introduction of the dingo four thousand years ago. Thylacines were eventually confined to the dingo-free island of Tasmania, where they gained a bad reputation as poultry thieves. The species was consequently wiped out during a large-scale eradication effort during the nineteenth and early twentieth centuries.

The Thylacine has traditionally been described as a marsupial wolf, although recent studies have suggested the animal's hunting habits were more akin to those of a big cat. A solitary, ambush predator that could not outrun its prey over long distances it is perhaps now better described as a marsupial tiger. Studies of skeletal remains reveal that the Thylacine had a cat-like ability to rotate its front legs so that the paw faced upwards, enabling it to subdue its prey after an ambush. In this respect it resembled the Tasmanian Devil, which is the largest carnivorous marsupial alive today. Dingoes and wolves are far more restricted in their paw movements, reflecting their strategy of hunting in pursuit packs rather than by surprise. Suffice to say there is nothing quite like the Thylacine alive today, the last captive specimen, known as Benjamin, having died in Hobart Zoo in Tasmania in September 1936.

Situated at Zurich University's Irchel site is the Anthropological Institute and Museum of the University of Zurich (Anthropologisches Institut und Museum der Universität Zürich) at Winterthurerstrasse 190 (Oberstrass). The museum aims to reconstruct man's evolutionary history, and to explain man's unique features with reference to primates and other animals both living and fossilised. Needless to say the collection is dominated by skulls and skeletons.

Other places of interest nearby: 19, 20, 21, 22

19 From the Desk of Thomas Mann

District 1 (Hochschulen), the Thomas Mann Archive
at Schönberggasse 15
Tram 5, 9 Kantonsschule, 6, 9, 10 ETH-Universitätsspital

In 1956 the heirs of German novelist Thomas Mann (1875–1955) donated his literary estate, personal effects, and the furniture from his last study to the Swiss Federal Institute of Technology (ETH) in Zurich, the city where he had died a year earlier. This led to the creation of the Thomas Mann Archive (Thomas-Mann-Archiv) in a cosy seventeenth century villa at Schönberggasse 15 (Hochschulen). Open limited hours

The Thomas Mann Archive on Schönberggasse contains the author's desk

each week it is a must not only for those interested in Mann's work but also for those appreciative of the literary process at work. And it has a lovely garden with wonderful views, too!

Thomas Mann was born in 1875 in Lübeck, the second son of a grain merchant. Following his father's death in 1891 the family relocated to Munich, where Mann entered university to study literature and art (during this period he wrote for the satirical magazine *Simplicissimus*). After university Mann devoted himself exclusively to writing, and in 1901 aged just twenty-five he published his first major novel, *Buddenbrooks*. Before being banned and burned by Adolf Hitler the book sold over a million copies in Germany alone. Its success, together with that of succeeding works such as *Der Tod in Venedig* (Death in Venice), enabled Mann to purchase a riverside villa in Munich, where he lived with his wife Katia and their six children between 1914 and 1933.

Mann's second great novel, *Der Zauberberg* (The Magic Mountain), was published in 1924, and in 1929 he was awarded the Nobel Prize for literature. The first volume of his tetralogy *Joseph und seine Brüder* (Joseph and his Brothers) followed in 1933, the same year that he exiled himself to Switzerland in opposition to Hitler becoming German chancellor. He lived in Küsnacht on the eastern shore of Lake Zurich until he was encouraged to move to America in 1939, where he took up a position at Princeton University, and wrote works such as *Doktor Faustus* (Doctor Faustus) and *Der Erwählte* (The Holy Sinner).

Mann returned to Switzerland after the war and in 1948 the ruins of his Munich villa were handed back to him. He sold it and never again lived in Germany, although he travelled there regularly. In 1953 he moved to Kilchberg on the shore opposite Küsnacht. It was in Kilchberg Cemetery that he was buried in 1955 after succumbing to blocked arteries in a Zurich hospital.

The Thomas Mann Archive was established in the villa on Schönberggasse in 1961. Known as the Bodmerhaus the villa was built in 1664 and named after the Swiss-German author and critic Johann Jakob Bodmer. He lived here between 1739 and 1783 during which time he was visited by several renowned literary figures, most notably the poet Goethe (1749–1832). The archive, which is located on the second floor of the building, is home to the majority of Mann's remaining hand-written works, including manuscripts, diaries, notebooks, letters, and other documents, revealing much about the manner in which he worked. To this raw material translations, letters, photographs, and press articles have been added.

The most affecting part of the archive is undoubtedly the memorial room, which includes Mann's own writing desk, furniture, library, as well as pictures and ornaments from his former study in Kilchberg. Mann himself would undoubtedly approve of the archive's reading room next door, which is used by both staff and visitors. Between them they have made Mann's works accessible to a new generation, spreading the word about one of the twentieth century's most important novelists through a journal, yearbook, and new translations.

Alongside Thomas Mann's remains in Kilchberg are those of his wife Katia (1883–1980), and four of his six children, most of whom became literary and artistic figures in their own right: Elisabeth (1918–2002), Erika (1905–1969), Michael (1919–1977), and Monika (1910–1992). Golo Mann (1909–1994) is buried in the same cemetery but outside the family grave according to the terms of his will. Klaus Mann (1906–1949) committed suicide and is buried in Cannes.

Other places of interest nearby: 18, 20, 21, 22, 26, 28, 59

20 The Sprayer of Zurich

District 1 (Hochschulen), a graffito by Harald Naegeli
at Schönberggasse 9
Tram 5, 9 Kantonsschule (Note: the graffito is accessible from
the rear of Schönberggasse 9, or from the top of
the Rechberggarten between Hirschgraben 40 and Florhofgasse 8)

Zurich in the 1970s did much to live up to its traditional image as a
cold-hearted financial centre, where straight-laced bankers worked se-
cretively and the trams always ran on time. All was not as it seemed
though and political activism amongst Zurich's youth movements
would culminate in major riots during the early 1980s (see no. 37). It
was against this backdrop that an enigmatic Swiss graffiti artist began
leaving his mark on the city's walls and buildings.

Dubbed the "Sprayer of Zurich" he commenced work in 1977. Under
cover of the night he used black spray paint to create human figures
on both public and private buildings. The distinctively spindly figures,
which looked as if they were made out of wire, quickly became recognis-
able as the Sprayer's work.

A university building on Schönberggasse retains an original graffito by Harald Naegeli

The graffiti soon provoked a heated controversy across Switzerland. Whilst the Swiss authorities and the majority of the general public decried the figures as illegal defacement of property, intellectuals and artists saw value in them. The Sprayer would later claim later that he saw himself as a political artist, using graffiti as a means of opposing the city's increasing anonymity.

Inevitably the Swiss authorities issued an arrest warrant and The Sprayer was eventually apprehended after returning to the scene of one of his works having forgotten his glasses. At this point The Sprayer was revealed as one Harald Naegeli (b. 1939), a classically trained artist who had studied in Zurich and Paris. At the time of his arrest Naegeli was responsible for around nine hundred graffiti across Zurich.

Prior to being tried Naegeli fled to Germany where he was sentenced *in absentia* to nine months in prison and a hefty fine. Despite an appeal from lawyers, Naegeli's sentence was confirmed by the Swiss Supreme Court in November 1981, as a result of which an international arrest warrant was issued. Seventy two Swiss artists signed a petition to have Naegeli pardoned but to no avail.

For the next few years Naegeli remained in Germany, where he continued spraying his characteristic figures in Cologne and Düsseldorf. His work there caused far less of a furore and was more generally accepted. In Cologne, for example, he produced a cycle of six hundred figures nicknamed the *Kölner Totentanz* (Cologne Dance of Death), although most were removed immediately by the city's cleaning department. The mayor of Osnabrück in Lower Saxony went so far as to offer money for Naegeli to come and spray in his city although the offer was declined by Naegeli on the grounds that his artistic talents couldn't be bought.

On 27th August 1983 Naegeli was arrested on the Baltic island of Fehmarn from where he was trying to enter Denmark. Released on bail he was eventually (albeit reluctantly) extradited by Germany to Switzerland, where he served his jail sentence, and then returned to Düsseldorf. In complete contrast to his spontaneous graffiti of old Naegeli now invented a new artistic style he called *Partikelzeichnungen*, consisting of thousands of tiny dots and lines. As a result he became a well-respected artist in Germany, and even received a professorship in Cologne. Not wishing to miss out on Naegeli's unexpected celebrity the authorities in Zurich decided to recognise the worth of Naegeli's early work (which they dubbed *Schmiererei* or Scribbling) by protecting a still extant graffito to the rear of a University of Zurich building at Schönberggasse 9 (Hochschulen). Created in 1978 and called

Undine (after the elemental water sprite) the graffito was restored in 2004, when the building was renovated. At the same time later graffiti was removed, a fate suffered originally by much of Naegeli's own work.

Other places of interest nearby: 18, 19, 21, 22, 26, 28, 59

Another Naegeli graffito on Römerhof

21 A Secret Baroque Garden

District 1 (Hochschulen), the Rechberggarten between
Hirschgraben 40 and Florhofgasse 8
Tram 3 Neumarkt; Bus 31 Neumarkt

Between Hirschgraben 40 and Florhofgasse 8 in the university district of Hochschulen there is a pair of ornate wrought iron gates. They are mentioned in few guidebooks, which seems odd, since immediately beyond them lies one of Zurich's hidden gems: the Baroque garden of the former Palais Rechberg. Open free of charge to the public the recently-restored garden provides an oasis of peace and tranquillity.

The area occupied by the Rechberggarten today is first documented in 1465 as monastic land, immediately outside the former Neumarkt Gate. In the 1530s a tavern called the Haus zur Krone was in business on the site, which at the time was in the possession of muslin manufacturer Hans Kaspar Oeri, one of the wealthiest men in Zurich. Between 1759 and 1770 his daughter replaced the tavern with the grand Baroque house seen today (the relatively long building time is a reminder that construction in these days only occurred during the summer months). In 1799 during the War of the Second Coalition waged by Britain, Austria and Russia against Napoleon the building served as a military headquarters.

In 1839 the house was purchased by the Schulthess von Rechberg family, under whose auspices the garden was replanted and further adorned. Both house and garden subsequently took the family's name and remained in their possession until 1866. In 1899 the building was taken over by the University of Zurich since when it has been used for educational purposes.

An engraving of 1772 shows that the Rechberggarten had been completed by this date, and in essentially the same form as it appears today. A courtyard directly behind the house gives access to an ornate well, either side of which a flight of stairs leads up to the first of several terraces stretching as far as what is today Rämistrasse. The use of terraces to maximise the area available for planting on a sloping site such as this is a typical solution in Italianate Baroque garden design.

On the first terrace a fountain is positioned at the end of a straight path defining the main axis of the garden, either side of which are ranged identically-sized *parterre* flower beds (symmetricality was another device by which Baroque gardeners brought order to naturally awkward plots). The left-hand perimeter of the first terrace is marked by an orangery, the *Jugendstil* greenhouse on the right-hand side was added later. Behind the fountain is a retaining wall masked by neatly espaliered trees, and topped with potted shrubs.

Further stairs lead from the first terrace upwards to more terraces. The lowest is defined by a row of dwarf cypresses imbuing the garden with a distinctly Tuscan feel. In the 1772 engraving the uppermost terrace was punctuated by a garden pavilion from where to gain an overview of the entire garden but this has subsequently been lost and is now planted with trees. Despite this the original longitudinal axis of the garden is still clearly defined, with the water and the steps bringing dynamism to an otherwise rigid design.

The Baroque Rechberggarten between Hirschgraben and Florhofgasse

Other places of interest nearby: 19, 20, 21, 22, 26, 28, 29

22 The Forgotten Walls of Zurich

District 1 (Rathaus), a fragment of medieval city wall at Chorgasse 22
Tram 4, 15 Rudolf-Brun-Brücke

The casual visitor to Zurich could be fooled into thinking that the city was never protected by a defensive city wall. This is because the tangible evidence can easily be overlooked, and because Switzerland's famed neutrality would seem to militate against the need for such a thing. Armed with the right addresses, however, the interested explorer can track down evidence for three major walling phases, representing five hundred years of city history.

Until recently it was thought that Zurich was unfortified prior to the thirteenth century, except for the sturdy walls of the Roman outpost of Turicum and the subsequent Carolingian-era royal palace *(Kaiserpfalz)* of Louis the German, the remains of which lie deep beneath the Lindenhof hill (Lindenhofhügel) (see no. 1). This view was altered in the 1990s by the chance discovery of walling during construction work in the basement of the Zurich Central Library (Zentralbibliothek Zürich) at Zähringerplatz 6 (Rathaus). It now seems that Zurich was first surrounded by a circuit wall *(Stadtbefestigung)* sometime during the eleventh and twelfth centuries, although its full extent still remains unclear.

Following the extinction of the main line of the ruling Zähringer family in 1218, Zurich was placed under the authority of the Holy Roman Empire, and became a free imperial city. To celebrate this new found status a second city wall was constructed during the 1230s. Enclosing an area of thirty eight hectares the wall ran northwards along what is now Bahnhofstrasse, and returned southwards along Hirschengraben on the east side of the Limmat, the word *Graben* referring to the ditch once used to protect it in which deer *(Hirsche)* were grazed.

A sturdy chunk of this second wall lies concealed behind a doorway at Chorgasse 22 (Rathaus) (a key can be obtained on production of a passport from the Building History Archive (Baugeschichtliches Archiv) at Neumarkt 4). The wall was 2400 metres in length, and constructed using stone taken from Louis the German's abandoned palace. It was punctuated at regular intervals by gates, cylindrical towers, and projecting bastions *(Bollwerke)*, ten on the east side and thirteen on the west, with the main entrance on Rennweg (Lindenhof). An excellent impression of the wall is given by Jos Murer's detailed city plan of 1576, including thc so-called Ketzerturm, a defensive tower erected in 1314 on what is today Gräbli-Gasse. A large chunk of the tower can still be found there incorporated into the corner of a modern building.

This fragment of Zurich's medieval city wall is hidden away on Chorgasse

Not to be confused with these cylindrical towers were ten square-planned towers known as *Adelstürme* (Nobles' Towers). These freestanding towers located inside the city were built as much for show as for protection, and were used by Zurich's knightly families. Still to be seen are the Bilgeriturm and Grimmenturm on Neumarkt, the Brunnenturm on Napfgasse, the Glentnerturm on Limmatquai, the Mülnerturm on Weinplatz, and the Steinhaus on Kirchgasse.

Zurich joined the Old Swiss Confederacy in 1351, which in 1515 lost a battle against a combined force of French and Venetians. This setback prevented any further expansion, and instead the Confederacy committed itself to an early form of neutrality. This was ratified in November 1815 by Austria, France, Prussia, Great Britain, and Russia following the Congress of Vienna, and has remained the basis of foreign policy in the Swiss Confederation to this day. Switzerland has not fought a foreign war since.

During the sixteenth and seventeenth centuries, Zurich adopted an isolationist attitude, and with the start of the Thirty Years War (1618–1648) its council embarked on the construction of a third and final city wall. Commenced in 1624 the wall took the form of fifteen angular projecting bastions, encompassing a space twice that of the second wall. Within the walls ran a series of casemates, along which troops and artillery could be deployed without being seen by the enemy. A twenty metre-wide zigzag moat called the Schanzengraben, which was fed by the Limmat, was excavated to protect the west wall and this can still be seen today, the section alongside the Zur Katz bastion now used for summer bathing (see no. 82). The new eastern wall ran along the terrace on which the Federal Polytechnic Institute (Eidgenössisches Poly-

The walls of Zurich are depicted in this city model in the Haus zum Rech on Neumarkt

technikum) was built. A unique bastion, known as the Bauschänzli, was built midstream at the point where Lake Zurich (Zürichsee) empties into the Limmat, and its enormous base is still visible. All this is depicted in a fascinating model (Stadtmodell) of the walls as they appeared around 1800 in the Building History Archive (Baugeschichtliches Archiv) in the Haus zum Rech at Neumarkt 4 (Rathaus) (a virtual version is available at www.stadtmodell-zuerich.ch). The house itself is an excellent example of a medieval middle class burgher's house.

In 1648, Zurich proclaimed itself a republic, shedding its former status as a free imperial city. Napoleon's short-lived Helvetic Revolution of 1798 brought about its fall, and in the early 1800s the city and canton separated their possessions. Following the so-called *Züriputsch* in 1839, the city walls were torn down to allay rural concerns over the city's hegemony. Their destruction enabled the city to develop leaving behind the few fragments seen today.

Other places of interest nearby: 18, 19, 20, 21, 23, 25, 26, 28, 29

23   A Herd of Fibreglass Cows

District 1 (Rathaus), the Adler Cow in the Hotel Adler
at Rosengasse 10
Tram 4, 15 Rathaus

The Hotel Adler is located in the heart of Zurich's Altstadt at Rosengasse 10 (Rathaus). Although it may not look particularly special from the outside it has several unusual features. These include a rainwater toilet-flushing system, murals of Old Town scenes in each of the rooms, environmentally friendly minibars, a cast iron water fountain for dogs commemorating Zurich animal painter Rudolf Koller (1828–1905) (he spent the first ten years of his life in the hotel), and one of the city's best *fondue* restaurants (see no. 45). Oddest of all is a full-size fibreglass cow peering out from one of the balconies!

The Adler Cow, known affectionately as Heidi, may look a little out of place today but back in 1998 she was just one of a herd of around eight hundred roaming the streets of Zurich. Known as *Land in Sicht* (Land Ahoy) this unusual public art exhibit was the brainchild of artist Walter Knapp, who commissioned his son Pascal to create clay sculptures of standing, grazing, and lying cows. These were then reproduced in fibreglass, and used as canvases by local artists and displayed across the city in public places, including train stations, shops, restaurants, parks, and squares. The paintwork on each cow was unique in reflecting a specific aspect of life and culture in Zurich.

Knapp's concept was based on a similar idea dating from 1986 in which lions – the symbol of Zurich – were commissioned by shopkeepers from local artists, and also displayed on the streets. However, whereas the lions of Zurich only ever spawned the cows of Zurich, the cows have conquered the world under the trademark CowParade. After appearing on the streets of Chicago in 1999, painted fibreglass cows have cropped up regularly in cities from Tokyo to Tunis and Moscow to Mexico City. All are based on Pascal Knapp's three original sculptures and in most cases were exhibited for a year or more and then auctioned off for charity. In the case of the Adler Cow it was commissioned by the hotel as an advertising gimmick, and has remained on the balcony ever since.

The cows of Zurich have prompted many copycat projects around the world, including camels in Dubai, elephants in Hannover, penguins in Liverpool, and pigs in Seattle. There was even a display of six hundred and thirty teddy bears mounted in Zurich in 2005 under the moniker "Teddy-Summer".

Heidi the Cow looks out from the Hotel Adler on Rosengasse

Perhaps the most interesting project to be inspired by the popularity of the fibreglass cows also occurred in Zurich. In 1999 a huge storm dubbed Lothar ripped through Switzerland, leaving thousands of fallen trees in its wake. With this sudden glut of timber the authorities in Zurich decided to create a thousand public benches, each of which was decorated by a local artist and sponsored by a local company or individual. Some were unusually shaped, for example a submarine, a cake, or a crocodile, but most were just painted, with designs ranging from desert islands to aliens. After the benches had remained in place for a year

Artist Jan Leiser sitting on his fountain pen bench

they were removed and again auctioned off for charity. One of them, however, which was adorned with a series of oversized fountain pens, was retained by its original artist, Jan Leiser (b. 1958). It is displayed in his studio in a former eiderdown quilt factory at Bändlistrasse 86 (Altstetten), and can be visited by appointment (www.janleiser.ch). Coincidentally, Leiser was also responsible for the dazzling paintwork of one of the original fibreglass cows, which stands outside Zurich's Restaurant blindekuh (see no. 68).

Inside the Hotel Adler are numerous Zurich scenes painted by the artist Heinz Blum, who was responsible for decorating Heidi the cow. Blum was also commissioned to brighten up the neighbouring Rosenhof-Passage, which he did by depicting the buildings on either side of the Limmat. On a rainy day the paintings offer the pleasures of an Old Town stroll without getting wet!

Other places of interest nearby: 21, 22. 24, 25, 26, 27, 28

24   An Evening at the Aelpli Bar

District 1 (Rathaus), the Aelpli Bar at Ankengasse 5
Tram 4,
15 Rathaus

Ankengasse (Rathaus) is but one of several narrow alleyways which since medieval times have led up from the Limmat into the area known by locals as Niederdorf (or Niederdörfli). What sets Ankengasse apart is the sign hanging outside the building at number five. It depicts an alpine gentleman sucking contentedly on his pipe, and it points the way to Zurich's Aelpli Bar, where Swiss folk music and good cheer go hand in hand many nights of the year.

Walking into the Aelpli Bar is like entering another world. One is suddenly no longer in Zurich but instead high amongst the Swiss Alps. The cosy rooms are fitted out like the living rooms found in alpine regions such as Appenzeller, with wood-panelled walls and rustic furniture. In the main room a long alpine horn hangs from the ceiling and on the far wall a mural of mountain scenery adds to the effect. Indeed it's worth remembering that as one is now officially in the mountains there is no television on the wall, and transactions are cash only. No credit cards are accepted here!

The Aelpli Bar is today managed by journalist and folklore expert Martin Sebastian, under whose watchful eye it was renovated in 2007. It quickly re-established itself as a unique cult music venue. During the bar's high season between September and April a programme of professional Swiss folk music is staged from Wednesday until Saturday between 8am and 11.30pm (communal singing of traditional Swiss songs takes place each first Tuesday of the month at 8pm); during May and June there are professional performances on Fridays and Saturdays only (for details see www.aelplibar.ch). The

The Aelpli Bar on Ankengasse is a Zurich cult

rest of the time it's a free for all, with a Swiss-style accordion, contrabass, and washboard always to hand. Whatever the time of year the main room is usually filled with a merry throng of all ages.

The Aelpli Bar is renowned not only for its music but also the food and drink that accompanies it. *Raclette* and other traditional Swiss specialities are available, including macaroni cheese with apple compote *(Älplermakkaroni mit Apfelmuus)*, cheese pie *(Chäschüechli)*, and chunky garlic bread *(Knoblibrot)*. There are hearty cold platters, too, including the Aelpli-Teller (Appenzeller Bauernspeck, St. Galler salami, and Emmentaler) and the Sennen-Platte (spicy smoked Knebeli sausage from the Säntis region accompanied by slices of Emmentaler, Tilsiter, Gruyère, and St. Paulin).

And it can all be washed down with some intriguing beverages unique to the Aelpli Bar, including *Verrückte Kuh*, *Heisse Geiss*, and *Durstige Sau*. Definitely worth trying is *Aelpli-Milk*, a unique and secret recipe of the house. A rack of hollow cow horns are available for those who don't wish to drink from a glass!

Zurich boasts several other distinctive café-bars, which make a pleasant alternative to the generic venues appearing with depressing regularity in many European cities. Restaurant Café Zähringer, for example, at Zähringerplatz 11 (Rathaus) has been in existence since 1981 and is run as a collective. This makes it one of Zurich's few catering enterprises in which the staff are responsible not only for kitchen duties and waiting on customers but also for setting workers' pay and conditions. Wherever possible the collective sources the freshest raw materials from responsible local sources guaranteeing food and drink that is both tasty and ecologically friendly. Down on the riverbank at Limmat-Quai 54 is the Wings Airline Bar & Lounge, a themed venue created by a group of Swissair pilots and flight attendants after their company went bankrupt in 2001. Similarly novel is My Place at Hottingerstrasse 4 (Fluntern), where punters sit on designer furniture which they can also buy. Further north in Wipkingen the Nordbrücke at Dammstrasse 58 occupies a renovated railway station buffet, the old sofas and nicotine-stained walls sitting comfortably alongside the newly fitted bar. Kafischnaps at Kornhausstrasse 57 occupies a former hundred year old butcher's shop, the tiles of which still hang on the walls. Equally historic but much larger is the Volkshaus at Stauffacherstrasse 60 (Langstrasse), established in 1910 as Switzerland's first alcohol-free community centre. Frequented originally by the city's workers' movements, social reformers and women's associations it is today a popular concert venue. This round-up finishes with Triibhuus at Salzweg 50 (Altstetten) housed inside a pair of plant-filled greenhouses and the refreshingly modest Helsinkiklub (Helsinki Hütte) at Geroldstrasse 35 (Escher Wyss), which is located under the Hardbrücke inside part of an old gasworks. It's the perfect place to enjoy a beer and in-house bands.

Other places of interest nearby: 22, 23, 25, 26, 27, 28

25 The Remains of Dada

District 1 (Rathaus), Cabaret Voltaire at Spiegelgasse 1
Tram 4, 15 Rathaus

Escapees, dissidents, and misfits have gravitated towards Zurich since the early sixteenth century, when the city declared itself neutral and it became the centre of the Swiss Reformation. As a major centre of intellectual life, and latterly of international socialist activity, it has drawn the likes of Rosa Luxemburg, James Joyce, and Vladimir Ilych Lenin (see nos. 26 & 56). But undoubtedly the most creative arrivals have been the band of émigré artists calling themselves Dada.

Dada or Dadaism was an informal international cultural movement that began in Zurich at the outbreak of the First World War, and peaked between 1916 and 1922. Its founders were expatriates primarily from Europe, who came to Zurich in search of political and artistic freedom. Dada embraced visual arts, literature, theatre, music, dance, and graphic design in its mission to oppose war through the rejection of prevailing art standards. The Dadaists expressed their disgust with the modern world by the creation of anarchic works of anti-art. Even the name 'Dada' was an act of anti-rationalism, a childish and nonsensical word said to have been selected by inserting a knife randomly into a dictionary.

For Dadaists the root cause of the war lay in prevailing capitalist, nationalist and colonialist interests, which were reflected in a cultural and intellectual conformity in art and society. Dada sought through anti-art to oppose war by rejecting traditional culture and aesthetics. As founder Hugo Ball (1886–1927) described it, Dadaism was "an opportunity for the true perception and criticism of the times we live in".

The impetus for the birth of Dada was probably the arrival in Zurich in 1916 of a group of Jewish artists from East Europe (particularly Romania), where there was already a vibrant modernist tradition. They included Tristan Tzara and Marcel Janco, who together with predominantly German artists such as Hugo Ball and his wife Emmy Hennings, Jean Arp and his partner Sophie Täuber, Richard Huelsenbeck, and Hans Richter began staging Dada art performances in Zurich. The venue was a nightclub called Cabaret Voltaire in an upstairs room at Spiegelgasse 1 (Rathaus), where according to Janco the belief was that "Everything had to be demolished. We would begin again after the tabula rasa. At the Cabaret Voltaire we began by shocking common

The upstairs room of Cabaret Voltaire on Spiegelgasse

sense, public opinion, education, institutions, museums, good taste, in short, the whole prevailing order". The performances, like the war they were mirroring, were often raucous and chaotic, and amongst the experimental artists on stage were the likes of Kandinsky, Paul Klee, and Max Ernst.

After Ball left for Bern, Tzara emerged as the new Dada leader, and he began a tireless campaign to spread the movement's ideals, publishing several issues of the *Dada* review in the process. With the end of the war, however, the original excitement generated at Cabaret Voltaire fizzled out. Some of the Zurich Dadaists returned home, whilst others continued Dadaist activities in other cities, such as Paris, Berlin, and Cologne. Their efforts eventually helped spawn new and equally con-

A Cabaret Voltaire motif

troversial artistic genres, such as Surrealism, Social Realism, and Pop Art.

The Cabaret Voltaire still courts controversy today, having been saved from closure in 2002 by a group of neo-Dadaists, who occupied the building illegally. Despite police eviction and an attempt by the Swiss People's Party to cut funding, the building still functions as an alternative arts space; it also contains the cosy duDA bar, and a well-stocked Dada giftshop. Alongside the fireplace in the original upstairs room can be seen a small black and white picture depicting the Cabaret Voltaire in full swing, with Hugo Ball and his friends on stage, and an enthusiastic Lenin in the audience, his arm outstretched in support.

The best place to see original Dada art is in the Kunsthaus at Heimplatz 1 (Hochschule), although much of the fragile paper remains are archived and can be seen by appointment only. A visit should also be made to the Museum Bellerive at Höschgasse 3 (Seefeld), where amongst a unique collection of twentieth century marionettes there are several examples created by Sophie Täuber for the Dadaist interpretation of the opera *König Hirsch (The Stag King)*.

Other places of interest nearby: 21, 22, 23, 24, 25, 26, 28, 29

26 Lenin's Swiss Non-Revolution

District 1 (Rathaus), the house where Lenin lived
at Spiegelgasse 14
Tram 4, 15 Rathaus

Zurich was the first Swiss city to embrace the Reformation, and with the abolition of the Catholic Mass in 1525 it became a centre for dissident intellectuals from across Europe. Strict neutrality during the First World War again made Zurich a refuge for dissidents, as well as pacifists, and for several months in 1916 and 1917

HIER WOHNTE
V.21.FEBR.1916 BIS 2.APRIL 1917
LENIN
DER FÜHRER DER RUSSISCHEN
REVOLUTION

Lenin lived here on Spiegelgasse

it was home simultaneously to the avant-garde novelist James Joyce (1882–1941), émigré artists the Dadaists, and revolutionary-in-waiting Vladimir Ilych Lenin (1870–1924) (see nos. 25 & 56). Earlier, in 1889, the socialist Rosa Luxemburg (1871–1919) fled detention in Poland to study in Zurich, and even today the canton courts controversy by being a centre for those seeking assisted suicide.

Lenin arrived in Switzerland from Austria with his wife Nadia Krupskaya in 1914, assuring the authorities that he was a political exile and not an army deserter. The couple initially settled in Bern, where Lenin tried unsuccessfully to convince his Swiss comrades of the need for international revolution. As the chairman of Russia's Bolsheviks he attended several clandestine socialist conferences where he suggested that the First World War was being fought by the workers on behalf of the bourgeoisie, and that it should be used as a catalyst for an armed uprising against capitalism. His plea fell on deaf ears, and for the duration of the conflict Europe's Social Democratic parties all supported their own respective governments' war efforts.

Disappointed with what he termed Bern's "Swiss social pacifists" Lenin moved in February 1916 to Zurich. With access to the city's central library he was able to finish his work *Imperialism: The Highest Stage of Capitalism*. During this time Lenin and his wife rented a modest, two-room apartment at Spiegelgasse 14 (Rathaus), marked today by a wall plaque. A trail of interested tourists can usually be seen winding their way up the street to see it. Lenin enjoyed Zurich and in letters to his mother he recounted pleasant afternoons spent with his wife on

Lenin took coffee in the Café Odeon on Limmatquai

the lakeshore. The pair were less enamoured with the smell of sausages from a nearby factory that filled their backyard!

Lenin still dreamt of an armed popular uprising, and he continued working on his theories. Zurich's Social Democrats were more radical than those in Bern, and Lenin hoped they would be more receptive. He attended party meetings and always arrived early so that he could sit on the front row. He was careful, however, not to alienate the authorities, and worked diligently to surround himself with supporters willing to spread the word.

One of Lenin's favourite haunts in Zurich was the Café Odeon at

Limmatquai 2 (Rathaus). The place still appears much as it did when Lenin – as well as James Joyce and Einstein – frequented the place, although the clientele has changed considerably since then. The décor remains Art Nouveau in style, with rich red upholstery, sparkling chandeliers, and brass and marble fittings.

Despite Lenin's best efforts little came of his recruitment drive, and by early 1917 he was disillusioned once again. In letters to friends he complained that Zurich's leftist sympathisers were as apathetic as those in Bern. Lenin then received news of the February Revolution in Russia, and the abdication of Tsar Nicholas II. With the help of leftist colleagues in Switzerland he was given permission to return to Petrograd (St. Petersburg). On 9th April 1917 Lenin left Switzerland for good, crossing Germany without stopping in a sealed one-carriage. Although Lenin was a citizen of a country at war with Germany – namely Russia – it was in Germany's interest to allow safe passage in the hope that he would destabilise Russia. Six months later the Bolsheviks seized control following the October Revolution, and Lenin entered the history books as the leader of the world's first Communist state.

Other places of interest nearby: 21, 22, 23, 24, 25, 27, 28, 29

27 The Fountains of Zurich

District 1 (Rathaus), the Napfbrunnen fountain on Napfgasse
Tram 4, 15 Rathaus

If one gets thirsty in Zurich there's no need to find a café or a supermarket because it is quite acceptable to drink from a public fountain. And one will never have to travel far to find one because there are few cities with more fountains than Zurich. Rome is often quoted as having the most – and Kansas comes a close second – but Zurich is up there with them, indeed at the last count the Swiss city boasted a total of around twelve hundred!

The perfect place to reflect on the fountains of Zurich is the Napfbrunnen, a charming old fountain on peaceful Napfgasse (Rathaus). Installed in 1568 the fountain stood for three hundred years directly in front of the so-called Brunnenturm, a medieval noble's tower

The Napfbrunnen fountain on Napfgasse

house *(Adelsturm)* at the top end of the street (this is known because the fountain appears as such in Jos Murer's city plan of 1576) (see no. 22). Not until 1876 was the fountain moved to its present position, and in 1911 its column was replaced (the original can be found in the Landesmuseum Zürich at Museumstrasse 2 (City)). The figure on top of the column was only added in 1937, demonstrating how a purely functional fountain over time became more ornamental.

The Napfbrunnen is also of interest because it is one of over three hundred fountains in Zurich that are fed exclusively by pure spring water (the rest offer an equally potable cocktail of 70% lake water, 15% ground water, and 15% spring water, which is the same as the water in the city's taps). Today's spring water is sourced from one hundred and sixty springs in the hills surrounding Zurich, and supplemented by water from another one hundred and twenty sources in nearby valleys. All this water is fed first into a chamber, where it is tested for quality, and then passed through biological sand filters and on into the spring water network.

Spring water fountains are naturally the most ecologically sound because their water requires neither pumping nor treating. They can also guarantee a dependable water supply in times of emergency, as they are fed by a 150 kilometre-long network of pipes that

One of Zurich's Cold War-era drinking fountains

is quite separate from the normal water system. During the Cold War era in the 1970s around eighty spring water drinking fountains were installed around the city for fears that Communist infiltrators might poison the mains water supply. An example of one of these sturdy bronze cylindrical fountains by interior designer Alf Aebersold can be seen at Promenadengasse 9 (Hochschulen).

The history of Zurich's extant fountains spans some five hundred years. The earliest were purely practical, serving to supply water whilst also acting as locations for social interaction. As was the case with the Napfbrunnen, many were only adorned subsequently, becoming beloved works of street art in the process. The Amazonenbrunnen on Rennweg is somewhat different. Installed in 1530 it was one of Zurich's first public fountains, and used spring water brought by pipeline from the Albisrieden hills. It is unusual in having been adorned with figures from an early date, and is depicted as such in Murer's plan. It is interesting to note that such figures from Greek mythology were often used to adorn Zurich's fountains after flamboyant religious adornments had been forbidden under the Reformation. As a result Zurich was for a time dubbed "Athens on the Limmat" (Limmat-Athen).

Other places of interest nearby: 22, 23, 24, 25, 26, 28, 29, 30

28   A Much Used Monastery

District 1 (Rathaus), the former Barfüsserkloster
on Obmannamtsgasse
Tram 3 Neumarkt; Bus 31 Neumarkt

An intriguing fragment of old Zurich can be glimpsed at through a glass foyer on Obmannamtsgasse (Rathaus). Consisting of an arcaded cloister surrounding a pretty garden it is all that remains of the so-called Barfüsserkloster, Zurich's former Franciscan monastery. In the eight centuries since its construction this once extensive structure has served a variety of very different purposes.

The Barfüsserkloster was founded by the discalced ('barefoot') Franciscan order during the 1240s (in reality they wore sandals). It was situated in the southeastern corner of the medieval walled city, between the Neumarkt and Linden gates. In 1336 Rudolf Brun (c. 1290–1360), Zurich's first independent mayor, established the city's guild laws *(Zunftordnung)* here, diluting the power of the nobles and empowering the city's workers (see no. 10).

The monastery as it appeared three hundred years later can be seen in the so-called Murerplan of 1576, a copy of which is displayed in the nearby Haus zum Rech at Neumarkt 4. This extremely detailed map of Zurich by Jos Murer (1530–1580) shows the aspect of all the town's buildings. Today's Gothic arcaded cloister installed during the fourteenth century is clearly depicted, flanked by multi-storey ancillary buildings on either side. In one of these was the monastery church with a three-aisled, columned basilica measuring sixty six by twenty two metres.

The Swiss Reformation of 1524 brought life at the flourishing monastery to a sudden end, and the buildings were secularized (see no. 3). For a while the monastery church suffered the ignominy of being used as a grain depot. Then, in 1532 the monastery buildings became the headquarters of those overseeing the nationalisation of Zurich's former monastic estates. The buildings remained more or less intact until 1807, when a neo-Classical building containing a concert hall and a ballroom was erected over part of the site.

The greatest change came in 1832 with the construction of the Aktientheater, Zurich's first municipal theatre, and the predecessor of Zurich's Opera House (Opernhaus Zürich). Built on the site of the church it resulted in the loss of much of the original monastic fabric. Later still, in 1874 the concert hall and ballroom was converted into

Zurich's cantonal High Court (Obergericht), and two sides of the cloister were lost (these have subsequently been replaced). This building is still in use as a court today and is the only post-monastic structure still in use on the original site. The theatre meanwhile was destroyed by fire in 1890, and its former location is now occupied by a car park.

All that remains of the Barfüsserkloster is this cloister on Obmannamtsgasse

Recent archaeological excavations have revealed numerous details regarding the various structures that have occupied the site, including the foundations of the medieval monastery church. Graves found inside the church are thought to be those of nobles, who according to medieval custom were buried inside rather than in the surrounding graveyard. Also revealed was evidence for the elaborate heating system once used to keep the audience warm in the Aktientheater. This would certainly have been appreciated by the eight hundred people who attended a performance of Mozart's *Magic Flute (Zauberflöte)* here on opening night in November 1834.

Historians have long valued the detailed maps and drawings of Zurich-born cartographer Jos Murer (1530–1580). His own home – the Haus zum Nägeli – is still standing on Rüdenplatz (Rathaus), where a likeness of Murer can be seen carved into the exterior woodwork. Needless to say, the house appears in Murer's Zurich map, the so-called Murerplan of 1576. Also clearly depicted is another of Zurich's former religious houses, the Frauenkloster Oetenbach, a Dominican convent erected in the 1280s and dissolved during the Reformation. It stood immediately north of the Lindenhof hill (Lindenhofhügel), where today stands the Urania underground garage, which contains an information board.

Other places of interest nearby: 20, 21, 22, 23, 25, 27, 29

29 The Prettiest House in Zurich?

District 1 (Rathaus), the Villa Tobler at Winkelwiese 4
Tram 3, 5, 8, 9 Kunsthaus, Bus 31 Kunsthaus

It says something about a city when there are too many candidates for its prettiest house. That's certainly the case with Zurich, where a dozen or more magnificent villas vie for pole position. A cluster of them are located on the east bank of Lake Zurich (Zürichsee), including the neo-Renaissance Villa Bleuler, the English-style Villa Egli, the neo-Classical Villa Wegmann, and the exotic Villa Patumbah (see no. 67). Others, such as the Villa Wesendonck, Park-Villa Rieter and the Villa Schönberg, stand in Rieterpark on the west bank (see no. 33). This author's favourite, however, is the Villa Tobler, and it can be found tucked away behind high garden walls at Winkelwiese 4 (Rathaus).

The Villa Tobler was built between 1852 and 1855 for the wealthy banker Jakob Tobler-Finsler (1810–1898), who contrary to urban myth had nothing to do with the similar-sounding Swiss chocolate bar! The location was on the so-called *Wallgelände*, the land where Zurich's medieval walls once stood (see no. 22). Architect Gustav Albert Wegmann (1812–1858) chose to render the building in the style of a neo-Classical mansion, with elegant iron balconies festooned today with trailing plants. Between 1898 and 1901 the house was reworked as an Italianate *palazzo* through the addition of a belvedere tower by Conrad von Muralt (1859–1928).

Little remains of the original interior because around the time the building was reworked so was the interior, for Tobler's son Emil (1850–1923). The Swiss artist Hans Eduard von Berlepsch-Valendas (1849–1921), who had been educated in Zurich under star architect Gottfried Semper (1803–1879), was commissioned to provide what would be Zurich's most beautiful *Art Nouveau* interior. All the main rooms – entrance hall, grand staircase, dining room, library, and smoking salon – were transformed by the addition of huge, petal-shaped window frames, gilded wallpapers, carved wooden ceilings, wall fountains, and other sumptuous details. Although the villa itself is not open to the public, a lucky few will get to glimpse the elegant interior since it is used today as offices. It is also possible to gain a glimpse the grand staircase through the windows in the main door!

The garden of the villa is also a joy, especially since it is open for

The delightful Villa Tobler on Winkelwiese

public viewing during office hours. Restored in 2000 it retains its original English-style layout, and is the perfect place to spend a quiet lunch break, reading a book beneath one of the venerable Copper Beech (Blutbuche) trees, or perhaps sitting at the edge of the fountain, with its exquisitely carved dragon's head. Above and behind the fountain is a pergola beneath which stands an accomplished bronze figure by Swiss sculptor Richard Kissling (1848–1919) (he is better known for the Es-

The dragon fountain in the garden of the Villa Tobler

cher fountain in front of the Zurich Main Station (Zürich Hauptbahnhof) (see no. 15)). Beneath the trees are planted shade-loving hellebores, foxgloves, cyclamens, and ferns, as would be found in an English garden a century ago.

It is difficult today to imagine that by the early 1960s both villa and garden were in a dilapidated condition and threatened with demolition. Fortunately, in 1964 the City of Zurich stepped in and rescued the property, handing over ownership to a Zurich art association, who rent out the building's *belle étage* for events. Also based at the villa is the Theater an der Winkelwiese, a small avant garde theatre group that has used the cellar for performances since the 1960s. The group was founded by the actress, feminist, and political activist Maria von Ostfelden (1896–1971), and a wall plaque to this effect can be found on an outside wall.

Other places of interest nearby: 25, 26, 27, 28, 30, 31

30 Some Stories from Trittligasse

District 1 (Rathaus), a walk along Trittligasse
Tram 4, 15 Ielmhaus; 2, 5, 8, 9, 11 Bellevue

Trittligasse is a narrow medieval passage lined with modest, two-storey houses. Documented as early as 1489 it is first mentioned by name in 1790, the word *Trittli* being the vernacular for steeply rising steps. It has been cobbled since the seventeenth century, and until the early nineteenth century it was a bustling centre for hand working and crafts. Although quiet today the street was once a densely populated area of town. Records for the house at Trittligasse 4, for example, show that it was once occupied by a couple with three children and several servants, another couple with four children, and a widow and her daughter. Medieval living conditions were obviously more cramped than they are today!

A parrot is perched over the doorway at Trittligasse 2

Of particular interest is the wooden parrot perched over the doorway at Trittligasse 2, which was placed there in the twentieth century. An accompanying inscription states that the house is called Zum Sitkust. The antiquarian Heinrich Fries in his book *Im Zürcher Oberdorf* (as the surrounding area between the Grossmünster and Rämistrasse is called) refers to *Psittacus*, the reason being that the first documented owner of the building, Jacobus Rufus (d. 1321), owned a real parrot, and another word for parrot in the German language is *Sittich* (meaning parakeet), whence *Psittacus* and *Sitkust* are both derived.

But there is more to this building than parrots. It was later inhabited by Heinrich Schüpfer and his son Rudolf, who opposed the power-greedy mayor of Zurich Rudolf Brun (c. 1290–1360) (see no. 10). In 1350 The Schüpfers were killed together with twenty six others during the *Zürcher Blutnacht*. Later still the Zurich mayor Hans Waldmann (1435–1489) occupied the house. He ruled Zurich harshly, enforcing austerity on the people whilst living his own life extravagantly (he owned Dü-

Trittligasse is a street full of history and charm

belstein Castle, the ruins of which lie on the northeastern slope of the Adlisberg, just outside Zurich's city boundary). Waldmann ordered that people living in the countryside surrounding Zurich kill the townspeople's dogs, lest they disturb Waldmann's hunting pleasure. Eventually the people rose up against him, and Waldmann was beheaded on 6th April 1489. Despite this a nearby street is named after him, and an imposing equestrian statue of the man rears up in front of the Fraumünster. When Waldmann's house was cleared out it was found to contain 30000 Gulden, 32000 litres of wine, 500 sacks of cereal, seventy pieces of silver cutlery, and plenty of fine clothes.

Elsewhere on Trittligasse are numerous other colourful house names: Rosenkranz, Sonnenzirkel, Sonnenberg, Drei Rosen, Rote Rose, Schwarze Linde, and Goldenes Lämmlein. One of them warrants special attention. During the 1560s the house Rehböckli at number 26 was home to Johannes Stumpf (1500–1577/78), author of the first history of Switzerland. Known as the Stumpf-Chronik it contains around four thousand wood engravings, and was printed by Christoph Froschauer (c. 1490–1564). Stumpf was a friend and admirer of the Swiss Protestant reformer Huldrych Zwingli (1484–1531), whose German translation of the Bible was also printed by Froschauer (see no. 2).

After leaving Trittligasse be sure to walk along charming Neustadtgasse, where at number 5 can be seen an old door adorned with three bell pulls, one for each of the building's three occupants!

Other places of interest nearby: 27, 28, 29, 31, 32

31 An Old Private Cemetery

District 1 (Hochschulen), the Hohe Promenade Private Cemetery
(Privatfriedhof Hohe Promenade) on Carolin-Farner-Weg
Tram 5, 8, 9 Kunsthaus; Bus 31 Kunsthaus

Until the early nineteenth century, Zurich's dead were sometimes laid to rest in a leafy cemetery on Anna-Gasse (City), within the city walls between Bahnhofstrasse and Sihlstrasse. The cemetery is long gone now, although a Chapel of St. Anna (St. Anna-Kapelle) is still there, with an empty green space concealed behind it.

Zurich's oldest extant public burial ground is the Hohe Promenade Cemetery (Friedhof Hohe Promenade), which opened in 1848 *outside* the city walls on the so-called Promenadenhügel. Graves once filled the space between Hohe Promenade and Promenadengasse (Hochschulen), the latter marked by a Gothic funerary chapel. Visitors to the site today, however, will find it much changed from how it appeared during the second half of the nineteenth century.

A headstone in the Hohe Promenade Private Cemetery (Privatfriedhof Hohe Promenade)

The funerary chapel at Promenadengasse 1, which formed the entrance to the cemetery, was designed by the Swiss architect Ferdinand Stadler (1813–1870). Stadler was the first teacher of structural design at Zurich's Federal Polytechnic Institute (Eidgenössisches Polytechnikum) – today the Swiss Federal Institute of Technology (Eidgenössische Technische Hochschule) (ETH) – and was particularly interested in church architecture. He was also an early proponent of the backwards-looking Historicist style, and as such enjoyed adorning his buildings with neo-Romanesque and neo-Gothic ornament. The funerary chapel on Promenadengasse was no exception, and being Stadler's first neo-Gothic building it featured characteristic tall Gothic windows and spiky rooftop finials.

Between 1881 and 1895 the chapel was rented by the Catholic church, at which time the stone-built structure received a smooth plastered finish. Then in 1895 a stone-built choir and vestry were added at one end of the building, in preparation for it being handed over to Zurich's English-speaking Anglican community for use as a church. Since the building would no longer function as an entrance to the cemetery the doorway on Promenadegasse was converted into an extra window on that side of the building. The chapel opened as a church dedicated to St. Andrew in 1896, and has been known as the English Church (Englische Kirche) ever since, although local residents quickly forbade the new incumbents from ringing any church bells!

Not long afterwards in 1912 the cemetery was closed down and much of it was cleared as larger municipal cemeteries were opened elsewhere. Beyond the church, where once mourners would enter the graveyard, a girls' school was built (Töchterschule). It is still there today albeit in a more up-to-date building and with a different name (Kantonsschule Hohe Promenade).

It would be easy to think that the old cemetery now exists only in the history books but this would be wrong. In a leafy glade between Hohe Promenade and Schanzengasse a part of the original burial ground still remains. It can be glimpsed at from Carolin-Farner-Weg, unmarked on most street maps. A pair of grand wrought iron gates can be found here, each adorned with a winged hourglass signifying the passage of time and the transience of life. But the gates are locked since this fragment of the old cemetery was always private. Known as the Hohe Promenade Private Cemetery (Privatfriedhof Hohe Promenade) it was the first cemetery in Zurich in which grave plots had to be acquired through the city's land registry and not rented. Still run that way today the cemetery is a peaceful corner of old Zurich that has held out against the encroachment of modern times.

Other places of interest nearby: 27, 28, 29, 30, 32

32 Burning the Böögg

District 1 (Hochschulen), the Sechseläuten festival
on Sechseläutenplatz
Tram 2, 5, 8, 9, 11 Bellevue; Bus 912, 916

Being Switzerland's financial capital may have given Zurich a staid reputation but when it comes to exciting street festivals it is more than a match for other European cities. Fasnacht in February, for instance, is a boisterous Lenten affair, followed by the triennial Züri Fäscht in July, and the colourful Street Parade in August, one of Europe's biggest street festivals. Zurich is also home to the Caliente, the largest celebration of Latin American culture in the German-speaking world. But it is the city's traditional spring festival, the curiously-named Sechseläuten, which is the most dramatic.

The origins of Sechseläuten stretch back to medieval times, when Zurich's trade guilds controlled the city (see no. 10). The length of the working day was strictly regulated, finishing at nightfall in winter, and in summer when the church bells tolled six o'clock. The first day of summertime working hours was a cause for celebration in the city's

guildhalls *(Zunfthäuser)* because it meant that workers gained a few precious hours of daylight leisure time each evening. This explains why the celebrations were called Sechseläuten, or Six O'Clock Bells.

Sechseläuten has been celebrated in its current form each April since the early twentieth century. The festivities commence with the Procession of the Guilds (Zug der Zünfte), which comprises several thousand men in historical costume, together with hundreds of horses, carriages, and musicians (despite Swiss women having gained the vote in 1971 they are still not permitted to join the guilds, and so cannot take part in the procession; their own

Burning the Böögg is the highlight of the Sechseläuten festivities

Fraumünsterzunft is not recognised by the traditional guilds). The procession winds its way through the streets of the Altstadt and arrives at 6pm in the suitably-named Sechseläutenplatz (Hochschulen) on the shore of Lake Zurich (Zürichsee). Guildsmen on horseback then gallop around a huge pre-prepared bonfire, on the top of which is a straw effigy in the form of a giant snowman. Known as the Böögg the effigy represents Winter, and its burning symbolises the welcome return of Spring. With the same etymology as the English word Bogeyman, a Böögg was originally a masked figure doing mischief and frightening children during the Lenten carnival season.

The combination of the Sechseläuten parade and the burning of a Böögg was introduced in 1902. Since then it is customary to stuff the Böögg's head with fireworks, and onlookers await eagerly the inevitable explosion. Popular tradition maintains that the length of time between the lighting of the fire and the explosion of the head is indicative of the coming summer: a quick explosion means warm, sunny weather, whereas a long wait signifies a wet and cold summer. The shortest time on record was 5:07 minutes in 1974, and the longest was in 2001 at 26:23 minutes.

Between 1902 and 1951 Sechseläuten was held on the first Monday following the vernal equinox. On that day the bell in the Church of St. Peter (St.-Peters-Kirche) on St.-Peter-Hofstatt tolled for the first time in the year, marking the change in working hours. From 1952 onwards the date of the celebration moved to the third Monday in April, and because of the introduction of Summer Time in 1981 the lighting of the fire now also occurs later than 6pm.

It is interesting to note that Sechseläuten often falls within a week of May 1st, creating a stark contrast between the guild-dominated Sechseläuten and the working class holiday of May Day. This has led to several confrontations including the abduction of the Böögg by Left Wing activists in 2006. Only in Zurich!

Other places of interest nearby: 29, 30, 31

33 When Wagner Came to Stay

District 2 (Enge), the villas of the Rieter-Park
at Seestrasse 110
Tram 7 Museum Rietberg

One of Zurich's loveliest public green spaces is the Rieter-Park at Seestrasse 110 (Enge) on the west bank of Lake Zurich (Zürichsee). Within this leafy parkland stand no less than three grand villas. Once private they are owned today by the City of Zurich, which uses them to house one of Switzerland's few museums dedicated to non-European art (Museum für außereuropäische Kunst). Fortunately for visitors the internationally-renowned collection is usually referred to by the easier-to-remember name of Museum Rietberg!

The magnificent neo-Classical Villa Wesendonck at Gabler-strasse 15 was erected in 1857 for the wealthy silk merchant Otto von Wesendonck and his poetess wife Mathilde. In 1852 the pair encountered the composer Richard Wagner (1813–1883) and his wife Minna, who had fled to Zurich following the 1849 May Uprising in Dresden. Otto was a great admirer of Wagner, and in 1856 offered him the use of a cottage on the Wesendonck estate. During this time Wagner became well acquainted with Mathilde Wesendonck and used her poems in his *Wesendonck Lieder*, a five-song cycle composed whilst working simultaneously on *Die Walküre*. Some commentators claim that Wagner and Mathilde had an affair. Whatever the truth their mutual infatuation

The Villa Wesendonck
is today a part of the
Museum Rietberg

This Japanese theatre mask is displayed in the Smaragd museum extension

contributed to the intensity of the first act of *Die Walküre*, as well as having a discernible effect on Mathilde's poems during this period. Incidentally, Wagner once sang the first act of his *Die Walküre* in Zurich's luxurious Baur au Lac hotel, accompanied by Franz Liszt on piano!

In 1872 the Wesendonck's sold their mansion and gardens to the family of cotton manufacturer Adolf Rieter; it was during this period that the German Emperor Wilhelm II (1888–1918) stayed for several nights as a guest. At the end of the Second World War the City of Zurich acquired the villa and park, and renovated both. Around the same time the City was bequeathed the private non-European sculptural collection of Baron Eduard von der Heydt (1882–1964), and it was decided to house it in the villa, as a result of which the Museum Rietberg opened in 1952.

The collection is today spread across four different buildings. The Villa Wesendonck is used to display religious and ceremonial objects from America, India, Oceania, and Southeast Asia (as well as some unsettling Shrovetide masks from Switzerland). In Room 28 amongst the wonderful Buddhist art from India and Pakistan is the bronze statue of a four-armed dancing Shiva, surrounded by a ring of fire.

An underground extension to the museum was opened alongside the villa in 2007, more than doubling the exhibition space. Designed by Alfred Grazioli and Adolf Krischanitz it is called the *Smaragd* (an allusion to a poem by Mathilde Wesendonck used in Wagner's third song), and is entered by means of a green glass pavilion. Of particular note amongst the African, Japanese and Chinese holdings is the Han Dynasty bronze horse in Room 2, the colourful glazed Tan Dynasty figurines in Room 4, the seventeenth century Noh theatre masks in Room 11, and the large cloisonné Ming jar in Room 7.

On the two floors of the nearby Park-Villa Rieter are displayed exquisite examples of Islamic, Persian and Indian paintings, prints, and calligraphy. The collection of North Indian miniatures is one of the world's finest.

In the northern part of the park at Gablerstrasse 14 stands the fourth and final element in the museum complex. The red-brick Villa Schönberg was built in the late nineteenth century by the Rieter family, and remained in private hands until the 1970s. Narrowly escaping demolition it too was acquired by the City of Zurich, and is used today as a specialist non-lending library. Worth noting are the orangery, grotto, and turret-shaped pavilion in the garden, as well as a bust of Wagner lurking amongst the shrubbery.

Another charming former private estate lies between Rieter-Park and Lake Zurich. Belvoirpark at Seestrasse 125 was purchased in 1826 by Heinrich Escher, who erected a neo-Classical villa there. His railway-building son Alfred (1819–1882), whose memorial fountain stands in front of Zurich Main Station (Hauptbahnhof Zürich), later occupied the villa, which like those in Rieter-Park was eventually acquired by the City of Zurich. The park is today open to the public and the villa serves as a restaurant and school of catering.

Other places of interest nearby: 34

34 A Centre for Succulents

District 2 (Enge), the Succulent Collection (Sukkulentensammlung) at Mythenquai 88
Tram 7 Brunaustrasse; Bus 161, 165 Sukkulenten-Sammlung

The suburban quarter of Enge lies on the western shores of Lake Zurich (Zürichsee). For the most part a residential area it numbers amongst its attractions the Museum Rietberg and the Seebad Enge lido (see nos. 33 & 82). On the same road as the lido, however, there is something quite unique for Switzerland: one of the largest and most important collections of succulent plants in the world!

Zurich's Succulent Collection (Sukkulentensammlung) at Mythenquai 88 is easy to find since the nearby bus stop is named after it. The collection was inaugurated in September 1931 after Jules Brann, a local department store owner, donated an already renowned collection of succulents to the City of Zurich, which still maintains it to this day.

The statistics for the current collection are impressive: 50 000 individual plants representing 6500 species from more than eighty botanical families, displayed across an area of 4750 square metres, including six show houses, 700 square metres of glasshouses (for acclimatization, breeding, over-wintering, and protection), 550 square metres of heated bedding frames, as well as open-air rockeries for frost-hardy plants. There is also an extensive seed collection and a herbarium containing 14 000 dried plant specimens for botanical reference and research. Little wonder that the collection is the official repository for the International Organisation for Succulent Plant Study (IOS)

The taxonomy of the plants on display can be complex but need not concern most visitors, who will be more than happy just to marvel at some of the most curiously shaped plants in the world. Representing every arid region on earth they include towering prickly cacti, lethally spiked *Agaves*, rosette-shaped *Aloes*, *Euphorbias* exuding bitter milky juice, and tropical *Epiphytes* suspended from the glasshouse ceilings. Probably the most curiously-shaped is the Blue Candle cactus (Myrtillocactus geometrizans) from Central America, which because it is prone to abnormal growth patterns at its tips is nicknamed "Dinosaur Back".

Some very basic botanical knowledge will certainly enhance a visit to the Succulent Collection. Most importantly it should be borne in mind that whilst cacti are classed as succulents, not all succulents are cacti. The word succulent is a descriptive term for plants living in dry areas of the tropics and subtropics, such as steppes, deserts, sea coasts, and dry lakes. They have adapted to high temperatures and low precipitation by storing water in their leaves or stems, enabling them to survive long periods of drought. Cacti form a distinct group of succulents known as *Cactaceae* but it is not their spines that create the distinction, since some cacti are smooth (like most *Lophophoras*) and there are some prickly succulents (such as *Agaves* and *Euphorbias*). Classification is made not on external characteristics such as the presence of spines or leaf shape but rather on the basis of their reproductive systems. All cacti have spine cushions known as areoles, which usually appear like small, fluffy cotton-like protrusions. The spines, hairs, branches, and flowers of a cactus will only grow out of these cushions, whereas the prickly parts of other succulents exhibit an entirely random growth pattern.

Twenty percent of the collection's plant holdings come from a variety of horticultural origins, with forty five percent hailing from the wild, mainly in the form of seeds. The rest come predominantly from seed obtained through controlled pollination and the propagation of plant cuttings. Flowering time for many of the plants in the col-

Sempervivum is a rosette-shaped succulent

A striking specimen in the Succulent Collection
(Sukkulentensammlung) in Enge

lection is between May and June, although some are still blooming in September. Most unusual of all is the night-blooming *Selenicereus grandiflorus* from Central America. Known also as the "Queen of the Night" it starts its annual bloom at dusk and has finished by dawn. It is considered so unusual that the blooming is announced on local radio, and the collection remains open all night for visitors (for blooming times visit www.foerderverein.ch).

Other places of interest nearby: 33

35 How Saffa Island Got its Name

District 2 (Wollishofen), the Island of Saffa (Saffa-Insel)
on Mythenquai
Tram 7 Bahnhof Wollishofen; Bus 161, 165 Bahnhof
Wollishofen

Just north of the Wollishofen shipyard, where the ferries of the Lake Zurich Shipping Company (Zürichsee Schifffahrtsgesellschaft) are docked, lies the tiny Island of Saffa (Saffa-Insel) (see no. 36). Connected to the shore by a bridge, and with little to distinguish it beyond a clump of trees, it's not much to look at. The island's unusual name, however, recalls a very interesting story.

Saffa today is an island for all seasons: in summer it is popular with bathers, in autumn it doubles as a theatre stage, and in winter, when the lake is frozen, it provides a welcome feeding ground for swans and ducks. Hard to imagine then that barely more than fifty years ago the island didn't exist at all.

So what does Saffa mean? Is it perhaps Greek, or has it some connection to Saffron? Definitely not. Saffa is an acronym for the Schweizerische Ausstellung für Frauenarbeit (Swiss Exhibition for Women's Work), which took place on the shoreline here between 17th July and 15th September 1958. Material excavated for the construction of the exhibition buildings was not taken away but rather dumped offshore, together with material from the excavation of the Enge road tunnel, creating Saffa Island in the process. The exhibition's landmark was a thirty five-metre high, eight storey tower erected immediately north of the island on the so-called Landiwiese. Visible for miles around the tower acted as an advertisement for the exhibition, which the locals dubbed *Frauenlandi* (Women's Land).

The exhibition, the second of its type after an earlier one staged in Bern in 1928, was organised by numerous women's groups and was a major national event. Its purpose was to illustrate the position and importance of Swiss women in the family, the workplace, and in Swiss society as a whole. With a daily programme of concerts, congresses, and other events it proved a great success, attracting two million visitors. Inside the tower were constructed a series of rooms in which the many and varied rôles of Swiss women in the 1950s were represented, from the young apprentice in her rented room and the well-to-do housewife in her detached family home to the retired lady in an old people's home.

The novel idea for the tower came from the exhibition's female chief architect, Annemarie Hubacher. Her celebration of womanhood was an early stab at Swiss feminism, although it may now appear tame to some. Notably it still clung to the traditional three-phase model laid out for women – training for a career, motherhood, and the return to gainful employment. Hubacher typified the situation for some women at the time in that she was thirty seven years of age, a mother of two and expecting a third, and a partner in her husband's architectural practice.

Men were also represented in the exhibition – and again in a stereotypical manner. Alongside the nearby railway a cable-car was erected for male visitors, as well as an artificial petrol station, a punch bag, and a rifle range. One must remember that women were still in the thrall of men, and that prior to the exhibition an attempt at granting Swiss women the right to vote had been rejected.

Hubacher was no political activist though and it seems unfair she was criticised for not pushing female emancipation farther with her exhibition. Her son, however, was incisive about her lot as a Swiss woman: "Sie war immer beides: Familien- und Berufsmensch, aber doch vor allem – mit Leib und Seele Architektin" (She was always both: a family and a career person, but above all with love and soul an architect). On a personal level he was referring to the fact that architecture ran in the family's blood, one of their ancestors being Zurich city architect Gustav Gull (1858–1942) (see nos. 13 & 14). On a broader level he was speaking for many Swiss women who juggled with varying degrees of success their rôles as wife, mother, and professional woman.

Swiss women eventually gained the right to vote in 1971 (despite it being one of the demands of a general strike as far back as 1918), and a triumphant bronze statue by Swiss sculptor Hermann Haller (1880–1950) entitled *Mädchen mit erhobenen Händen* (Girl with Raised Hands) still reminds the passer-by of the part Saffa Island played in the process (see no. 71). Quite by coincidence, an equally triumphant but far smaller work called *Mädchen im Wind* (Girl in the Wind) by German artist Otto Münch (1885–1965) has graced the nearby main road since 1936, when it was placed there by the City of Zurich. It is one of the most charming but little-known public sculptures in Zurich.

Against the odds several Swiss women have left an important impression on their country during the twentieth century, especially in

Zurich. They include Paulette Brup-bacher (1880–1967), who promoted the rights of mothers and wives despite a ban on her speaking publically; she is recalled together with her husband in a monument in the church cemetery in Höngg (see no. 80). Another woman who encountered problems in her work was Emilie Kempin-Spyri (1853–1901), niece of the *Heidi* author Johanna Spyri. She was the first Swiss woman to graduate in Law but denied access to the bar because of her gender; an artwork in her memory by the artist Pipilotti Rist (b. 1962) can be found in the courtyard of the University of Zurich (Universität Zürich). Despite these events being a long time ago women are still not allowed to join Zurich's guilds *(Zünfte)* (see no. 32).

Hermann Haller's triumphant sculpture identifies the Island of Saffa (Saffa-Insel)

It was the brave women of Zurich who defended the Lindenhof against attack by the Habsburg Duke Albrecht I (1282–1308) as far back as 1292; at the time the men of Zurich were away waging a battle in Winterthur. The episode is recalled by the Hedwig Fountain (Hedwig-Brunnen) on the Lindenhof (1688), which since 1912 has included the helmeted figure of a female warrior.

Other places of interest nearby: 33, 34, 36, 37

36　The Emperor's Paddle Steamer

District 2 (Wollishofen), the *Stadt Zürich* paddle steamer
at Wollishofen shipyard on Mythenquai
Tram 7 Bahnhof Wollishofen; Bus 161, 165 Bahnhof
Wollishofen

It is a little-known fact that Europe's first iron-hulled ship was the steam ferry *Minerva*, which made its inaugural cruise across Lake Zurich (Zürichsee) on 19th July 1835. Many vessels have worked the lake since then, and the ferries of the Lake Zurich Shipping Company (Zürichsee-Schifffahrtsgesellschaft) are still an iconic part of the Zurich scene. In amongst the modern ferries, however, there is one especially historic vessel. Built a little over a century ago the *Stadt Zürich* is the oldest paddle steamer *(Raddampfer)* on the lake and a piece of floating history.

When not racing from port to port the *Stadt Zürich* can be found moored at the shipping company's harbour on Mythenquai in Wollishofen (Wollishofen Schiffstation). A visit to the dock around 7am or 7pm provides the opportunity of having the vessel to one's self (albeit viewed from the path overlooking the harbour) as opposed to sharing it with the 750 passengers it can hold when in service.

The *Stadt Zürich* was built for the Lake Zurich Shipping Company by the Zurich engineering firm Escher, Wyss & Cie. Launched on 8th May 1909 she was the thirty second commercial ferry on Lake Zurich after the *Minerva*. Her maiden voyage took place on 12th June and immediately it was clear she was something special. Like her sister vessel the *Stadt Rapperswil* (1914), also built to satisfy the increasing popularity of lake steamers, she had several novel features, including a spacious Art Nouveau-style First Class saloon on the upper deck, and short smoke stacks. In her first year of service the *Stadt Zürich* sailed over twelve thousand kilometres, and burned over two hundred and fifty thousand kilos of coal.

Although many cantonal and municipal dignitaries sailed on the maiden voyage of the *Stadt Zürich*, undoubtedly the vessel's most famous passenger was German Emperor Wilhelm II (1888–1918). On the evening of 4th September 1912 he boarded the steamer with his retinue and made a tour of the lake. The vessel was adorned with flowers, strict dress regulations were applied, and tea and German beer were

The paddle steamer *Stadt Zürich* in the harbour at Wollishofen

served. Fireworks were let off along the shoreline as the vessel steamed by. It is interesting to note that stoker Jakob Stampfer was replaced for the evening because of his anti-imperial and Social Democratic political views.

During the First World War ferry services on Lake Zurich were reduced, and in December 1918 stopped altogether by the Swiss Federal Council because the country was unable to import coal. Services resumed in 1919, and between 1922 and 1939 the *Stadt Zürich* was overhauled on several occasions, receiving new boiler tubes and new paddle wheels. In 1938 the vessel was fitted for the first time with electric heating.

During the Second World War the boilers of the *Stadt Zürich* were kept filled around the clock and her engines in perfect running condition in readiness for possible military activity. Her services were not required and instead she was upgraded from coal to oil in 1951, at which point her original crew of eight was reduced. It was also during the 1950s that the sun awning on the upper deck was replaced by a solid roof, and the original Art Nouveau salon fittings stripped out.

By the 1980s the two paddle steamers were the last of their type, and had been replaced for daily ferry services by modern diesel-powered vessels. The old steamers were not to be abandoned though, and

The engine room of the *Stadt Zürich*

instead the Lake Zurich Shipping Company decided to preserve and restore them, and to use them for special services. It was at this time that the interior of the *Stadt Zürich* was lovingly restored to its original appearance. Further upgrades occurred in 2003 with the result that today both vessels offer the thrill of travel by paddle steamer combined with all the comforts of a modern ferry. Still going strong a century after her launch the *Stadt Zürich* has now travelled more than seven hundred thousand kilometres!

Another relic of the steam age is the little locomotive *Schnaagi Schnaagi* built in 1899. It runs on the last Sunday of the month between April and October along the Sihl Valley between Bahnhof Wiedikon and Sihlwald (www.museumsbahn.ch).

Other places of interest nearby: 35, 37

37   When Zurich was *Zureich*

District 2 (Wollishofen), the Rote Fabrik at Seestrasse 395
Bus 161, 165 Rote Fabrik

On 30th May 1980 a protest staged by youth activists outside Zurich's Opera House (Opernhaus Zürich) turned violent. Months of rioting between police and protestors ensued and the orderliness for which the city was renowned was turned upside down. By the time peace was restored, shops were wrecked, cars burned, thousands arrested, many injured, and one woman had died after setting herself on fire in protest. Zurich was like a war zone and the outside world was stunned. Most surprising of all the cause was less about political ideology and more about the lack of government support for the city's alternative arts scene.

The Zurich riots were played out against a backdrop of a society in flux. A rebellious European youth counterculture was manifesting itself in punk music, anarchistic art movements, and squatting protests. The conservative authorities in straight-laced Zurich struggled to accommodate it – and little wonder since at the time there was an eleven o'clock curfew in place across the city and dancing was forbidden on religious holidays. One of several watering holes that defied the curfew was the Helvti Bar in the basement of the Hotel Helvetia at Stauffacherquai 1 (Werd). Students, artists, musicians, and journalists from the leftist newspaper *Tages Anzeiger* regularly discussed the countercultural revolution here well into the early hours. They also assembled here to take part in the great street marches that defined the era.

Since the early 1970s Zurich's youth movement had been growing steadily more frustrated at the lack of public funding and work space for a new generation of artists. Pleas for the establishment of youth centres were repeatedly turned down and so instead the counterculture focussed itself on two big community squats.

The first took place in 1980 inside a former silk mill at Seestrasse 395 (Wollishofen) on the shore of Lake Zurich (Zürichsee). Constructed in 1892, the building had been set for demolition before the council earmarked it for use by the opera, which was about to be renovated at the taxpayers' expense. It was this that triggered the protest in May 1980 by those who felt ignored in favour of "elitist" venues. Whereas squats in municipal premises elsewhere in Switzerland have remained illegal it is indicative of Zürcher pragmatism that in 1987 the so-called Rote Fabrik collective voted to apply for permanent legal status, and an arts

Rote Fabrik: where old meets new

subsidy from the city council. They were successful, and today the alternative heart of the Rote Fabrik still beats loudly by providing studio and performance space for artists thanks to public funding. Indeed, even Zurich's most conservative newspaper the *Neue Zürcher Zeitung* has been known to review the avant-garde dance and drama performed at the venue!

The second great squat occurred in 1991 when a group of artists moved into the newly empty Wohlgroth gas meter factory on Zollstrasse (Gewerbeschule), alongside the city's main railway line. The squatters quickly erected a sign on the building to greet arriving trains that imitated an official Swiss Federal Railways sign. Instead of "ZÜRICH" it read "ZUREICH" (Too rich) and guaranteed fury from the establishment. The Wohlgroth squat became a *cause célèbre* and quickly developed into a thriving alternative arts centre. Concerned at not being able to generate income from the building the owner eventually offered to relocate the squat elsewhere but his offer was rejected. Shortly afterwards in 1993 the building was cleared by police using tear gas and water cannons. It might have pleased the squatters to know that the so-called Industrie-Quartier (District 5) to the west of Zollstrasse would later be transformed into Zürich-West, the pulsating heart of the city's new subculture.

Other places of interest nearby: 35, 36

38 A Thoroughly Modern Housing Estate

District 2 (Wollishofen), the Neubühl Housing Estate
(Neubühlsiedlung) at Ostbühlstrasse 33–79
Tram 7 Morgental, then Bus 66 Neubühl

Europe in the late 1920s and early 30s was a time of economic crisis highlighted by unemployment, inflation, and a chronic housing shortage. City architects were tasked with creating new social housing to replace the dark and insanitary tenements of the nineteenth century. The solutions included large-scale complexes for the masses, as well as comfortable yet affordable family homes for the middle classes. Consequently new housing estates appeared in many European countries and Switzerland was no exception.

In Zurich the Neubühl Housing Estate (Neubühlsiedlung) on Ostbühlstrasse (Wollishofen) is a fine example of how Swiss architects envisaged communal middle class living in the second quarter of the twentieth century. Its construction, as with similar estates elsewhere, was inspired by the success of the Weissenhofsiedlung, a housing exhibition mounted in Stuttgart in 1927 by the Deutsche Werkbund (German Work Federation). The Werkbund was a group of enterprising designers founded by architect Hermann Muthesius (1861–1927) in Munich in 1907. Similar in ethos to the Viennese Wiener Werkstätte and the English Arts and Crafts Movement in their production of quality products, they differed only in being unopposed to reaping the financial rewards made possible through industrialised mass-production.

Under the patronage of the Swiss Werkbund, a group of young Swiss architects attended the Stuttgart exhibition, where a row of six dwellings was put at their disposal by the renowned Bauhaus architect and exhibition manager Mies van der Rohe (1886–1969). The dwellings consisted only of simple steel frames giving the architects complete freedom to practice their design skills. The following year the same architects took part in the Congrès International d'Architecture Moderne near Lausanne under the auspices of Swiss-born architect Le Corbusier (1887–1965). By the end of the decade the Swiss group were firmly established amongst those architects practising what later became known as the International Style of modern architecture.

For the Neubühl Housing Estate in Wollishofen the group selected a low ridge near Zurich's southern border, which at the time was open

A view of the Neubühl Housing Estate (Neubühlsiedlung) on Ostbühlstrasse

country. Here, between 1930 and 1932, they designed and constructed one hundred and ninety four dwellings. Financed both publically and privately the houses provided a stark contrast to Zurich's lofty nineteenth century apartment blocks with their gloomy inner courtyards. Instead, the new houses were built in low, flat-roofed rows running at right-angles to the road, so as to minimise the intrusion of dust and traffic noise. Using the pared-down Bauhaus style pioneered by Walter Gropius (1883–1969) the geometric houses of Neubühl appear as modern today as when they were first built.

The first occupants at Neubühl included many creative people (the photographer Hans Finsler, for example, and the art historian Sigfried Giedion), who were drawn not only by the radical new look of the houses but also by the advertising material created by renowned Abstractivist designer Max Bill (1908–1994) (see no. 83). Moreover, between each row, which was painted brilliant white and positioned so as to catch the sun, were placed gardens to promote health and vitality. Walking between the rows today allows the visitor to appreciate the estate's still vital original vision.

Although the Neubühl Housing Estate is the work of several architects – including Max Ernst Haefeli (1901–1976) who designed the similar Rotach-Häuser estate at Wasserwerkstrasse 27–31 (Unterstrass) – the group as a whole provided a cohesive blueprint for the planning and designing of housing estates elsewhere in Switzerland.

39   The Ruins of Castle Manegg

District 2 (Leimbach), the ruins of Burg Manegg
(Ruine Manegg) on the Uetliberg above Leimbach
S4 Bahnhof Leimbach or Bus 70 Frymannstrasse,
then walk up Frymannstrasse and turn left at the top,
from where a track leads to the ruins

Lying 623 metres above sea level on the slopes of the Uetliberg are the enigmatic ruins of Burg Manegg (Ruine Manegg). The remains of this medieval castle can be reached by following Frymannstrasse out of Leimbach, on the banks of the River Sihl, and then turning left onto a track through dense forest from where the ruins are signposted. Without leaving the boundaries of the city one is able to experience a real sense of nature and history here. Amongst the storm-blasted trees, and with glimpses of the city and Lake Zurich (Zürichsee) spread out below, this is indeed an atmospheric place.

During the fourteenth century Burg Manegg was occupied by the Manesse family. This explains why visitors arriving at the base of the gloomy castle mound today will find a water trough dedicated to the memory of the family (a far more impressive fountain, the Manessebrunnen on Hirschengraben (Rathaus), recalls how in 1351 the family helped the people of Zurich outwit the Habsburgs at the Battle of Dättwil). The castle is first documented in 1303 and for a hundred years it was the headquarters of the Manesse knights. Whether the family name inspired that of the castle or vice versa is unknown, as is the name of the castle's architect. Protected by a precipitous slope as well as a ditch the castle was probably entered by means of a long-vanished wooden bridge.

The Manesse family is well documented and were ennobled as a result of commercial success. Founded by Rüdiger I (c.1224–1253), a prominent Zurich councillor, the family shouldered loans given to Zurich's Fraumünster and Einsiedeln Abbey, and became a renowned Zurich dynasty. The family also used its wealth to create a collection of courtly songs *(Minnelieder)*, which Rüdiger's son, Rüdiger II (1252–1304), eventually bequeathed to the Chorherrenstift, an ecclesiastical institution in Zurich.

In 1393 Burg Manegg was sold at auction to "the Jew Visli or Vifli", whose widow sold it a few years later to the monastery at Selnau. Uninhabited at this time the castle fell victim to fire in 1409, which according to local legend occurred on Ash Wednesday as a result of a

Grotesquely-shaped stones mark the approach to Burg Manegg (Ruine Manegg) on the Uetliberg

carnival stunt. Significant pieces of walling remained in place until the seventeenth century although today there are only a few loose stones where once stood sturdy towers. The magic of Manegg resides today in the imagination.

On top of the castle mound is an inscribed stone recalling the hundredth anniversary of the birth of Zurich writer Gottfried Keller (1819–1890), who used Manegg and its dynasty as inspiration for his *Züricher Novellen* (see no. 43). In *Der Narr auf Manegg* (The Fool on Manegg), for example, Keller describes the fall of the family, and the fictional adventurer Butz Fallät, who makes the old castle his base. He also mentions the torching of the castle. In *Hadlaub* Keller states that the family spent much of their time in the city, inspired perhaps by the fact that as First Official Secretary of the Canton of Zurich, Keller himself was based in the so-called Steinhaus, a former medieval tower house at the top of Kirchgasse, which during the thirteenth century had been been owned by the Manesse knights (see no. 22).

In *Der Narr auf Manegg* Keller relates how a pleasure excursion was made to the castle ruins, and indeed such trips were popular during the nineteenth century. Not so many make the effort today, and the views Keller would have recognised have now been obscured by trees. But the memories linger and one in particular concerns a farmer's daughter seduced by one of the knights. She succumbed to his charms at a place called Drei Buchen (Three Beeches) only to be later rejected by him. Heartbroken she returned to the spot and hung herself, and for years it was said that whenever a storm broke over the Uetliberg a bolt of lightning would ignite the woodland, creating the frightful form of a hanging woman. Only when the trees were felled did the ghostly apparition finally disappear.

A second ruined castle also looks out over Zurich from the slopes of the Uetliberg. Like Burg Manegg the ruins of Burg Friesenberg (Ruine Friesenberg) date to the thirteenth century, and were once home to a knightly family (see no. 42).

40 Exploring Brocki Land

District 3 (Alt-Wiedikon), Brocki-Land
at Steinstrasse 68
Tram 9, 14 Schmiede Wiedikon; Bus 33, 67, 76
Schmiede Wiedikon, Bus 33, 72, 76 Manesseplatz

How is it that Zurich appears so neat and tidy when compared with other cities in Europe? Where are the piles of outmoded furniture and other unwanted domestic debris that litter the streets elsewhere? The answer is simple: much of it ends up in junk shops called *Brockis*.

The name *Brocki* is derived from *Brockenhäuser*, the general term used to describe Switzerland's countrywide organisation of junk dealers. The name was first coined in Germany in 1872 by Pastor Friedrich von Bodelschwingh (1831–1910). As founder of the charitable Bodelschwingh Bethel Institute (Bodelschwinghsche Anstalten Bethel) he began selling other people's junk to raise money for those suffering with mental health problems. Bodelschwingh called his business *Brockenhaus* after the passage in the Bible (John 6:12) in which Jesus, having fed the five thousand with heavenly manna, says "Sammelt die übrig gebliebenen *Brocken*, damit nichts verloren gehe!" (Gather up the fragments that remain, so that nothing is lost). In other words waste not, want not for one man's rubbish is another man's treasure.

The *Brockenhaus* concept spread subsequently to Switzerland, where it has become especially popular with young people and immigrants. *Brockenhäuser* can today be found across Zurich, and Brocki-Land at Steinstrasse 68 (Alt-Wiedikon) is a prime example. Located inside a former underground garage the enormous array of crockery and picture frames, cutlery and clothes is displayed neatly on row upon row of wooden shelves. Everything that isn't to be found underground will be found above ground in Brocki-Land's three subsidiary depots: Antik-Shop also at number 68 contains jewellery and collectibles, Bücher-Land at Steinstrasse 68a is where books can be found, and Musik-Land at number 70 is a haven for records, cassettes, and CDs.

Another good example of a Zurich *Brockenhaus* can be found behind Zurich Main Station (Hauptbahnhof Zürich) at Neugasse 11 (Gewerbeschule). Called Zürcher Brockenhaus it is a little more upmarket and therefore more expensive, offering designer furniture and lamps, a café, and regular parties and cultural events. Book lovers, meanwhile, will definitely want to visit the Bücher-Brocki at Bederstrasse 4 (Enge).

Clocks galore at Brocki-Land

Those wishing to explore more of Zurich's *Brockenhäuser* should visit www.nichtneu.ch, which contains an exhaustive list of more than eighty *Brockenhäuser*, as well as a useful function enabling the user to search by specific categories, price, and area. The site also contains details of two annually published guidebooks (*Zürcher Brockis* and *Zürcher Secondhand*).

A *Brockenhaus* with a difference is Zurich's lost and found property office (Fundbüro der Stadt Zürich) at Werdmühlestrasse 10 (Lindenhof). It is here that the more than twenty thousand items lost annually on the city's transport system are stored in the hope their owners will retrieve them. Those unclaimed are eventually auctioned off.

Saturday flea markets are also popular in Zurich offering everything from sneakers and screwdrivers to trumpets and televisions. One of the best is the year-round Flohmarkt Kanzlei at Kanzleistrasse 56 (Langstrasse). Another is the Flohmarkt am Bürkliplatz (Lindenhof) from May until October (it is a fruit and vegetable market on Tuesday and Friday mornings). Both are open between 8am and 4pm. The Kuriositätenmarkt Rosenhofmarkt (Rathaus) includes ethnic arts and crafts and is open from March until December, 10am–8pm on Thursday and 10am–5pm on Saturday.

41 The Story of the Eight-Twentyfivers

District 3 (Friesenberg), the Oberer Friesenberg
Jewish Cemetery (Israelitischer Friedhof Oberer
Friesenberg) at Friesenbergstrasse 330
Tram 9, 14 Schaufelbergerstrasse, then Bus 89
Friesenbergstrasse, then Bus 73 Friedhof Uetliberg
(Note: men must cover their heads when visiting
the cemetery)

The earliest evidence for the Jews in what is now Switzerland comes from the Roman province of Germania Superior, where a finger ring adorned with a seven-branched candelabrum *(Menorah)*, the symbol of Judaism, was found in the ruins of Augusta Raurica, east of Basel. Today there are around eighteen thousand Jews living in Switzerland and their story is every bit as interesting as anywhere else in Europe.

The first documentation of the Swiss Jews dates from 1214, and within a century there was a thriving medieval Jewish community in Zurich, centred on the streets around Rindermarkt (Rathaus). As elsewhere during the Middle Ages they suffered frequent persecution, and in Zurich they were accused of having poisoned a public well at Predigergasse 15. All that remains of the community today is the name Synagogengasse, where the medieval synagogue once stood, and some fragmentary Gothic wall paintings of around 1330 on the first floor of what was once a Jewish merchant's house – the Haus zum Brunnenhof – at Brunn-Gasse 8 (a key for the house can be obtained on production of a passport from the Building History Archive (Baugeschichtliches Archiv) at Neumarkt 4).

In 1291 the Old Swiss Confederacy was founded, a loose federation of small, largely independent states called cantons. During the 1620s Jews were again banished from Swiss towns, and from 1776 they were permitted only to reside in the villages of Endingen and Lengnau, in what is now the Canton of Aargau, west of Zurich. This explains why some old houses in Endingen have two doors: one for Christians and the other for Jews.

With the arrival of French forces under Napoleon in 1798 the Old Swiss Confederacy was transformed into the short-lived puppet state known as the Helvetic Republic. Swiss reformers took the opportunity to press for Jewish emancipation but there was little support from either the French or the Swiss, and in 1802 the Jews of Aargau were

This fourteenth century mural adorns a former Jewish merchant's house at Brunn-Gasse 8

persecuted. Not until 5th May 1809 were the Jews permitted to engage in trade and agriculture. The right of settlement, however, remained restricted to the two-village ghetto until 1846, when Jews were allowed to live anywhere within the canton. The right to settle outside Aargau (which was not granted under the terms of the Swiss Constitution of 1848) was only granted with the revised constitution of 1874. Until this time those Jews wishing to do business in Zurich had to take the 8:25 train from Aargau and return the same day. As a result the Aargau Jews were referred to as the *Achtfuenfundzwanziger* (Eight-twentyfivers), a name recalled today by the Eight 25 kosher restaurant at Lavaterstrasse 33 (Enge). Only in 1877 did a resolution from the Grand Council of Aargau finally grant full and effective citizens' rights to the Jews of Endingen and Lengnau.

Freedom of travel saw Switzerland's Jewish population rising to a peak of twenty one thousand in 1920, bolstered by immigration from Alsace, Germany, and Eastern Europe. Temporary fluctuations followed as refugees arrived during the Second World War, Ashkenazic Jews fled the Hungarian (1956) and Prague (1968) uprisings, and Sephardic Jews arrived from North Africa and the Middle East.

Zurich is now home to Switzerland's largest Jewish population of around seven thousand, and a dozen of the country's thirty eight synagogues are located here. One is the synagogue of the orthodox Agudas Achim community (Jüdische Orthodoxe Gemeinde Agudas Achim) at Freigutstrasse 37 (City), which also contains a ritual bath for women *(Mikvah)*. Another is Zurich's oldest synagogue opened in neo-Roman-

A grave in the Oberer Friesenberg Jewish Cemetery (Israelitischer Friedhof Oberer Friesenberg)

esque style in 1884 at Löwenstrasse 10 (City). It is used by Liberal Jews of the Jewish Congregation of Zurich (Israelitische Cultusgemeinde Zürich), who are also responsible for Zurich's Oberer Friesenberg Jewish Cemetery (Israelitischer Friedhof Oberer Friesenberg) at Friesenbergstrasse 330 (Friesenberg). Established in 1952 this peaceful corner at the foot of the Uetliberg is a testimony to Zurich's more recent Jewish past, and includes the graves of conductor Otto Klemperer (1885–1973), tenor Joseph Schmidt (1904–1942), and the author of *Bambi*, Felix Salten (1869–1945). It is well worth a visit.

42 Footpath Through the Solar System

District 3 (Friesenberg), a walk along Planetenweg
on the Uetliberg
Tram 9 or 14 Triemli, and then walk, or S10 Uetliberg

The Uetliberg is Zurich's very own mountain and is the highest point in the city. Rising to 873 metres above sea level it marks the end of the Albis chain of hills, which stretch nineteen kilometres to Sihlbrugg in the south. Locals and visitors alike come here throughout the year, taking full advantage of the many hiking, picnicking, sightseeing, and sledging possibilities. What sets the Uetliberg apart, however, is an unusual summit trail, which whilst providing some breathtaking views, also provides a lesson in astronomy.

There are several ways to reach the summit of the Uetliberg. The energetic explorer might want to alight Tram 9 or 14 at Triemli, and then strike out southwards into the foothills. From here a path initially follows the bed of the Döltschlibach along Hohensteinweg, and onto Studentenweg. A half hour detour along Friesenbergweg (an unmarked track crossing a bridge to the left) provides an opportunity to visit the enigmatic ruins of Burg Friesenberg (Ruine Friesenberg). The castle is thought to have been constructed in the first half of the thirteenth century for a Zurich family of knights (as was Burg Manegg farther south), and then to have passed to the barons of Regensberg and the counts of Habsburg (see no. 39). Returning to Studentenweg the path rises to join Hohensteinstrasse, which in turn joins Uetlibergstrasse – and the summit.

Alternatively, the S10 railway (Uetlibergbahn) delivers visitors every half hour directly from Zurich Main Station (Hauptbahnhof Zürich) to just near the summit in only twenty minutes. Whether arriving by foot or by train, the starting point for this particular trail is a little way uphill from the Uetliberg railway terminus. The trail, which was laid out in 1979 under the patronage of Zurich's Urania observatory, is known as the Planetenweg (Planet Path), and it soon becomes clear why (see no. 13). Between the station and the summit to the south-east, the path is lined with a number of boulders on which are models of the planets of the solar system. Each planet is rendered at a scale of 1:1 billion, as are the distances between them. Consequently, the Sun is represented as an unmissable yellow ball about a metre in

A miniature Sun heralds the start of the Planetenweg on the Uetliberg

diameter, and mounted prominently on a steel pole. By comparison Mercury, Venus, Earth, and Mars are little more than steel ball bearings set inside perspex panels. When viewed this way the colossal size of the Sun (and the tiny size of Earth) can be truly appreciated.

The summit offers a panoramic view of the entire city of Zurich, as well as Lake Zurich (Zürichsee) beyond. The public observation tower increases the summit height to a vertigo-inducing 900 metres of altitude. Alongside the tower is a 132 metre-high television mast, as well as the Uto Kulm Hotel, where refreshments can be taken before continuing along the Planetenweg. That the summit has long been an important vantage point is confirmed by various mounds and ditches from the Roman, Bronze Age, and even Stone Age periods, the latter dating back to around 3000 BC (look out for the information panels alongside the footpath).

By this stage it is quite possible that the visitor has forgotten the fact that only Mars has been reached on the planetary trail. As has been said, the planets and their relative distances are all to scale, which means that Pluto, the most distant planet in the Solar system, still lies a long way away. Indeed it can be found on the Felsenegg mountain approximately five kilometres to the southwest!

The panoramic trail to the Felsenegg in the district of Horgen follows a forested ridge, and takes in a succession of glorious views; on a clear day it is possible to see eastwards all the way into Austria, and

A detail of the observation tower on the summit of the Uetliberg

southwestwards as far as the Jungfrau. The Felsenegg is also home to the hilltop terminus of the Luftseilbahn Adliswil-Felsenegg, established in 1954 and the only aerial cable-car in the Canton of Zurich. Known as the Felseneggbahn, or simply LAF, it transports the weary walker all the way down into the village of Adliswil in the Sihl Valley, from where it is only a short walk to Adliswil railway station, and the regular-running train back to Zurich. (The cable-car runs daily every fifteen minutes, May-Sep 8am–10pm, Oct-Apr 9am–8pm.)

43 Heidi and the Nobel Prize Winner

District 3 (Sihlfeld), the Sihlfeld Cemetery (Friedhof Sihlfeld) at Aemtlerstrasse 151
Tram 2, 3 Zypressenstrasse; Bus 33 Friedhof Sihlfeld

Sihlfeld Cemetery (Friedhof Sihlfeld) is the largest burial ground in Zurich. Opened in 1877 it has been extended several times, and today covers an area of 28.8 hectares (71 acres). However, since only a third of the area is actually occupied by graves, Sihlfeld Cemetery is also Zurich's largest park. With its variety of landscapes both natural and manmade it is anything but a mournful place to visit.

Following a revision of Switzerland's Federal Constitution in 1874 the responsibility for burial grounds was transferred from church to municipality. With city centre burial grounds full it was decided to open new and larger ones in the suburbs. Sihlfeld Cemetery was one of these new burial grounds, and the first in Zurich where the denomination of the deceased was irrelevant. It was also the first cemetery in Switzerland to be equipped with a crematorium, erected in 1889 to a design by Albert Froelich. Like city architect Arnold Gieser's main gateway on Albisriederstrasse, from which an avenue of chestnuts leads to the crematorium, it is realised in imposing neo-Classical style.

There are two ways to explore the cemetery. One can wander aimlessly, taking in peaceful vistas as they appear, stopping at random graves, and enjoying the birdsong from the sixty or more species that live here amongst the Cypresses and other trees. Alternatively, one can request a free map at the cemetery office inside Gate A at Aemtlerstrasse 151 (Sihlfeld), and make a tour of those graves where the great and good of Zurich are buried. The renown of some of these people is limited to Zurich, for example Hulda Zumsteg (1891–1985), the colourful former manageress of the Restaurant Kronenhalle at Rämistrasse 4 (Hochschulen), and city engineer Arnold Bürkli (1833–1894), after whom Bürkliplatz is named. Others achieved countrywide renown, including Marie Heim Vögtlin (1845–1916), the first female doctor in Switzerland and founder of the country's first hospital for women; artist Rudolf Koller (1828–1905), whose vivid *Gotthardpost*, a study of a horse-drawn coach in full flight through a herd of cattle, hangs today in the Kunsthaus Zürich; Carl Seelig (1894–1962), Albert Einstein's first biographer; and Susanna Orelli-Rinderknecht (1845–1939), founder of

Painted pebbles on the grave of Henry Dunant in the Sihlfeld Cemetery (Friedhof Sihlfeld)

the Zurich women's temperance movement and the first woman to appear on a Swiss stamp (her alcohol-free *Kurhaus* founded in 1900 at Orellistrasse 21 (Fluntern) is today the Hotel Zürichberg).

Then there are those whose significance in life extended far beyond the borders of Switzerland. They include the "Red Emperor" August Bebel (1840–1913), one of the founders of German Social Democracy, whose funeral was attended by fifty thousand mourners including Rosa Luxemburg and Clara Zetkin, and artist Richard Paul Lohse (1902–1988), who together with Verena Loewensberg (1912–1986) (also buried here) was a member of the Zürcher Schule der Konkreten, an Abstractivist art movement founded by Max Bill (1908–1994) in the 1930s (see no. 83). Perhaps not surprisingly Lohse's grave is marked by a yellow- and red-painted steel square. Down the road in Section D of the cemetery is the grave of social reformer Henry Dunant (1828–1910), creator of the Geneva Convention and winner of the first ever Nobel Prize; the pebbles painted with red crosses remind the onlooker that Dunant's book about the Battle of Solferino in 1859 prompted the formation of the International Committee of the Red Cross.

The world of literature is represented by Berlin-born Walter Mehring (1896–1981), a prominent satirical writer in the Weimar Republic, whose books were burned by the Nazis; Johanna Spyri (1827–1901), the authoress of *Heidi*, one of the best-loved pieces of Swiss children's literature; and Swiss national poet Gottfried Keller (1819–1890), whose works rooted in bourgeois Swiss life are also popular in Germany; a plaque marks his birthplace at Chorgasse 37 (Rathaus), his writing desk is preserved in Zurich Central Library (Zentralbibliothek Zürich) at Zähringerplatz 6 (Rathaus), and there is a monument to his memory on the lakeside in Enge.

This selection is completed by a couple of architects. Karl Culmann (1821–1881) was a professor at Zurich's Federal Polytechnic Institute (Eidgenössisches Polytechnikum), where he lectured on the principles of steel construction to Maurice Koechlin, one of the designers of the Eiffel Tower. Also at the Polytechnikum and buried here is architect Alfred Friedrich Bluntschli (1842–1930), who succeeded Gottfried Semper (1803–1879) as professor, and who together with Karl Jonas Mylius planned the Central Cemetery in Vienna. De-

The grave of *Heidi* author Johanna Spyri

spite this the Viennese famously snubbed Bluntschli's hometown by claiming that despite it being twice the size of Vienna's new cemetery it was only half the fun ("Zürich ist doppelt so groß wie der Wiener Zentralfriedhof, aber nur halb so lustig")!

Other places of interest nearby: 44

Silver Screen Zurich

District 4 (Werd), the Uto-Kino at Kalkbreitestrasse 3
Tram 2, 3 Kalkbreite; Bus 32 Kalkbreite

Switzerland has never supported a large film history, and like other small European countries is heavily dependent on state support. For Switzerland, however, subsidies are not sufficient to maintain an industry that produces films in three languages. Consequently output has lagged behind the rest of Europe. But this is not to say that Switzerland has not left its mark on cinema. The French-born *avant-garde* director Jean Luc Godard spent his early years here, and Swiss director Xavier Koller won the Oscar for Best Foreign Language Film in 1990 with his film *Reise der Hoffnung* (*Journey of Hope*), about a Turkish family trying to emigrate illegally to Switzerland. The most successful Swiss film is Rolf Lyssy's *Die Schweizermacher* (1978), a satirical comedy dealing with similar issues. One of the most popular Swiss directors was Kurt Früh (1915–1975), whose *Bäckerei Zürrer* was filmed along Zurich's Langstrasse (see no. 46).

Zurich plays a special role in Swiss cinema. Not only has it provided the backdrop for many international films (notably the 1988 version of *The Bourne Identity*) but also since 2005 it has played host to the Zurich Film Festival. As Switzerland's cultural metropolis and a base for numerous producers, distributors and filmmakers perhaps it is not surprising that Zurich also lays claim to having the world's highest concentration of cinemas. Of these several have a story to tell.

Many old cinemas survive in Zurich albeit with modernised interiors. These include the ABC at Waisenhaustrasse 2–4 (Lindenhof), which was founded as the Orient in 1913, the Walche at Walchestrasse 11 (Unterstrass), established in 1922, and the Piccadilly at Mühlebachstrasse 2 (Mühlebach), which opened in 1929. Others include the Capitol at Weinbergstrasse 9 and the Corso at Theaterstrasse 10 (both in Hochschulen).

Two old Zurich cinemas warrant special attention. The first is the Uto-Kino at Kalkbreitestrasse 3 (Werd), located alongside the Wiedikon tram depot. It opened in the 1920s to offer a couple of hours' escapism to the neighbourhood's factory workers: most nights the cinema's five hundred seats would have been occupied. Today the factories are gone, and the programme is focussed squarely on arthouse films. The two hundred seats now available are more luxuriously upholstered than in former times, having been salvaged from more upmarket cinemas elsewhere. But the memories linger, and the foyer with its starry cupola still reeks of nostalgia. The wonderful Art Deco façade is preserved in all its faded glory, too, and appears especially glamorous at night, when the 1950s-era neon lighting is switched on. The rather frightening sculptured head at the corner of the building is Uto, the old Germanic god, after whom the cinema is named.

A second old cinema of note is the former Radium Kino at Mühlegasse 5 (Rathaus); opened in 1907 the cinema was Zurich's first. In 1928 the building was given an unusual Expressionist painted façade, which is still in place today. After the cinema closed its doors in 2008 a team of archaeologists moved in temporarily to conduct an excavation during which they revealed not only the original

The foyer of the Uto-Kino on Kalkbreitestrasse

painted walls of the cinema but also evidence for timber-framed walls and fireplaces dating back to the tenth century! They also stumbled upon an unexpected stash of old film posters hidden behind a wooden panel. Dating back a century they included one for Louis Feuillade's popular French film *Fantomas* (1913), although it is unknown why the posters were hidden there. Their survival is all the more remarkable when one learns that at the time such advertising materials were considered tasteless in some circles and rarely saved for posterity.

Zurich also has many innovative small cinemas screening art house films. The cooperative-run Riff Raff at Neugasse 57 (Gewerbeschule), for example, which despite its modern look once screened silent movies, premiered the documentary *Electro Pop Made in Switzerland* (2005) about the Swiss electronica band Yello and its charismatic singer Dieter

The façade of the former Radium Kino on Mühlegasse

Meier. The ground floor bar is partly illuminated by a re-directed beam from the cinema projector. The ultra relaxed Kino Xenix and Xenix-Bar at Kanzleistrasse 52 (Langstrasse) has its origins in Zurich's banned anti-establishment youth centres of the 1980s (see no. 37). Forced to move on several occasions it eventually came to rest here in a wooden former barracks building in the grounds of a school. Not so colourful quite literally is Le Paris at Gottfried-Keller-Strasse 7 (Hochschulen), which has a foyer lined with black and white film stills, and where lunch is served during midday film screenings.

Other places of interest nearby: 43, 45, 46

45 The Secret History of Fondue

District 4 (Langstrasse), the Fribourger Fondue-Stübli
at Rotwandstrasse 38
Tram 2, 3, 8, 9, 14 Stauffacher

Fondue isch guet und git e gueti Luune! (Fondue is good and puts you in a good mood!). So ran a fondue marketing campaign in Switzerland during the early 1980s. The jury seems permanently out as to whether eating large quantities of cheese in a single sitting is a good thing – but it can't be denied that sharing fondue with friends is one of the most convivial ways of dining. It really does put you in a good mood!

Derived from the French verb *fondre* meaning to melt, *fondue* is a Swiss/French winter dish of melted cheese, wine and seasoning served in a communal pot *(caquelon)* over a small burner *(rechaud)*; it is eaten by dipping cubes of bread on long-stemmed forks into the cheese. Whilst the *fondue* technique is first documented in 1699 – as *Käss mit Wein zu kochen* (to cook cheese with wine) in a book published in Zurich – only in 1735 is the name *fondue* attached to the recipe, in Vincent la Chapelle's *Cuisinier moderne*. Even then the dish called for the inclusion of eggs.

The first known recipe for cheese *fondue* without eggs was published in 1875. Despite the modern equation of the dish with rustic mountain life *fondue* was in reality first popularised in the towns of French-speaking west Switzerland. The earliest recipes called for sophisticated cheeses such as Gruyère (*Greyerzer* in Swiss Deutsch), which those living in the mountains could rarely have afforded.

The introduction of corn starch *(Maizena)* to Switzerland in 1905 made it easier to blend the cheese and wine smoothly, and probably contributed to the growth in popularity of *fondue* at this time. During the 1930s the Swiss Cheese Union (Schweizerische Käseunion) promoted *fondue* as a national dish, in an attempt to increase cheese consumption, and by the 1950s it had become popular in North America. The Swiss restaurateur Konrad Egli is credited with first applying the name *fondue* to a variety of other dishes in which food is dipped into a hot liquid. In 1956 in his New York restaurant Chalet Suisse he pioneered *fondue bourguignonne* (meat dipped in hot oil), and then in the 1960s he introduced *chocolate fondue* (fruit dipped into melted Toblerones!).

The best place to eat *fondue* in Zurich is much debated. A good place is the cosy and long-established Fribourger Fondue-Stübli at

Fondue is a national dish and a social pastime

Rotwandstrasse 38 (Langstrasse), where the *fondue* is made either from pure Vacherin Fribourgeois (a speciality cheese from the Jura region of Vaud) or from a mixture of Vacherin and either Gruyère or Emmentaler, known as *Moitié-Moitié* ('half-and-half'). Vaudois *fondue* is also available in the historic surroundings of the Restaurant Le Dézaley at Römergasse 7 (Rathaus). A traditional *fondue* restaurant in the Rathaus quarter is Adler's Swiss Chuchi at Rosengasse 10.

There are several traditions associated with fondue, for example if a man loses his bread in the pot he must buy a round of drinks, whereas if a woman does the same she must kiss her neighbours. It should also be remembered that protocol dictates no item be double dipped. Best of all, if the *fondue* is maintained at the right temperature, a thin crust of toasted but not burnt cheese known as *la religieuse* (French for 'the nun') will remain at the bottom of the pot. It should be eaten at the very end and is delicious!

Another cheesy dish from French Switzerland is *raclette*. A large half round of cheese is held in front of a fire and as it melts it is scraped (*raclé*) onto a plate, and served with boiled potatoes and pickles. Good raclette is available at Raclette Stube at Zähringerstrasse 16 (Rathaus).

Other places of interest nearby: 8, 9, 44, 46

46 Hotels with History

District 4 (Langstrasse), a tour of historic
hotels finishing with the Hotel Rothaus
at Sihlhallenstrasse 1
Bus 31 Militär-/Langstrasse

It can be said with confidence that for a relatively small city, Zurich offers one of the widest selections of distinctive hotels in Europe. From basic to luxurious there is something here to satisfy all tastes – and many offer not only a bed but also a history lesson to go with it. Here are a few of them.

Not surprisingly for a moneymaker's town there is some superlative accommodation for those lucky enough to be able to afford it. The Dolder Grand at Kurhausstrasse 65 (Hottingen), for example, is a nineteenth century turreted palace perched on a hill, with its own cogwheel railway for access (see no. 53). Built in 1899 and revamped in 2008 at a cost of over two hundred million Euros the hotel includes a spa powered by geothermal probes beneath the building. The hotel's ice rink created in 1930 is one of the largest in Europe and its 173 rooms and public spaces all contain original art works (an ipad tour is available chronicling the entire collection including works by Andy Warhol, Salvador Dali and Man Ray). The Dolder Grand is matched in opulence by the Baur au Lac at Talstrasse 1 (City), which has been managed by the same family since opening in 1844. Luminaries from Richard Wagner to Henry Kissinger have stayed here and enjoyed its private lakeside park.

Other hotels provide a more intimate lesson in luxury. The Widder at Rennweg 7 (Lindenhof) is a design hotel created by joining together nine ancient town houses dating back to the eleventh century (including that of the medieval Guild of Butchers). The buildings' exposed stonework, timbers and wall paintings act as a backdrop for modern art and classic furniture (see no. 10). The Hirschen at Niederdorfstrasse 13 (Rathaus), which has been a guesthouse since 1703, is of a similar age and origin, and boasts a medieval well and wine cellar. The Romantik Florhof at Florhofgasse 4 (Hochschulen) is part of a former sixteenth century merchant's house where muslin and silk were once manufactured.

The Alden Hotel Splügenschloss at Splügenstrasse 2 (Enge) is rather more modern, being a neo-Baroque townhouse from 1897, its original stucco ceilings and parquet flooring now enhanced by sleek,

The Hotel Rothaus on Sihlhallenstrasse

contemporary furnishings. Of a similar age is the Lady's First Design Hotel inside a stuccoed townhouse at Mainaustrasse 24 (Seefeld); once a finishing school for girls, the upper floors are now reserved for use by women only. Most modern of all is the Greulich at Hermann-Greulich-Strasse 56 (Langstrasse), a renovated industrial building offering minimalist rooms centred on a Japanese-inspired courtyard planted with silver birch trees.

When all this luxury and design gets too much, there is one hotel in Zurich that offers the perfect antidote. The refreshingly unpretentious Hotel Rothaus at Sihlhallenstrasse 1 (Langstrasse) has been in business in one way or another for over a century. From the late nineteenth century until the 1980s it stood at the heart of working class Zurich. As such the hotel has witnessed the ebb and flow of history in this always vital part of the city.

The hotel was founded as the 62-bed Gasthaus z'Rothaus in 1891, and in 1896 it was taken over by Emma and Ernst Huber-Morf. For more than fifty years they made it available as a meeting place for the area's numerous workers' associations and clubs. Between the wars circus performers and variety artists took rooms or kept a *Stammtisch* here, including the comedian Fredy Scheim (1892–1957). He starred in several popular Swiss films during the 1950s, including *Oberstadtgass* directed by Kurt Früh (1915–1975). Früh's 1957 film *Bäckerei Zürrer* is a sympathetic portrayal of the bums, boozers, small criminals, prostitutes, and migrant workers for which the area surrounding the hotel was renowned. At this time a double bedroom with wash basin and water jug cost twelve Swiss Francs; by contrast, a night in a six-bed room for the unemployed up on the fourth floor cost two Swiss Francs fifty.

During the 1970s several renowned artists were drawn to the hotel, including Zurich-born photographer Robert Frank (b. 1924). Thereafter it passed through several hands and gained an increasingly sordid reputation as the surrounding district witnessed unemployment and drug problems. In the 1980s the hotel bar became a strip club, the name Rothaus now referring not only to the red brick from which it was made – but also the activities going on inside! Rooms were offered on an hourly basis.

The courtyard of the Hotel Greulich in Langstrasse

With the arrival of the new millennium the area began reinventing itself. As old buildings have been refurbished so red light activities have begun sharing the streets with multicultural and avant-garde activities (the area is said to be home to 140 different nationalities) (see no. 83). In 2006 the Rothaus joined the throng and was reopened as a clean, well-run 43-room hotel offering value for money, occasional live events, and a very decent brunch.

Other places of interest nearby: 44, 45, 47

47 These Shops Are Different!

District 5 (Escher Wyss), a tour of unusual shops beginning
with Freitag Zürich at Geroldstrasse 17
S3, S5, S6, S7, S12, S16 Bahnhof Hardbrücke; Bus 33, 71, 72
Bahnhof Hardbrücke

The high streets of Europe look increasingly similar these days. Fortunately Zurich has managed to retain a healthy number of individual
and independent specialist retailers. These idiosyncratic bastions of
local colour are manned by knowledgeable staff, each with a passion
for their products. This shopping tour – *Lädälä* or *Lädeli* to the locals –
takes in just a few of them.

The tour begins in the former Industrie-Quartier (District 5),
which is being reinvented as Zürich-West. This part of the city is increasingly renowned for its trend-setting social and cultural amenities, so much so that there is a German-language website devoted to it
(www.kreislauf4und5.ch) (see no. 83). Most unusual is the shop Freitag
Zürich at Geroldstrasse 17 (Escher Wyss), which is constructed from
seventeen reused freight containers. Ideally suited to its location alongside the busy Hardbrücke, over which freight lorries thunder on their
way from Germany to Italy, it appears like a mini skyscraper. It is the
brainchild of Daniel and Markus Freitag, who wanted a unique space
from which to sell their bags, wallets, footballs, and other accessories
made out of recycled truck tarpaulins. Old seat belts are used for the
straps and bicycle inner tubes for the seams. Freitag bags are now considered design classics, and they are made in Zurich by a sixty-strong
workforce in a nearby factory. Although the shop only occupies the
lower four storeys, it is possible to climb right to the top of the remaining nine stacked containers.

Zurich has plenty of other highly individual fashion outlets, including Amok at Ankerstrasse 61 (Langstrasse), which specialises in skirts
for men, Edo Popken at Bärengasse 10 (City), which provides bespoke
men's shirts, and Sonja Rieser at Neumarkt 1 (Rathaus), the home of
outlandish hats. For outsize men's clothing there is Bovet at Talacker
42 (Lindenhof), with its window mannequins with famous faces, and
for the latest trends in alpine and urban chic visit Alprausch at Werdmühleplatz 1 (Lindenhof). And if it's fine silks you're after then visit
the elegant Fabric Frontline at Ankerstrasse 118 (Langstrasse), or the
old-fashioned Spitzenhaus Degiacomi at Börsenstrasse 14 (Lindenhof) for table linens from Zurich and Bern, and lace from St. Gallen

and Appenzell (around the corner from the latter is the excellent Rena Kaufmann music shop at Fraumünsterstrasse 9, founded in 1909 and where the first phonographs in Zurich were sold).

Zurich's penchant for modern design also applies to furniture and interior design. Bord at Badenerstrasse 123a (Werd), for example, occupies a former courtyard garage and offers furniture by Swiss and other modernist designers. Other design shops include Bogen33, an excellent secondhand outlet located inside a railway arch at Geroldstrasse 33 (Escher Wyss), and the eponymous Neumarkt 17 (Rathaus), an old four-storey town house containing items from a hundred or more interior design companies. For distinctive antique furniture visit the atmospheric Antik Marangoni at the end of a narrow alley at Rindermarkt 26.

The Freitag store occupies a pile of freight containers on Geroldstrasse

When it comes to food and drink, Zurich offers some wonderful shops. Delicacies not only from Switzerland but also from around the world are available in the city's two great department stores, Jelmoli at Seidengasse 1 and Globus-City at Schweizergasse 11 (City). But for a more traditional experience visit Schwarzenbach at Münstergasse 19 (Rathaus). This old fashioned grocery shop advertises *Colonialwaren* on its façade, that is exotic goods redolent of the colonial era: tea, coffee, nuts, dried fruits, and spices. The shop dates back almost a hundred and fifty years, and still retains its original gilt and wood fittings. Coffee beans ground freshly in one of the windows are served in the cosy café next door.

A Pavarotti mannequin in the Bovet clothing store on Talacker

Another product with colonial connotations is chocolate – and Switzerland is famous for it! Zurich has two famous *chocolatiers* both of which have cafés attached: the legendary Confiserie Sprüngli at Bahnhofstrasse 21 (City), with its handmade *Truffes du Jour* and *Luxemburgerli* (cream-filled coloured meringues), and the cosy Café Schober at Napfgasse 4 (Rathaus), renowned for its hot chocolate.

Zurich contains numerous shops selling quintessentially Swiss products. Cheese is one of the country's great exports, and there's a wonderful variety of it at Chäs Vreneli at Münsterhof 7 (Lindenhof), including Tilsiter, Appenzeller, Emmentaler, and, for *fondue*, Gruyère and Vacherin Fribourgeois. For *fondue* pots visit Schweizer Heimatwerk at Bahnhofstrasse 2 and Uraniastrasse 1 (Lindenhof). Other Swiss favourites include sausages from Pretôt Delikatessen at Kuttelgasse 3 (Lindenhof), multi-functional Swiss-made army knives from Dolmetsch at Limmatquai 126 (Rathaus), and antique wristwatches from Greenwich at Rämistrasse 2 (Hochschulen). Most intimate of all is the Bäckerei Vohdin at Oberdorfstrasse 12, a hole-in-the-wall bakery selling Swiss bread and pastries since the 1620s.

Other places of interest nearby: 46, 48

48 Bookshops and Backstreets

District 5 (Escher Wyss), a tour of bookshops finishing
with Sphères bookshop and café-bar at Hardturmstrasse 66
Tram 17 Förrlibuckstrasse

The first port of call for book lovers in Zurich should be the Old City
(Altstadt) on the east bank of the Limmat. For secondhand books one
should explore the old medieval streets that criss-cross Niederdorfstrasse
and Oberdorfstrasse (Rathaus). Those clustered around the Grossmünster provide the perfect backdrop for some of Zurich's many antiquarian booksellers. They include Altstadt-Antiquariat Rita H. Schnellmann
at Oberdorfstrasse 10, EOS Buchantiquariat Benz at Kirchgasse 17, and
Biblion Antiquariat Leonidas Sakellaridis at Kirchgasse 40, which between them offer some five hundred years' worth of fascinating books.

Buchhandlung Medieval Art & Vie at Spiegelgasse 29 is a singu-
lar shop, offering not only books and music on a medieval theme but
also a selection of Moroccan art, including tagines and a nice line in
slippers! Meanwhile, Sportantiquariat at Frankengasse 6 is the place
to go for sports-related books and ephemera, and the Comic Shop at
Froschaugasse 7 is a haven for those interested in the art of the comic
book (the premises once housed the bookshop of celebrated Jewish left
wing activist and publisher Theo Pinkus (1909–1991)). Froschaugasse
is also home to book and art dealer Gerhard Zähringer at number 5 and
bookbinder Beatrice Wetli at number 22, as well as craftspeople such as
Musikhaus Thurnheer at number 28, where brass instruments are lovingly repaired, and engraver Jürg Bosshart at number 30.

The venerable Travel Book Shop at Rindermarkt 20 is sure to in-
spire wanderlust in all who enter it. This is the place to come not only
for books about Zurich, Switzerland, and the rest of the world but also
for alpine trekking guides and mountaineering maps. Founded in 1975
by travel expert Gisela Treichler it is said to be the oldest travel bookshop in the German-speaking world.

Buchhandlung im Licht at Oberdorfstrasse 28 caters for readers
interested in spirituality and meditation. Almost next door is another
specialist, Kinderbuchladen Zürich at Oberdorfstrasse 32, which as
its name suggests is a haven for young readers. For the scientific and
culturally minded there is the well-stocked Caligramme at Häringstrasse 4, and KLIO at Zähringerstrasse 41–45 for history and philoso-
phy. Des Balances at Kruggasse 12, meanwhile, stocks books for the
modern witch!

Rita H. Schnellmann's antiquarian bookshop on Oberdorfstrasse

It would be wrong, however, to think that book lovers shouldn't stray across to the other side of the Limmat. In Lindenhof, for example, Anglophiles will find mainland Europe's largest selection of English-language books, at a branch of the bookshop chain Orell Füssli at Bahnhofstrasse 70. The company, whose main branch is at Füsslistrasse 4 (City), was established as Orell Gessner Füssli in the late eighteenth century, at which time it specialised in disseminating literature of the French Enlightenment. One of the company partners, Salomon Gessner (1730–1788), founded the *Zürcher Zeitung* newspaper in 1780 (from 1821 the *Neue Zürcher Zeitung* or *NZZ*). Also on Bahnhofstrasse is Barth Bücher at number 94, offering a wide selection of travel books, whilst Zurich's oldest bookshop is Buchhandlung Beer at Peterhofstatt 10, founded in 1832 and located in one of the city's loveliest squares.

Not as charming but no less interesting are the former industrial areas of Districts 4 and 5, which have given rise to a less traditional form of bookselling, spearheaded by Paranoia City at Ankerstrasse 12 (Langstrasse). This anarchist bookshop was founded in 1975 by a collective comprising members of the anti-capitalist *Jugendunruhen* youth movement. Equally passionate but for a very different subject are the staff at alpine and climbing specialist Piz Buch & Berg at Müllerstrasse 25.

This area is also home to what is perhaps Zurich's most unusual bookshop, namely Sphères at Hardturmstrasse 66 (Escher Wyss), which is a combined book and magazine shop, publishing company, café, bar, and theatre. It is located in what was once the dispatch depot of a porcelain factory, indeed the theatre stage was once the ramp

Sphères bookshop occupies a former porcelain factory in Escher Wyss

from which finished goods were loaded onto waiting trucks. The stage doubles as the main display area for what is always an eclectic array of books.

Sphères typifies the recent trend in this part of Zurich – the Industrie-Quartier (District 5) which is being reinvented as Zürich-West – to reuse former industrial-era premises for social and cultural purposes (see no. 83). The café is especially popular in the summer, when outside tables are set up along the riverbank. Breakfast, light lunches, and afternoon snacks are available, and the beer comes courtesy of the TurbinenBräu on nearby Badenerstrasse (see no. 78). Whatever the drink it will definitely be best enjoyed with some good literature to hand!

Downstream from Sphères, and on the same side of the river, can be found the Hardturm, a fairytale medieval watchtower *(Wehrturm)*. It was built during the second half of the thirteenth century to guard the nearby river crossing. Since a third storey was added during the seventeenth century it has served as a private house.

Other places of interest nearby: 47, 81

49 The Forgotten Mrs. Einstein

District 6 (Unterstrass), the memorial to Mileva Marić
in Nordheim Cemetery (Friedhof Nordheim)
on Käferholzstrasse
Tram 11, 15 Bucheggplatz, then Bus 40 Krematorium Nordheim

All guidebooks to Zurich mention the fact that Albert Einstein (1879–1955) spent time in the city during the years leading up to the First World War. Seven years and eight months, to be precise, at six different addresses. Einstein's name is now synonymous with genius and his face has become a twentieth century icon. But what about his wife during this time, the gifted mathematician Mileva Marić (1875–1948)? Few books mention her name, and even fewer reveal that she was buried in an unmarked grave in Zurich. It is time her story was told.

Einstein arrived in Zurich in October 1896 to study at the Federal Polytechnic Institute (Eidgenössisches Polytechnikum) – today the Swiss Federal Institute of Technology (Eidgenössische Technische Hochschule) (ETH). A wall plaque at Unionstrasse 4 (Hottingen) marks one of the addresses where he lived during this period. In the same year Marić attended the same institution and the two soon became close friends.

Born to wealthy parents in Titel (at the time under the rule of the Austro-Hungarian Empire and today a part of Serbia) Marić was a brilliant student from primary school onwards. Despite the Empire disapproving of high school education for girls her father gained special dispensation, enabling her to attend an all boys' school in Zagreb. From there she was sent to Zurich, where she was the only female in the department of physics and mathematics. She would eventually gain the same score in physics as Einstein.

In 1900 Einstein presented his first published paper – on the capillary forces of a straw – in which his lifelong quest for a unified physical law is already apparent. A year later Marić became pregnant by Einstein and the pair left for Bern, where on 6th January 1903 they were married (the fate of the child remains unknown). After gaining his doctorate in 1905 Einstein had high hopes for a teaching position but instead found work in the Swiss Patent Office, assessing the worth of electromagnetic devices. It was in the same year, however, that he also wrote four groundbreaking articles, one concerning the photoelectric effect (for which he would receive the Nobel Prize for Physics in 1921) and another containing his now famous mass-energy equivalence equation, $E=mc^2$.

In 1909 Einstein and Marić together with their first son moved back to Zurich, where Einstein was made associate professor of physics at the University of Zurich (Universität Zürich). By this time Marić had long given up any academic ambitions of her own, and there is little evidence to suggest she helped Einstein with his theories. The family lived on the second floor at Moussonstrasse 12 (today 10) (Fluntern), where in 1910 their second son was born. Then in March 1911 the family relocated to Prague, where Einstein became full professor at the Charles University.

In 1912 the family returned once more to Zurich, where Einstein took up a pro-

The memorial to Mileva Marić in Nordheim Cemetery (Friedhof Nordheim)

fessorship at the Polytechnikum. This time they lived at Hofstrasse 116 (Hottingen), where they remained until February 1914, when Einstein took German citizenship and became professor at Berlin's Humboldt University.

From 1912 onwards the marriage was in trouble, which goes some way to explaining why Marić was unhappy in Berlin, and returned to Zurich with her sons soon afterwards. Einstein returned to Zurich one more time in January/February 1919 to lecture on his Theory of Relativity. In the same year he divorced Marić and she filled her time giving private lessons in mathematics, physics, and piano playing. Her situation improved when Einstein gave her the proceeds from his Nobel Prize although his ulterior motive was to receive Marić's blessing to re-marry.

Marić invested the money in three properties in Zurich, occupy-

The former home of Mileva Marić on Huttenstrasse

ing one of them herself at Huttenstrasse 62 (Oberstrass) (the house has been identified by a memorial plaque since 2005). By the 1930s, however, the costs of treating one of her sons for schizophrenia at Zurich's Burghölzli psychiatric hospital had overwhelmed her (see no. 64). She was forced to sell her two investment properties, and to transfer the rights of her own home to Einstein so as not to lose it. Although he made regular payments to her she died penniless in 1948.

Marić was buried in an unmarked grave in Zurich's Nordheim Cemetery (Friedhof Nordheim) (Unterstrass) and gradually forgotten about. Not until 2009 was a memorial gravestone erected there by the Serbian Diaspora Ministry, just inside the cemetery entrance on Käferholzstrasse. It's worth visiting to remember a highly intelligent woman who placed family above fame.

Other places of interest nearby: 83

50   An Old School for Farmers

District 6 (Oberstrass), the Strickhof on Strickhofstrasse
Tram 9, 10 Universität Irchel; Bus 39 Strickhof

The Irchel is a small hill in the northern part of Zurich, on the border between the quarters of Oberstrass and Unterstrass. From the Middle Ages until the late eighteenth century the area was farmland, belonging to the wealthy Predigerkloster on Spitalgasse (Rathaus). By contrast the Irchel today is the site of a bustling campus of the University of Zurich (Universität Zürich).

This old barn was once part of the Strickhof school for farmers

During the intervening period, however, it was home to the Strickhof, Switzerland's first agricultural college, the remains of which can still be seen.

With the dissolution of the Predigerkloster and other monasteries in Zurich during the Swiss Reformation the fields on the Irchel came into the possession of the Canton of Zurich. Fast forward to 1853 and it was decided to open here the canton's first agricultural school. At the time the Swiss government wanted greater productivity from the land, and one way of doing this was to prepare the sons of farmers for their future profession.

Known as the Strickhof the school was laid out exactly like a large farm, where around fifty would-be farmers could be trained each year in everything from crop growing and animal husbandry to machine maintenance and accountancy. The workings of a real farm were replicated down to the tiniest detail, from the cows grazing in the meadows to the fruit-heavy orchards and open fields planted with cereals. By 1976 when it was decided to relocate the school to Lindau around seven thousand young farmers had been trained at the Strickhof.

Where once fields were the new university was built. The former farmers' boarding school was converted into a library, the old bedrooms became offices, and the stables became research stations. From the outside, however, the old buildings still retain their rustic charm, especially at the far end of Strickhofstrasse, where there is an ornate

The old farm buildings are now used by the University of Zurich (Universität Zürich)

wooden barn, and a flower and vegetable garden. The remaining land was landscaped thereby transforming the old agricultural landscape into a park.

Not far from the Strickhof, along a footpath off Krattenturmstrasse, is a forest glade called Vrenelisgärtli. Surprisingly it is manmade and dates from 1882, when a reservoir was excavated here. It was connected by an underground pipeline to the Letten Waterworks, where until 1914 the water was used to generate electricity. The access road to the reservoir was landscaped by the Association for the Beautification of Zurich and its Surroundings (Verschönerungsverein Zürich und Umgebung), and originally afforded a distant view of the snow-capped Glärnisch Mountain. After 1914 the water was redirected to turbines beneath the Strickhof until the reservoir was abandoned in 1942. It has subsequently become a natural feature.

Krattenturmstrasse is named after a fourteenth century watchtower and signal station that once stood on the hill above the Resiweiher (*Kratten* being the baskets used to hold the resin used to make smoke signals). The site is today marked by a glacial boulder. Attached to it is a plaque recounting how the tower was destroyed during the Old Zurich War of 1444, when Zurich fought against fellow members of the Old Swiss Confederacy in a doomed attempt to seize land from the Count of Toggenburg, who had died intestate. Zurich was readmitted to the confederacy in 1450.

Other places of interest nearby: 51, 52

51 The Gnomes of Zurich

District 6 (Oberstrass), the MoneyMuseum at Hadlaubstrasse 106
Tram 9, 10 Seilbahn Rigiblick or Bus 33 Seilbahn Rigiblick,
then Seilbahn Rigiblick Hadlaubstrasse

During the twentieth century Switzerland became attractive as a financial centre for a number of reasons: the Swiss Franc could be exchanged for gold and other currencies, the country was politically stable, and in the wake of the foundation of the Swiss National Bank in 1907 Switzerland offered banking services of the highest quality. In the decades following the Second World War Zurich's foreign exchange speculators gained a reputation not only for success but also secrecy (it would later be revealed that some had honed their skills by accepting gold and other assets looted from Nazi-occupied countries in return for the foreign currency needed by the Nazis to finance their war machine). This irritated politicians elsewhere in Europe, especially British politicians during the sterling currency crisis of 1964. At the time the British labour politician George Brown, whose party had inherited an unusually large deficit on the country's balance of trade, referred to Zurich's bankers as "gnomes". He pictured them scurrying about in the hidden vaults of private banks, manipulating the finances of the outside world, and forever counting their gold. This reference to the "gnomes of Zurich" stuck, and even today journalists use the phrase when reporting on Switzerland's banking industry.

Zurich today hosts the world's most important market for trading gold and precious metals, and also boasts the fourth-largest stock market (after New York, London, and Tokyo). Although now transparent in its trading activities, the city's private banks are still there, focussed on and around Bahnhofstrasse. Like a scene from Robert Ludlum's *The Bourne Identity* clients at Credit Suisse at Paradeplatz 8 are still greeted (and vetted) by a *huissier de banque* in the foyer before being allowed to view the contents of their safety-deposit boxes. For the less wealthy there is a collection of safe deposit boxes displayed in the Landesmuseum Zürich at Museumstrasse 2 (City), which can be opened by anyone just for fun!

A display in the MoneyMuseum
on Hadlaubstrasse

With such a long-established interest in money it comes as no surprise to find that one of Zurich's numerous specialist museums is devoted to the history of money. The MoneyMuseum at Hadlaubstrasse 106 (Oberstrass) originated in a private coin collection started in 1995 by banker and historian Dr. Jürg Conzett. The aim from the beginning was to illustrate the history of currency across the world from antiquity to the present day. Within a couple of years it was decided to make the entire collection available to an interested public online. This was achieved in 1999 with the launch of www.moneymuseum.com, the world's first virtual money museum.

In 2002 Dr. Conzett's Sunflower Foundation, of which the MoneyMuseum is a part, acquired the leafy suburban property on Hadlaubstrasse in which the museum is now based. It opened its doors to visitors in February 2003, and has since embarked on an ambitious and regular timetable of currency-related exhibitions, lectures, and other events. With the help of state-of-the-art digital galleries and audio stations these events are far more fascinating than at first might be imagined. An exhibition staged in 2005, for example, was entitled *Womit Casanova in Zürich zahlte*, in which coins and documents were used to illustrate purchasing power, exchange rates, and wages prevailing when Casanova passed through Zurich in the 1760s, whilst he himself was avoiding unpaid debts!

Both the foyer and the gold-painted subterranean Treasure Chamber are given over to semi-permanent exhibitions highlighting specific aspects of the MoneyMuseum's extensive holdings. These include coins from Greek, Roman and Byzantine antiquity, as well as items illustrating the various stages in the development of Switzerland's national currency. Especially interesting is the display of traditional currencies from Africa, Asia, and Oceania, including seashells from Papua New Guinea, Ashanti gold weights, tea bricks from Tibet, Chinese silver ingots, and bronze armlets from Congo. All in all the museum provides a fascinating history of mankind from the point of view of money. After all, currencies are contemporary witnesses: they speak of power and powerlessness, of war and peace, of crises and glory.

Other places of interest nearby: 50, 52, 53

52 The Grave of Georg Büchner

District 6 (Oberstrass), the grave of Georg Büchner
at Germaniastrasse
Tram 9, 10 Seilbahn Rigiblick, then Seilbahn Rigiblick

During the tourist season a steady flow of visitors make their way along narrow Spiegelgasse (Rathaus) in Zurich's Old Town (Altstadt). Many are on their way to see the house at number 14, where a wall plaque recalls that Vladimir Ilych Lenin lived here until the outbreak of revolution in Russia in 1917 (see no. 26). Only a few onlookers, however, bother with another plaque at number 12. It was here in the house next to Lenin's that German dramatist, author and polyglot Karl Georg Büchner died in 1837.

The grave of Georg Büchner at the top of Germaniastrasse

The story of Georg Büchner (1813–1837) is a short and a tragic one. He was born near Darmstadt, the son of a doctor, and attended a Humanist secondary school that focussed on modern languages. An idealist at heart in an age of conservative repression Büchner penned a revolutionary pamphlet in 1834 criticizing social grievances in the Grand Duchy of Hesse. Charged with treason and facing imprisonment he fled across the border to Strasbourg, where he studied medicine instead and wrote a dissertation on the cranial nerves of fish! Simultaneously Büchner immersed himself in utopian Communist politics, Shakespearian drama, and translated two plays by Victor Hugo.

After receiving his doctorate Büchner was appointed lecturer in anatomy by the University of Zurich's Department of Natural Sciences (Departement Erdwissenschaften), and he relocated to the city in October 1836. Büchner spent his last months there teaching and writing. His first play, *Danton's Death*, about the French Revolution had already been published in 1835, followed by the novella *Lenz*, based on the life of *Sturm und Drang* poet Jakob Michael Reinhold Lenz (1751–1792). His second play, the romantic comedy *Leonce and Lena*, was published in 1836 and portrayed the nobility. His most famous work, however, is

Woyzeck, which he began writing in December 1836. It is remarkable for being the first literary work in German whose main characters were members of the working class. A deeply pessimistic tale of alienation, paranoia, murder, and suicide it is today considered a standard in the theatrical repertoire.

In early February 1837, while still working on *Woyzeck*, Büchner was taken ill with typhus. He died aged just twenty three in his room on Spiegelgasse, in the arms of his young bride Louise Wilhelmine Jaegle. Büchner was buried in a graveyard where the present day Kunsthaus Zürich stands, and his work largely forgotten. Fortunately, Büchner's papers, including the unfinished manuscript for *Woyzeck*, survived and during the 1870s they were edited and published. Büchner's talent was thus revealed to a new audience, and the plaudits were unanimous in their praise. Writer Arnold Zweig (1887–1968) described Büchner's *Lenz* as the "beginning of modern European prose", whilst Bertolt Brecht considered *Woyzeck* to be the birth of German Expressionism. *Woyzeck* was first staged in 1913 and later became the basis for the opera *Wozzeck* by Viennese *avant-garde* composer Alban Berg (1885–1935), which premiered in Berlin in 1925.

When the Kunsthaus was built in 1910 Büchner's grave was relocated to the top of Germaniastrasse (Oberstrass), which winds its way up the Zurichberg. Visitors can walk up or else take the Rigiblick Seilbahn, the upper terminus of which is located alongside the grave site (see no. 53). Here Büchner rests in peaceful isolation, beneath a headstone surrounded by iron railings and trees.

Similar in appearance to Büchner's gravestone but much larger is a war memorial (Schlachtendenkmal) farther up the Zürichberg on Hanslinweg. It recalls how Russian and Austrian troops drove French forces back across the Limmat following their occupation of Switzerland in 1798 and the establishment of the highly unpopular Helvetic Republic.

Other places of interest nearby: 50, 51, 53

53 Switzerland's First Automatic Funicular

District 6 (Oberstrass), the Seilbahn Rigiblick on Rigiplatz
Tram 9, 10 Seilbahn Rigiblick; Bus 33 Seilbahn Rigiblick

The concept of a funicular railway – from the Latin word *funis* meaning 'rope' – dates back to the sixteenth century. A cable attached to a pair of carriages on rails is used to move them up and down a steep slope, where friction alone would be insufficient to give traction. The ascending and descending vehicles counterbalance each other. Some early funiculars used the so-called Water Overbalance System in which the carriages are equipped with water tanks emptied at the bottom and filled at the top: as the heavier car descends so the lighter car is pulled upwards. The world's oldest example of a water counterbalanced funicular can be found in the Portuguese city of Braga, and was constructed in 1882 to a design by the engineer Niklaus Riggenbach (1817–1899). It probably comes as no surprise to learn that Riggenbrach was Swiss, since his alpine homeland had great need of funicular railways, too, and Zurich boasts a pair of them.

The newest is the Seilbahn Rigiblick (designated Line 23 by the Zurich transport operator Verkehrsbetriebe Zürich), which departs every six minutes during daylight hours from Rigiplatz (Oberstrass) up to Rigiblick on the Zürichberg. Inaugurated in 1901 it represented a refinement of the Water Overbalance System by using instead a powered winch to provide enough force to overcome the difference in weight between the two cars (namely the weight of the passengers they contain). The line was overhauled in 1951, when the original wooden carriages were replaced, and during the late 1970s the track was extended upwards from its original endpoint on Germaniastrasse to Rigiblick (Germaniastrasse thereafter became the third of three halts on the journey). Renamed the Seilbahn Rigiblick and reopened on 29th May 1979 it became Switzerland's first fully automated funicular

The Seilbahn Rigiblick is hauled by a cable

with halts. The journey time today is just over two minutes (excluding the halts) during which the 385 metre-long track covers a rise of ninety four metres. Averaging 160 journeys a day the Seilbahn Rigiblick carries around 600 000 passengers annually.

The Seilbahn Rigiblick was originally envisaged as an extension to Zurich's oldest funicular, the Polybahn (designated Line 24 by the VBZ). Originally water-powered, this funicular was opened for service by the Zurich Mountain Railway Company in 1889, and was converted to electricity in 1897. It connects the city square known as Central (Rathaus) with the Swiss Federal Institute of Technology (Eidgenössische Technische Hochschule) (ETH) on the Polyterrasse forty metres above. In the 1950s the Polybahn began losing money and faced an uncertain future but fortunately during the 1970s the Union Bank of Switzerland stepped in and rescued it. In 1990 the line was rebuilt, automated, and new carriages installed, giving the funicular a new lease of life after its reopening as the UBS Polybahn in 1996 (the quaint timber-built upper station has been retained and contains defunct equipment and old photos). The journey time is one minute and forty seconds during which the 176 metre-long track covers a rise of forty one metres. It is used by more than two million people annually.

Another technique used to haul carriages up steep gradients is the rack-and-pinion or cogwheel railway, in which a toothed rack rail is placed between conventional tracks and the locomotive fitted with a cog wheel that engages with it. The first mountain cog railway was built in the American state of New Hampshire in 1868, followed shortly afterwards by one on Mount Rigi in Switzerland in 1871. Zurich's own cogwheel railway, the Dolderbahn (today designated Line 25 by the VBZ), was laid in 1895 as a means of connecting Römerhofplatz (Hottingen) with the Dolder Waldhaus Hotel and later the Dolder Grand Hotel, both on the slopes of the Adlisberg. The 1328 metre-long track, which covers a rise of one hundred and sixty two metres, was originally a cable-driven funicular until it was converted to a cogwheel mechanism in 1973. The Dolderbahn was fully renovated in 2004.

Other places of interest nearby: 51, 52, 54, 55

54 The Moulage Museum

District 6 (Oberstrass), the Moulage Museum (Moulagenmuseum) at Haldenbachstrasse 14
Tram 9, 10 Haldenbachstrasse

Until the 1950s, when high
quality colour photography
became affordable, anatomy
students were sometimes
taught using accurate, life-
sized wax models. Known as
medical *moulage*, from the
French word for 'casting' or
'moulding', such models were
undoubtedly more appealing
to handle than real bodies.
The last professional *moula-
geuse*, Elsbeth Stoiber, retired
in 1963 from the University of
Zurich (Universität Zürich),

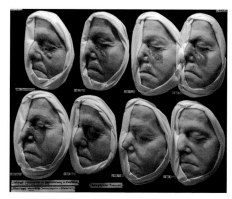

A display in the Moulage Museum
(Moulagenmuseum) on Haldenbachstrasse

leaving behind some 1800 examples of her art. Since 2005 these have
been on permanent display in what is undoubtedly Zurich's most curious museum: the Moulage Museum (Moulagenmuseum) at Haldenbachstrasse 14 (Oberstrass).

The technique of medical *moulage* was pioneered in Renaissance
Italy during the late 1600s by Gaetano Giulio Zummo (1656–1701).
Zummo worked first in Naples, then Florence, and finally Paris, where
he was granted a monopoly on the technique by King Louis XIV. Later
the technique spread as far as Russia, Japan, America, and England, by
which time medical *moulage* was being used not only in anatomy but
also to reproduce the physical manifestations of various diseases (such
as tuberculosis) and dermatological conditions (such as eczema).

To protect their livelihood practitioners of *moulage* were often
secretive about their methods. In general terms, however, the technique involved taking a plaster cast of the relevant body area from a
living patient, which was then filled with wax, resin, and sometimes
Calcium Carbonate. To render in lifelike detail the particular stages
of a disease or injury different coloured wax was used to render scars
and sores, with glass bubbles for blisters. Finally, hairs were inserted
individually for added realism. A laborious and expensive process

the technique of medical *moulage* was usually only available to the wealthiest clinics.

The moulage collection in Zurich was begun in 1917, shortly after the German dermatologist Bruno Bloch founded a clinic there. A problem for museum staff later tasked with documenting the collection was that many of the *moulages* were labelled only with the patient's name and date of birth, the relevant medical records having been long since destroyed. Fortunately, during the golden age of *moulage* great value was placed on publishing case studies, and so long hours in the university library have since reunited many of the exhibits with their individual histories.

Investigations also revealed that the Zurich *moulages* had not only been made for teaching purposes but also for medical research. Consequently many pieces in the museum record the results of laboratory experiments (for example into the causes of cancer), as well as the side effects of drugs, and the consequences of developing surgical techniques (including varicose vein removal and plastic surgery). One such *moulage* was taken from a seventeen year old girl, whose hands had been deliberately infected with a virus to demonstrate sensitization of the immune system. Another example documents the cancer-causing effects of early X-rays on human skin. The collection also includes *moulages* made of the experiments Bruno Bloch conducted on himself, demonstrating that eczema can sometimes result from an allergic reaction to external agents. Medical *moulage* served other purposes, too, as is the case with the disturbing examples showing the symptoms of venereal diseases, which were used in propaganda campaigns to discourage promiscuity.

Zurich's medical students still enjoy practising their skills of recognition in the museum, the *moulages* sometimes engendering greater intuition than even computer images in identifying subtle differences in the surface manifestation of diseases. Nor is the art of *moulage* yet dead since one of Elsbeth Stoiber's colleagues, Michael Geiges, a professor of dermatology and director of the museum, still makes the occasional *moulage*, whilst also restoring the old ones in the museum.

Other places of interest nearby: 18, 55

55 Journey to the Centre of the Earth

District 6 (Oberstrass), focusTERRA in the Department
of Natural Sciences (Departement Erdwissenschaften)
of the Swiss Federal Institute of Technology (Eidgenössische
Technische Hochschule) (ETH) at Sonneggstrasse 5
Tram 6, 9, 10 ETH-Universitätsspital

The Swiss Federal Institute of Technology (Eidgenössische Technische Hochschule) (ETH) is amongst Europe's most highly regarded technical colleges, and was founded in Zurich in 1854. It opened in 1855 as the Federal Polytechnic Institute (Eidgenössisches Polytechnikum) and was renamed in 1911, although it is still known locally as the Poly. As a federal institute the Poly is under direct administration by the Swiss federal government, whereas the neighbouring University of Zurich (Universität Zürich), which was founded in 1833, is a cantonal institution (see no. 18). Conservatives of the day were up in arms that the Poly might give free reign to dangerous liberal thoughts!

The main building (Hauptgebäude) of the Poly was erected in the early 1860s to a neo-Classical design by German architect Gottfried Semper (1803–1879); he became the Poly's Professor of Architecture after fleeing Dresden, where he had taken part in the May Uprising of

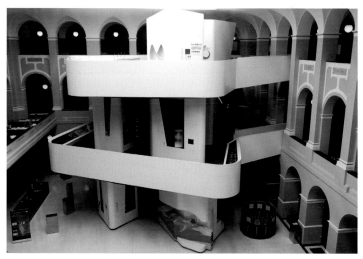

The focusTERRA in the Swiss Federal Institute of Technology (Eidgenössische Technische Hochschule)

1849. Overlooking the city centre the building sits high on the so-called Polyterrasse, which was once the site of the city walls (see no. 22).

Between 1912 and 1916 the Poly was extended northwards onto Sonneggstrasse by city architect Gustav Gull (1858–1942) (see nos. 13 & 14). The new four-storey building became home to the Department of Natural Sciences (Departement Erdwissenschaften), and an imposing covered inner courtyard was used to display its geological collection in row-upon-row of old fashioned wooden showcases. When the courtyard was renovated in 2005 the opportunity was taken to rework the display, the result being a novel exhibition space called focusTERRA.

Although the university's geological collection was first assembled during the sixteenth century by natural scientists such as Conrad Gessner (1516–1565), the concept behind focusTERRA is as old as Earth itself. Designed by the Zurich firm of architects Holzer Kobler in conjunction with the staff of the Department of Natural Sciences it takes the form of a three-storey tower reaching up to just beneath the courtyard's glass roof. A spiralling staircase, with a continuous ribbon of showcases alongside it, connects the levels seamlessly, taking the visitor on a journey to the centre of the Earth and back again.

The story starts at ground level with the internal dynamics of Earth, explaining what makes volcanoes erupt, how earthquakes are triggered, and the forces that create mountains. On the second and third levels, visitors can discover the many geological treasures of the Earth by viewing an archive of specimens spanning millions of years. The formation of crystals, gems, and minerals is explained, and the many ways in which man uses them is highlighted. Sedimentary deposits rich with fossils are used to demonstrate how past environmental conditions can be studied, and there are also media stations highlighting important issues such as climate change and geothermal energy sources. Visitors to focusTERRA on a Sunday have the added thrill of being able to experience the department's earthquake simulator (Erdbebensimulator), which is activated at 11am, 1pm, and 3pm.

The Poly's main building at Rämistrasse 101 is home to the Collection of Prints and Drawings of the Swiss Federal Institute of Technology (Graphische Sammlung der Eidgenössischen Technischen Hochschule). It is one of Switzerland's largest collections of graphic art, and includes mainly sixteenth to eighteenth century European masters, including Canaletto, Dürer, Goya, Mantegna, Piranesi, and Rembrandt.

Other places of interest nearby: 18, 19, 55

56 In the Footsteps of James Joyce

District 7 (Fluntern), a literary tour finishing at Fluntern Cemetery (Friedhof Fluntern) at Zürichbergstrasse 189
Tram 6 or Bus 39 Zoo

Amongst most people's top ten greatest novels is *Ulysses* (1922) by James Joyce (1882–1941), which chronicles the passage of the protagonist Leopold Bloom through Dublin on the 16th June 1904. One of the unusual things about the work is that not a single word of it was written in Dublin but rather most was penned in Zurich, and it makes for an interesting outing to follow in Joyce's footsteps during his time in the city.

This tour starts at Zurich Main Station (Hauptbahnhof Zürich), where Joyce first arrived in October 1904 en route to Trieste. He was newly married to Nora Barnacle and the couple stayed for a week at the nearby Gasthaus Hoffnung at Reitergasse 16 (Langstrasse) (the building has unfortunately been demolished). A decade later and the Joyces were back at the same guesthouse with their two children, Giorgio and Lucia, having pawned their furniture in Trieste to escape wartime Austria (Joyce was delighted that the guesthouse proprietor's name was Döblin!). Zurich in 1915 was a haven away from the war not only for writers but also revolutionaries and artists (see nos. 25 & 26). Indeed, so many refugees arrived at this time that Bahnhofstrasse was dubbed "Balkanstrasse".

After walking down Bahnhofstrasse a left turn onto Augustinergasse reveals the first of Joyce's favourite Zurich watering holes, the Restaurant Augustiner (now the Cantinetta Antinori) at Augustinergasse 25 (Lindenhof). Joyce was fascinated by the Old Catholic Church that worshipped in the Augustinerkirche on nearby Münzplatz (Lindenhof), with its rejection of papal infallibility, as well as the presence of Greek immigrants in the area, which inspired him when he later wrote *Ulysses*. Fans of the author will want to visit the James Joyce Foundation at Augustinergasse 9, with its old fashioned reading room, helpful staff, and public readings (*Ulysses* Tue 5.30–7pm); the eighteenth century building also contains the Strauhof Museum of Literature.

Crossing the Limmat by means of the Rathausbrücke reveals another of Joyce's regular haunts, the Café Terrasse (now a smart restau-

This statue marks the grave of James Joyce in Fluntern Cemetery (Friedhof Fluntern)

rant) at Limmatquai 3 (Rathaus), where he liked to meet friends. Joyce was also a regular at the Café Odeon over the road at Limmatquai 2. Lenin liked it here, too, although nothing suggests the pair ever met, despite Tom Stoppard writing a play in which they do!

Opposite the Odeon is the venerable Restaurant Kronenhalle at Rämistrasse 4 (Hochschulen). Finances prevented Joyce being a regular here during the war years but it became a favourite during the 1930s, when he visited Zurich to see his ophthalmologist (at the time Joyce was living in Paris). Long popular with artists the walls of the restaurant are still hung with canvasses, and there is a Joyce Table, too, where the author ate his last meal in January 1941. Other Joyce favourites included the Café Pfauen at Rämistrasse 32 (today the Restaurant Santa Lucia), where the author recited tracts from the manuscript of *Ulysses*; Zum Weissen Kreuz at Falkenstrasse 27, which was the meeting place of the Club des Étrangers; the Zunfthaus zur Zimmerleuten at Limmatquai 40, where Joyce occasionally dined with friends in the 1930s; and the Museumsgesellschaft at Limmatquai 62, where he read the English newspapers. As manager of the English Players Joyce also frequented the Kaufleuten Theatre at Pelikanstrasse 18 (City).

To see where Joyce and his family lived during the war years head to Seefeldstrasse. Joyce occupied four addresses in this area, all of which are still standing, commencing from July until October 1915 with two cramped rooms at Reinhardstrasse 7 (Mühlebach). Money was tight but fortunately Joyce secured a literary grant with help from colleagues Ezra Pound and W.B. Yeats. As a result the family moved to a third floor apartment at Kreuzstrasse 19, then a ground floor apartment at Seefeldstrasse 54, and then to the third floor in the same house. They remained here until October 1917, when they relocated to Locarno for a few months.

Time to return to the Altstadt and Pelikanstrasse 8 (City) where stands the James Joyce Pub. It is a real curiosity since the interior comes from Jury's Hotel in Dublin, of which Joyce was a patron, which was shipped to Zurich in the 1970s after the hotel was demolished.

Returning northwards pass the Landesmuseum Zürich at Museumstrasse 2 (City), behind which is Platzspitz-Park at the confluence of the Limmat and Sihl. Joyce said this was his favourite spot in all Zurich and it is today marked with an inscription (see no. 17). From here it is three stops on Tram 6 to Universitätstrasse, and two addresses where the Joyce family lived after returning from Locarno. On the first floor at number 38 between January and October 1918 he wrote five chapters of *Ulysses*, and on the third floor at number 29 between October 1918 and October 1919 he wrote another four. Mrs. Joyce complained of too many mice here and not enough kitchen utensils!

When Joyce returned to Zurich during the 1930s he stayed at two hotels on Bahnhofstrasse, the St. Gotthard at number 87 and the Hotel Carlton Elite at number 41, where he worked on a chapter of *Finnegan's Wake*. Fleeing the Second World War Joyce stayed between December 1940 and January 1941 at the long-demolished Pension Delphin at Mühlebachstrasse 69 (Mühlebach). It was here that he was taken ill and admitted on 10th January to the Schwesternhaus zum Roten Kreuz at Gloriastrasse 14 (Fluntern). He died three days later and was buried in Fluntern Cemetery at Zürichbergstrasse 189 (Fluntern), his wife consoled by the fact that the lions in the nearby zoo could be heard roaring. Joyce was always fond of lions. A statue of Joyce by American artist Milton Hebald marks the site today, where Joyce's wife, son, and daughter-in-law are also buried.

The novelist Elias Canetti (1905–1994) who also lived in Zurich requested that his remains be buried close to those of Joyce in Fluntern Cemetery. Also buried here are: Emil Oprecht (1895–1952) and his wife Emmie, Zurich-based publishers of émigré authors; the German actress Therese Giehse (1898–1975), who left Germany for Zurich when Hitler came to power in 1933; the Swiss artist Warja Honegger-Lavater (1913–2007), who designed the 'three keys' Swiss Bank Corporation logo; nuclear physicist Paul Scherrer (1890–1969); and Franklin Bircher, whose father Maximilian (1867–1939) invented the breakfast cereal Bircher-Müesli. A good place to sample this popular oats, fruits, and yoghurt cereal is the hundred year old Honold La Confiserie at Rennweg 53 (Lindenhof).

Other places of interest nearby: 57, 58

57 A Procession of Penguins

District 7 (Fluntern), the Zoo Zürich at Zürichbergstrasse 221
Tram 6 or Bus 39 Zoo; Bus 751 Zoo/Forrenwied

Zoo Zürich may not be the largest zoo in Europe (that honour goes to Berlin) nor is it the oldest (Vienna came first in 1779) but what it lacks in historical superlatives it more than makes up for in ambition and novelty. The Zurich Zoological Garden, as it was known originally, opened in 1929 and is located on Zürichbergstrasse (the street was originally part of the medieval route over the Zürichberg and down into the Glatt Valley). The zoo today contains more than three hundred and fifty species and encompasses many of the world's major ecosystems, from the grasslands of India and the highlands of Africa to the South American cloud forest and the wetlands of Brazil.

Zoo Zürich offers several unusual experiences to its visitors, the most popular of which is a daily parade between October and March of King Penguins *(Aptenodytes patagonicus)*. So long as the temperature is less than 10 °C the penguins waddle around the zoo quite happily from 1.30pm onwards. Despite their comic appearance, however, the King Penguin should be taken seriously as it is a creature that has adapted supremely to hostile conditions. It has four layers of feathers to keep warm, is capable of diving to well over two hundred metres on foraging trips, and can drink seawater by expelling excess salt through its nostrils.

It is less well known that Zoo Zürich offers a variety of opportunities for visitors to experience wildlife in ways rarely made available in other zoos. Both adults and children, for example, can take part in a night hike after the zoo has closed its doors. The venue is the Masoala Hall, a self-contained biosphere mimicking a Madagascan rainforest, which is unusual since most rainforest exhibits focus on South America. Opened in 2003 and covering an area of eleven thousand square metres the hall is heated to a balmy 85º, with humidity nearing a hundred percent. The hike commences at 7pm and enables participants to see what the occupants of the rainforest, including lemurs, birds, and reptiles, get up to at night. Accommodation is in tents, with sleeping mats provided by the zoo (participants must bring their own sleeping bags), and it's strictly lights out at 11pm.

Children also have the opportunity to make a trek through the forest surrounding the zoo, in the company of a Lama and a pair of Alpacas. Both species are highly domesticated in their native Andes, where they are used as beasts of burden. The treks take place most afternoons and include the chance to examine indigenous Swiss species of plants and animals, with a picnic thrown in for good measure. For those younger children happy to stay within the confines of the zoo there is the popular Zoolino, a dedicated area where children can feed and touch wild animals under supervision.

A parade of King Penguins at Zoo Zürich

For adults Zoo Zürich offers an array of highly unusual wining and dining opportunities. Guided tours of the zoo, for example, are available including a stop for apéritifs and appetizers. This raises the possibility of enjoying a glass of Champagne overlooking the elephants, or nibbling Antipasti alongside the tigers. Parts of the zoo can also be hired out after hours for banquets, so that up to twenty people can dine in the Lion House.

On a more serious note, Zoo Zürich has an internationally renowned breeding programme for several endangered species, including the Arabian Oryx *(Oryx leucoryx)*, Siberian Tiger *(Panthera tigris altaica)*, Snow Leopard *(Panthera uncia)*, and Galapagos Giant Tortoise *(Chelonoidis nigra)*. The latter, despite being the longest lived of all vertebrates, have seen their numbers reduced from an estimated two hundred and fifty thousand during the sixteenth century to just twenty thousand today as a result of human disturbance. One of the most interesting breeding programmes at Zoo Zürich concerns the European Otter *(Lutra lutra)*, which is currently believed extinct in Switzerland. Favouring unpolluted bodies of freshwater it feeds on a diet consisting predominantly of fish, which emerging evidence suggests it may be able to hunt through the ability to smell underwater. A combination of hunting, the use of pesticides, and a decrease in fish stocks are to blame for its disappearance. The long term aim of the zoo therefore is to return the European Otter to Switzerland through a concentrated breeding programme. It is hoped they succeed.

Other places of interest nearby: 56, 58

58 The Modern Home of Football

District 7 (Hottingen), FIFA Headquarters at FIFA-Strasse 20
Tram 6 Zoo

A football-inspired sculpture in the garden at FIFA

There is little love lost between Zurich's two football teams, the Grasshoppers and FC Zürich, founded in 1886 and 1896 respectively. The two are currently sharing FC Zürich's Letzigrund Stadium (Stadion Letzigrund) on Herdernstrasse (Hard), following the demolition of the Grasshopper's Hardturm Stadium (Stadion Hardturm) on Hardturmstrasse (Escher Wyss). It is hoped that both teams will eventually move to a new stadium on the site, after which the Letzigrund Stadium will be used for athletics and concerts.

Whether you are a football fan or not, the Letzigrund Stadium is worth visiting for its aesthetic merits alone. Designed by contemporary Swiss architects Bétrix & Consolascio the sleek structure appears like a flying saucer half embedded in the ground, its discoid roof clad beneath in wood and made ecologically sound with the planting of vegetation on top. Impressive as it is, however, the stadium's combination of football and modern architecture is not unique in Zurich. In Hottingen in the eastern part of the city are the headquarters of international football's governing body FIFA, and the building is an architectural gem.

FIFA was founded in Paris on 21st May 1904 as the Fédération Internationale de Football Association, giving rise to the acronym still in use today even outside French-speaking countries. FIFA has been based in

Zurich since 1932, from where it governs football's major international tournaments, notably the FIFA World Cup. The need for a single body to oversee the game first became apparent at the start of the twentieth century with the increasing popularity of international fixtures. The founding members were Belgium, Denmark, France, Germany, the Netherlands, Spain, Sweden, and Switzerland (England signed up shortly afterwards and by 1913 membership had expanded as South Africa, the United States, and Argentina).

In 2007 FIFA unveiled its new headquarters in Zurich, at what is now FIFA-Strasse 20 (Hottingen). The complex is approached through a surprisingly beautiful garden over which towers a wooden sculpture depicting a troupe of footballers, each standing on the others' shoulders, and supporting a giant football. A broad flight of steps beyond leads through the garden, each step carved with the name of a different FIFA member state.

The headquarters cost 240 million Swiss Francs and were constructed to a design by local architect Tilla Theus (b. 1943). Using concrete, steel and aluminium she adopted a simple, low-level rectangular form and placed many of the amenities in five underground levels. Referring to the unexpected presence of a meditation room the FIFA president Sepp Blatter (b. 1936) described the building as being "like a home where people can meet, talk, rest and retreat in silence and contemplation". He added that the glass walls would "allow light to shine through the building and create the transparency we all stand for", a none too veiled reference to allegations of corruption and legislative interference made against Blatter around the same time.

It is only possible for members of the public to enter the lobby of the building but this is enough to afford a glimpse of the interior. To the south the building looks onto a full-size international football pitch. And at night the external walls of the building, which are covered in a textile-like mesh (called "dancing walls" by Tilla Theus), are used to display the work of American light sculptor James Turrell (b. 1943).

Other places of interest nearby: 56, 57

59 A Library Like No Other

District 7 (Fluntern), the Law Institute Library
of the University of Zurich (Bibliothek des Rechtswissenschaftlichen Instituts der Universität Zürich) at Rämistrasse 74
Tram 5, 9 Kantonsschule

Architects beware! Switzerland's living star architects – Mario Botta, Jacques Herzog, Pierre de Meuron, Peter Zumthor – have been busy adorning cities around the globe but none of them have yet contributed anything significant to Zurich. That is not to say, however, that the city is devoid of significant modern architecture. Le Corbusier's final commission is here, and local architect Tilla Theus has made a stab at international stardom with her new headquarters for FIFA (see nos. 58 & 70). Fortunately, architects from other nations have made their mark, too, and the most significant of them is the Spaniard Santiago Calatrava (b. 1951).

Calatrava, who was born in Valencia, has been fascinated by architecture since he was a child. Whilst still at school he and some friends published a pair of books on the vernacular architecture of Valencia and Ibiza. Inevitably he studied architecture at university, and after graduating in 1975 enrolled at the Swiss Federal Institute of Technology (Eidgenössische Technische Hochschule) (ETH) in Zurich. After completing his doctoral thesis ("On the Foldability of Space Frames") in 1981 he established his own architectural and engineering practice, and has been busy ever since.

Calatrava's early career was devoted mainly to bridges and railway stations. A significant commission was the remodelling of Zurich's Stadelhofen Station on Stadelhofstrasse (Hochschulen). Completed in 1990 the project involved inserting a new third track alongside an existing late nineteenth century station that occupied an awkward site on a curving hillside. Calatrava's ingenious solution involved excavating the hillside to insert the new track, and then recreating the hillside's former profile by means of a concrete promenade above the platforms. These are supported by impressive three-armed supports every nine metres, designed so that even if two were removed by a wayward train, the structure would remain standing.

It has been said that Calatrava continues a tradition of Spanish modernist engineering that includes Antonio Gaudí and Félix Candela, combined with his own personal style derived from studies of the human body and the natural world. This is apparent in projects such

The Law Institute Library of the University of Zurich (Bibliothek des Rechtswissenschaftlichen Instituts der Universität Zürich) on Rämistrasse

as the Allen Lambert Galleria in Toronto (1992), which from the inside appears like a colossal ribcage. It is also demonstrated by Calatrava's second project in Zurich, the Law Institute Library of the University of Zurich (Bibliothek des Rechtswissenschaftlichen Instituts der Universität Zürich) at Rämistrasse 74 (Fluntern), which was unveiled in 2004. In a quest to create more space for the university without acquiring new land, Calatrava added two storeys in steel and glass to an existing building of 1909. More inventively he roofed the inner courtyard and inserted six huge elliptical steel balconies. Appearing to float (but in reality supported on steel columns) the balconies are timber-clad, their balustrades used to conceal reading stations. As the rings rise so they increase in diameter, the whole creating a magnificent atrium, flooded by natural light from an overhead skylight. The library is quiet enough to hear a pin drop and is a wonder to behold – even if you're not interested in law!

Calatrava's other commissions include the Quadracci Pavilion of the Milwaukee Art Museum (2001), the fifty four-storey *Turning Torso* tower in Malmö (2005), and a new transportation hub at the site of the World Trade Centre in New York City (2014).

Other places of interest nearby: 19, 20, 21, 22, 26, 28

60 Communing with Krishna

District 7 (Hottingen), the Hare Krishna Temple Zurich
(Hare-Krishna-Tempel Zürich) at Bergstrasse 54
Tram 5, 6 Kirche Fluntern, then Bus 33 Hofstrasse or walk
(Note: shoes must be removed before entering the building)

One of the more surprising persecuted minorities to find a haven in Zurich are Tamils. Fleeing civil war in Sri Lanka they began arriving in Switzerland during the early 1980s, where around thirty five thousand of them are now based (twenty thousand in the Canton of Zurich). It is interesting to note that since the arrival of the Tamils, Hinduism has overtaken Judaism as the third largest religion in Switzerland (after Christianity and Islam).

The community is well served by more than twenty Hindu temples of which the Hare Krishna Temple Zurich (Hare-Krishna-Tempel Zürich) was founded in the spring of 1980 inside a crumbling former mansion at Bergstrasse 54 (Hottingen). It was commissioned by the Swiss Krishna Community (Krishna-Gemeinschaft Schweiz) under the auspices of the International Society of Krishna Consciousness (ISKCON), known more commonly as the Hare Krishna Movement.

The core beliefs of this non-sectarian movement are based on traditional Hindu scriptures such as the *Bhagavad*-gītā and the *Śrīmad Bhāgavatam*, both of which date back more than five thousand years. The distinctive characteristics of the movement find their origins in the monotheistic *Gaudiya Vaishnava* tradition, which has had adherents in India since the late fifteenth century, and Western converts since the early 1930s. At the heart of the tradition is the devotional worship *(bhakti)* of Krishna and his lover Radha (avatars of the Supreme God Vishnu), which is realised by singing their holy names in the form of the well-known Hare Krishna *mantra* (known also as *kirtan*).

ISKCON was founded in 1966 in New York City by the charismatic A.C. Bhaktivedanta Swami Prabhupada (1896–1977). His aim was to promulgate the practice of *bhakti* yoga, in which aspirant devotees *(bhaktas)* train their thoughts and actions exclusively on pleasing the Supreme Lord, Krishna. Today, ISKCON is a worldwide confederation of over four hundred temples, schools, restaurants, and farms, including the Hare Krishna Temple Zurich. The focus is set squarely on universal respect, tolerance, and freedom: the goal is to encourage outsiders to open themselves to the worship of Krishna, and to incorporate it into their daily life and work. A few go so far as giving up their previous life entirely, like the thirteen monks who make up the permanent community in Zurich.

The best time to visit the temple is on Sunday afternoon. It is at this time that a true taste of the Hare Krishna way of life can be experienced by anyone, regardless of their creed, colour, gender, or profession. The Sunday Celebration *(Sonntagsfest)* commences at 3pm with an hour of Hindu devotional songs *(Bhajan)*, followed by a lecture and discussion. A veg-

Sacred statues *(Murtis)* in the Hare Krishna Temple Zurich (Hare-Krishna-Tempel Zürich)

etarian buffet follows at 5pm, after which there is a session of *mantra* meditation at 6.15pm (*mantra* is Sanskrit for sacred utterance). This is followed by a *Vedic* temple ceremony at 7pm (*Vedic* is Sanskrit for knowledge and refers to the oldest scriptures of Hinduism). At this time the sacred statues *(Murtis)* through which the eighty or so worshippers make their invocations to the spiritual world can be examined more closely (the statues are decorated, dressed, and worshipped each day between 5am and 7am by the monks). The celebration concludes with sung *mantras* at 8pm.

Zurich's Buddhist Centre (Buddhistisches Zentrum Zürich), which was established in 1991, can be found at Hammerstrasse 9 (Hirslanden). So-called 16th Karmapa meditation – defined as the path to the realization of the nature of the mind through identification with the Lama – is available here daily at 7.30pm.

61 An Elephant in the Woods

District 7 (Hirslanden), a walk across the Adlisberg starting on Witikoner Strasse
Tram 3, 8, 15 Klusplatz, then Bus 34 Schlyfi and walk

The hills around Zurich – the Uetliberg to the west and the Zürichberg/ Adlisberg to the east – provide ample walking opportunities for those wishing to escape the bustle of the city. Many good starting points can be reached by tram or bus without having to cross the city boundary. One such walk, which traverses the southwestern slopes of the Adlisberg, combines natural beauty with a handful of unusual manmade sights.

The walk begins where Bus 34 stops, at Schlyfi on Witikoner Strasse. The curious name 'Schlyfi' is derived from a water-powered grinding shop (Schleiferei) that stood hereabouts from 1852 until its demolition in 1968 (it ceased working in 1933). From here walk uphill along the Stöckentobelweg, which follows the swift-flowing Stöckentobelbach, a stream skirting the southern flank of the Adlisberg. Along the way can be seen various weirs and waterfalls, constructed to channel rainwater safely off the hillside and thus protect the road from landslides and floods.

The locals hereabouts have long called the stream the Elefantenbach, and before long it's easy to see why: sitting in the riverbed is a large stone elephant with water jetting out of its trunk. One would assume that the stream took its name from the sculpture but this would be wrong. The sculpture, which was originally accompanied by a pair of playful stone sea lions, was only installed in 1898. The Elefantenbach, however, appears marked on maps as early as 1850, so historians assume that the stone elephant merely reflects an already existing name. The origin of the name therefore remains a mystery, with local legend claiming that the sculpture is one of Hannibal's famous elephants turned to stone after its retirement from walking across the Alps!

Continue eastwards along the Stöckentobelweg and after a while a charming little stone bridge will be reached. Look carefully and on the outside of the parapets will be made out the letters VVZU in stone. This recalls Zurich's bygone beautifying association (Verschönerungsverein Zürich) led by its industrious president, Emil Näf-Hatt, who was responsible not only for the bridge but also the elephant. Continuing onwards and after passing a reedy meadow, the quiet community of Looren will be reached.

A stone elephant sits in the Stöckentobelbach on the Adlisberg

Turn left now onto Loorenstrasse to join Eschenhaustrasse, passing a tennis court from where there is an expansive view. Loorengutweg on the right leads to the so-called Loorenkopfturm, a thirty three-metre high wooden lookout tower erected in 1954. At a height of 694 metres above sea level it is said that on a clear day one can see not only the Glatt Valley to the east but also the peaks of the Eiger, Mönch, and Jungfrau. Be warned though: to get to the top necessitates climbing one hundred and fifty three steps!

Continuing along Eschenhaustrasse one passes the Restaurant Degenried. Directly northwards from here runs Breitweg, a track off it to the right leading to Zurich's earthquake monitoring station (Erdbebenwarte). Northwestwards from the restaurant runs Degenriedstrasse, passings meadows and an extensive golf course belonging to the nearby Dolder Grand Hotel at Kurhausstrasse 65. This journey ends at Waldhaus Dolder, a station on the Dolderbahn cogwheel railway, from where trains can be taken back down into the city (see no. 53).

62   Discovering Historic Mills

District 7 (Witikon), the former Trichtenhausermühle
at Trichtenhauserstrasse 60
Tram 11 Rehalp, then cross the road and follow the path
down a steep track to join the Pfadi-Weg signposted
"Trichtenhusen"; alternatively Bus 91 Trichtenhausermühle

During medieval times the many rivers and streams that criss-cross the river valley in which Zurich is located were harnessed to drive water-mills. It is difficult to imagine today, for example, that the Limmat be-tween Bahnhofbrücke and Rudolf-Brun-Brücke was once choked with watermills. They were constructed in two lines right across the river and used for several purposes, including paper manufacturing and stone cutting. Demolished in 1950 only archive photographs and the name of the Mühlesteg bridge recalls their former presence.

Today it is only away from the city centre that vestiges of Zurich's milling industry can still be found. A particularly enchanting example is the Trichtenhausermühle, which stands at Trichtenhauserstrasse 60 in Zollikerberg, just outside the city boundary. It is possible to get there directly by bus but for a sense of the mill's rural location it is far better to walk to it from the terminus of Tram 11 (Rehalp). Across the road a track leads down steeply to the Pfadi-Weg, which follows the Wehren-bach upstream to Trichtenhusen. After half an hour's brisk walking the path emerges from the gorge at a sawmill. Just beyond, at a sharp bend where the main road crosses the river, stands the Trichtenhauser-mühle, or Trichti as it is known for short.

The Trichtenhausermühle is first documented as *Truhtil Husa* (the house of Truchtilo) in a church document of 946, in which the Grossmünster and Church of St. Peter agree to cease receiving income from the mill. Until 1218 the Zollikerberg region in which the mill stands was administered by the Dukes of Zähringen, then the Bar-ons of Regensberg, and later the Abbey of Rüti. The mill remained in operation until the 1920s, and then in 1932 its two waterwheels were removed. The building was renovated in 1963 and has since served as a cosy and traditional restaurant. As a reminder of its former function a reconditioned waterwheel from elsewhere was installed in the restau-rant garden in 1984.

The waterwheel serves to remind visitors of the once great impor-tance of rivers such as the Wehrenbach in powering mills. The nearby sawmill, for example, was water-driven until 1970, as was the Farbholzmühle Burgwies farther downstream at the junction of Forchstrasse and Wasserstrasse (Hirslanden). This particular mill is documented as a timber mill during the late seventeenth century, although the structure seen today dates from the nineteenth century, when it was used to extract cloth dyes from timber (hence the name Farbholzmühle). Again its waterwheel has been removed, as has the one from the Hirslanden Mühle over the road, founded in 1296, which was also powered by the Wehrenbach. Both mills can be reached by following the Pfadi-Weg westwards to Burgwies from the tram terminus at Rehalp. The Pfadi-Weg itself is of interest being a 2.4 kilometre-long trail inaugurated in 2002 in honour of Lord Baden-Powell, the founder of the Pathfinder (Pfadfinder) movement.

A waterwheel at the former Trichtenhausermühle in Witikon

To learn about the workings of a mill visit Mühlerama at Seefeldstrasse 231 (Mühle-bach). This hands-on museum is housed inside the sprawling four-storey Mühle Tiefen-brunnen, a former brewery constructed in the late 1890s, which was converted into a flour mill by Wehrli Brothers in 1913. The mill closed in 1983 and reopened in 1986 as a cultural centre, of which the museum is a part. Up to 10000 kilos of flour are still produced here annually using the original electrically-powered equipment, although this hardly compares with the 2000 kilos produced each hour when the mill was in full commercial production.

63 The Oldest Mosque in Switzerland

District 8 (Weinegg), the Mahmud Mosque
(Mahmud-Moschee) at Forchstrasse 323
Tram 11 Balgrist

Standing at Lenggstrasse 75 in the suburb of Balgrist (Weinegg) is the sturdy belfry of a Swiss Protestant church. There is nothing unusual in this, since Christians are by far the largest faith group in Zurich. What is unusual is that directly across the street at Forchstrasse 323 is the Mahmud Mosque (Mahmud-Moschee), and its slender eighteen metre-high minaret topped with a green crescent is one of only four minarets in the country. Both symbols of the call to prayer, the juxta-position of belfry and minaret would be an important one for many European cities, but it is especially so in Switzerland, where the con-struction of minarets has been banned since November 2009.

Although Arabs and Berbers settled briefly in the Valais during the tenth century, the first significant appearance of Islam in Switzerland occurred during the 1950s and 60s, with the arrival of international diplomats and rich Saudi tourists. Substantial Muslim immigration from the Balkans and Turkey began during the 1980s, and accelerated greatly during the 1990s, as a result of war in the former Yugoslavia. There are now around 400 000 Muslims living in Switzerland, where on average they account for five percent of the population. Their great-est concentration is in the cantons of the German-speaking Swiss Pla-teau, with Zurich currently home to 26 000 of them. Islam is the third biggest faith group in Zurich, accounting for 7% of worshippers after Catholicism (32%) and Protestantism (27%).

There are today more than one hundred and fifty mosques across Switzerland (including eighteen in Zurich) servicing twenty or so predominantly Sunni communities. Only two of them predate the 1980s, the oldest of which is Zurich's Mahmud Mosque. It was built in 1962 for the Ahmadiyya Muslim Community, which was founded in the Punjab in 1899 by Mirza Ghulam Ahmad (1835–1908). Ahmad proclaimed himself to be two messianic figures rolled into one, namely the 'Second Coming of the Prophet Jesus', predicted by the Holy *Quran* to return to Earth in the final days to defeat the antichrist, as well as the *Mahdi*, predicted to transform the world thereafter into a perfect Islamic society.

Ahmad believed that his message of peace had special relevance for the West, which he felt had slipped into materialism. Consequently, several Ahmadiyya communities were founded in Europe, including the one in Zurich in 1946. The foundation stone of the Mahmud Mosque was laid by Ahmad's own daughter, and the opening was attended by both the mayor of Zurich and the president of the UN General Assembly.

That the Ahmadiyya Muslim Community is not acknowledged by many Muslims, who view Ahmad's claims as heretical, serves as a reminder that Islam, like the other great Abrahamic faiths (Christianity and Judaism), contains several factions.

The Mahmud Mosque (Mahmud-Moschee) on Forchstrasse is the oldest mosque in Switzerland

Even the Ahmadiyya movement itself became divided after Ahmad's death, the Ahmadiyya Muslim Community believing him to be a genuine prophet, the Lahore Ahmadiyya Movement seeing him as no more than a *Mujaddid* or scholar of God. Visiting the Mahmud Mosque (or indeed any of Zurich's other mosques) on a Friday is a good way for a non-Muslim to grapple with such complexities.

Switzerland's three other mosques with minarets are in Geneva (1978), Winterthur (2004), and Wangen (2009). It should be said that until planning permission was sought for the minaret at Wangen there was very little opposition to the presence of minarets or indeed mosques in Switzerland. Fortunately in Balgrist relations are still harmonious, where for example the church is happy to allow visitors to the mosque the use of its car park during Friday prayers. Whilst the Muslim call to prayer has never been permitted from the minaret, the volume of the church bells opposite has been reduced by the installation of plastic screens in the belfry. Muslims don't absolutely need their minarets

This sturdy church belfry stands opposite the slender minaret of Zurich's Mahmud Mosque (Mahmud-Moschee)

(the earliest mosques lacked them) any more than Christians absolutely need their belfries – and the peace of non-believers must be taken into account, too. What is important is that the followers of both faiths have the freedom to worship in peace and harmony.

A more modest example of a mosque in Zurich is the Merkez Mosque (Diyanet Merkez Camii/Merkez-Moschee) at Kochstrasse 22 (Hard). Lacking a minaret this prayer hall is managed by the Zurich Turkish-Islamic Cultural Association (Zürcher Türkisch-Islamischer Kultur-verein). The word 'Merkez' means central in both Turkish and Arabic.

Other places of interest nearby:
64, 65

64 "Burghölzli eifach!"

District 8 (Weinegg), the Zurich University
Psychiatric Hospital (Psychiatrische
Universitätsklinik Zürich) at Lenggstrasse 31
Tram 11 Balgrist

Should one start exhibiting signs of mental fragility in Switzerland someone will probably recommend that he should "vom gälbe wägeli abgholt werdä" (be collected by the little yellow car). The yellow car, of course, is the ambulance that will take you to the nearest psychiatric hospital. In Zurich the recommendation is even more specific: "Burghölzli eifach!" (Burghölzli one-way!). Burghölzli-Hügel is the name of a wooded hill in Weinegg on the slopes of which the Zurich University Psychiatric Hospital (Psychiatrische Universitätsklinik Zürich) is located – and a visit there can be therapeutic even for those in robust health.

From the tram stop in the suburb of Balgrist (Weinegg) it is only a short walk to the hospital grounds. One is immediately struck by how green the place is, with fields and trees all around. Turn left along August-Forel-Strasse and soon the façade of the main hospital building reveals itself. It is possible for the visitor to take a peep inside the foyer and to pause there a while to reflect on the important work done here past and present.

The history of the hospital began in the early 1860s, when the university physician Wilhelm Griesinger proposed the building of a modern psychiatric hospital in Zurich, where the mentally ill could be treated in a humane way. This would set it apart from its predecessor, which was a traditional asylum *(Irrenhaus)* that stood on Predigerplatz (Rathaus). Although Griesinger died before the opening of the new hospital at Burghölzli he is still considered its founder.

Between 1870 and 1879 the hospital had three directors, namely Bernhard von Gudden, Gustav Huguenin, and Eduard Hitzig. All three practised medicine from a biological standpoint, with brain pathology and physiology being the focus of their research. The fourth director at Burghölzli was Auguste-Henri Forel, and it was under his leadership between 1879 and 1898 that the hospital began gaining an international reputation. With over three hundred patients under his care Forel combined the dynamic approach of contemporary French psychiatry with the biological orientation of the German school of psychiatric thought.

A sundial marks the church of the Zurich University Psychiatric Hospital (Psychiatrische Universitätsklinik Zürich)

Es schreitet die Zeit
Es schwindet das Leid
Es kehret die Freud

The most illustrious period at Burghölzli came with the director-ship of Eugen Bleuler between 1898 and 1927. This period witnessed the advent of psychoanalysis in Europe, and the emergence of Freud-ian psychiatric theories. Bleuler's assistant at Burghölzli between 1900 and 1909 was the psychologist Carl Gustav Jung (1875–1961), the father of analytical psychology. Having met Freud in 1907 he implemented many of his concepts at Burghölzli, together with his own ideas on word association, personality types, and dream analysis (for more in-formation visit the C. G. Jung Institute in Küsnacht). Bleuler and Jung together created a new standard of doctor-patient relationship, one in which the latest treatment therapies could be practised. And Burghölzli today continues to be an important centre for psychiatric research and the treatment of mental illness.

Continuing around the outside of the main building one notices how unlike a psychiatric hospital it appears. Indeed, with its wooden shutters, graceful ironwork, and pretty gardens it appears at times more like a French chateau! The effect is enhanced by the presence of the Weinberg Riesbach, a vineyard growing grape varieties such as Blauburgunder, Gewürztraminer, and Riesling, as

A well-stocked orchard surrounds the hospital at Burghölzli

well as Räuschling, which is only found in the German-speaking parts of Switzerland.

Walk down the side of the hospital now, beneath an arch festooned with Laburnum, to where the path divides. Straight ahead is the Burghölzli-Hügel through which a series of paths have been cut. Accompanied only by birdsong a walk here is truly a therapy in itself. The path to the right passes the rear of the hospital and the clinic church (Spitalkirche), outside which hangs a sundial. On it are inscribed the following wise words: "Es schreitet die Zeit, Es schwindet das Leid, Es kehret die Freud" (Time is passing, pain is diminishing, joy is returning".

Having almost returned to our starting point one last surprise awaits. On the left is an orchard of old and rare varieties of apples, pears, plums, cherries, quince, greengages, and walnuts. The almost six hundred trees in one hundred and thirty two varieties were planted by the hospital gardener Kurt Zurbrügg, and are best seen during the annual spring Fruit Blossom Festival (Obstblütenfest). The bucolic scene is made complete by the flock of sheep grazing beneath the boughs.

Other places of interest nearby: 63, 65, 75

65 Where Old Trams Go to Rest

**District 8 (Weinegg), the Zurich Tram Museum
(Tram-Museum Zürich) at Forchstrasse 260
Tram 11 Burgwies**

Zurich's tram system is one of Europe's finest. With fifteen urban routes (Lines 2–17) serving most city neighbourhoods it is supplemented by bus, trolleybus, and S-Bahn routes, as well as two funicular railways, and a cogwheel railway, too (see no. 53). The tram network is also used by Zurich's so-called Cargotram, which is used to transport freight and waste materials. All are operated by the city-owned public transport operator Verkehrsbetriebe Zürich (VBZ).

A restored tram in the Zurich Tram Museum
(Tram-Museum Zürich) on Forchstrasse

Plans to introduce trams to Zurich were proposed as early as the 1860s but it wasn't until 1882 that the first tram appeared on the city's streets. Operated initially by several private companies, they were acquired in 1896 by the municipal tramway operator Städtische Strassenbahn Zürich (StStZ), and by 1931 had been integrated into a single network. In 1950 StStZ was renamed VBZ.

In 2007 to mark the 125th anniversary of the city's tram system the Zurich Tram Museum (Tram-Museum Zürich) was opened at Forchstrasse 260 (Weinegg). The same year also marked the fortieth anniversary of the founding of the Zurich Tram Museum Society (Verein Tram-Museum Zürich), whose volunteer members have worked tirelessly to save Zurich's old trams from being scrapped.

Inside a restored tram

Long before the present museum was opened the greatest problem faced by the society was finding the space to restore their trams. The next challenge was where to display them when finished, and the first answer came in 1989, when a tiny depot with space for just five tram-cars was secured in the district of Höngg. Public support for the little museum grew quickly, and on open days it was not unusual to see refur-bished vintage trams trundling in and out of the depot. Space was lim-ited though and in 2005 Zurich City Council voted unanimously that the city's oldest preserved tram depot (1897) on Forchstrasse be made available to the museum.

At the heart of the present collection are twenty two tramcars, including six trailers and three maintenance vehicles. Dating from as far back as 1897, most of the vehicles are fully operational. On the last weekend of the month between May and October two of the trams operate every half hour along the specially designated Museumslinie 21, picking up passengers at Hauptbahnhof, Paradeplatz, Bellevue, and other city-centre stops, and transporting them to and from the museum. The thrilling experience is often enhanced by the personnel donning historic uniforms.

Whilst the majority of vehicles sport Zurich's iconic blue and white livery, a pair of early trams have been painted in the colours of the private companies that once operated them (a green car of Zürich Oerlikon Seebach (1897) and a yellow car of Limmattal Strassenbahn (1900)). Later vehicles represent important milestones in Zurich's tram history as the city responded to increasing urbanization and industrialisation. These include the development of the four wheeler, the 1930s *Elefant*-type bogie car, and the Swiss Standard Tram. More modern additions include examples of the *Karpfen* and *Mirage* trams, which were replaced in 2006 by the low-floor *Cobra* type.

The Zurich Tram Museum is a hands-on place, and children and adults alike will enjoy climbing on board the vehicles and pretending to be a driver. One of the trams contains a small cinema showing archive film of old trams, and in another a recording of street sounds adds to the atmosphere. The collection is rounded out with displays of drivers' and conductors' uniforms, tram tickets, and ticket machines, as well as a mezzanine floor containing a model tramway and a study area with old documents and photographs. A shop on the ground floor sells all manner of tram-related gifts including books, postcards, and scale models.

Alongside the Tram Museum is a charming ensemble of half-timbered farm buildings know as the Quartierhof. Such buildings are known in Swiss German as *Riegelhäuser*, and surrounding these ones are some charming old kitchen gardens.

Other places of interest nearby: 63, 64, 66

66 A Treat for the Senses

District 8 (Weinegg), the New Botanical Garden
of Zurich University (Neuer Botanischer Garten
der Universität Zürich) at Zollikerstrasse 107
Tram 11, 31 Hegibachplatz, then Bus 33, 77
Botanischer Garten or walk

In 1976 the University of Zurich relocated its botanical garden from a cramped former medieval bastion in the city centre to a new location in the suburban quarter of Weinegg (District 8) (see no. 9). Formerly the private park of the Villa Schönau the new garden covers an area of approximately thirteen acres (5.3 hectares). With over nine thousand plant species it offers visitors a botanical tour of the world without leaving Zurich. It is also a real treat for the senses.

The New Botanical Garden of Zurich University (Neuer Botanischer Garten der Universität Zürich) was laid out by local garden architect Fred Eicher. His well-considered design provided a modern research base for the university's Institute of Systematic Botany (Institut für Systematische Botanik) whilst preserving the overall feel of the original English-style park (note the venerable Copper Beech (Blutbuche) by the main entrance). This has resulted in a very special recreation area in which visitors can get lost for hours.

An important consideration when establishing the garden was that its ten thousand plant species should be grouped together according to their growing conditions. Accordingly, within the garden there are thirteen distinct plant habitats (biotopes) representing global plant diversity, three of which occupy futuristic-looking greenhouses. Two of the biotopes contain plants native to Zurich, namely the *Einheimischer Wald* (which includes indigenous forest trees such as beech and spruce, and forest-floor plants such as larkspur and wood anemones), and the *Einheimische*

The botanical garden contains many
secret corners

Wiese (including clover, dandelion, and a hundred or more species of meadow herbs and grasses). The mountainous regions of Switzerland, as well as the rest of the world, are represented by the *Alpinum* biotope, a rock-strewn garden with hardy shrubs such as rhododendron and azalea, and delicate flowers such as pulsatilla and fritillary, all of which have adapted to the harsh climatic conditions above the tree line.

Hotter climes are represented by the *Mittelmeergarten* biotope, with its shrubby pungent herbs, such as rosemary, thyme and lavender, and trees such as cork oak, fig, and cypress. Harsher still is the *Trockenfluss* biotope, in which the plants of the world's dry river valleys are represented, including specially-adapted poppies and lilies. At the other extreme is the *Wasserpflanzengarten* biotope, a water garden containing higher aquatic plants such as South American water lilies.

Especially interesting is the *Nutzpflanzengarten* biotope, in which one hundred and fifty cultivated plants useful to mankind are represented, and the *Färberpflanzen* biotope, which contains natural dye plants such as woad, indigo, and chamomile, which man has used since Neolithic times.

The other two outside biotopes are the *Frühlingsgarten*, which is obviously at its best in spring when it is ablaze with bulbs and fruit blossoms, and the *Fleischfresser*, which consists of carnivorous plants displayed in cabinets during the summer months. These curious plants eat flies to gain the salt that is missing in the nutrient-poor soils in which they grow.

The remaining three biotopes are housed in the garden's three glasshouses. Unique in Switzerland at the time they were constructed they consist of tinted Plexiglas hemispheres on an aluminium frame. The largest containing epiphytes and orchids represents the tropics *(Tropenhaus)*, whilst the two others represent the sub-tropics *(Subtropenhaus)*, with its tree ferns, and the savanna *(Savannenhaus)*, with its succulents.

Another botanical garden is the Stadtgärtnerei at Sackzelgasse 25–27 (Sihlfeld), which contains an abundance of native and exotic flowers, shrubs, and trees. Worth looking out for is the Chinese Paperbark Maple *(Acer Griseum)*, renowned for its decorative exfoliating bark, translucent pieces of which often stay attached to the branches until worn away.

Other places of interest nearby: 65, 67, 68, 70, 71, 72, 73

67 A Villa Built on Tobacco

District 8 (Mühlebach), the Villa Patumbah at Zollikerstrasse 128
Tram 11 or Bus 31 Hegibachplatz

A preferred address for Zurich's well-heeled during the nineteenth century was the municipality of Riesbach on the eastern shore of Lake Zurich (Zürichsee). It was incorporated into Zurich in 1893 and is today administratively a part of District 8 (Seefeld, Mühlebach and Weinegg). Running the length of the area is Zollikerstrasse and along it a number of imposing private villas were erected. They include at number 32 the Villa Bleuler designed by renowned Zurich architect Alfred Friedrich Bluntschli (1842–1930) for a colonel in the Swiss army, and at number 107 the Villa Schönau built for the Bodmer-Abegg family, the garden of which is now home to the New Botanical Garden of Zurich University (Neuer Botanischer Garten der Universität Zürich) (see no. 66).

Perhaps the most interesting of all Zurich's grand villas stands across the road from the Villa Schönau at Zollikerstrasse 128. Known as the Villa Patumbah it was built for the wealthy Zurich entrepre-

The Villa Patumbah on Zollikerstrasse

neur Karl Fürchtegott Grob (1823–1893), who made his fortune from a tobacco plantation in Sumatra. Grob paid tribute to the source of his wealth with the name of his villa, the word *Patumbah* being Malay for "desirable country".

The Villa Patumbah was designed by the architects Alfred Chiodera and Theophil Tschudy, and was constructed between 1883 and 1885. It is one of Zurich's outstanding examples of Historicism, an architectural style that fused elements and ornaments from the past – notably Classical, Romanesque, Gothic, and Baroque – in a nostalgic and eclectic combination. The style was popular during the late nineteenth century for both grand private homes and public buildings.

The exterior of the villa is neo-Renaissance, consisting of a base of rusticated masonry above which rises a delicate *piano nobile*. Between the windows, balcony doors, and sculptural niches are panels painted to give the impression of marble. The windows, doors and niches themselves are framed with real marble from Carrara and Verona. The balcony is flanked by statues of Mercury and Flora, the former representing Grob's commercial acumen and the latter the wealth resulting from it. Over the *piano nobile* is a similarly decorated upper floor punctuated by a series of oculi. The façade facing the street is particularly impressive, with the name *PATUMBAH* inscribed boldly beneath the roof line.

An ornate, single-storey glazed corridor connects the villa to a rustic ancillary building once used by the family as stables. This explains the horses' heads carved onto the gables and the equestrian motifs on the ceramic tiles. The building can also be considered Historicist since the fretwork gables *(Laubsägestil)* hark back to traditional Swiss country forms.

Inside the villa the main public rooms face the garden, and again they are realised in eclectic Historicist style. The drawing room and gentlemen's salon are neo-Renaissance with wainscotting and floral wallpaper on the walls, and wood-panelled ceilings. The neo-Gothic salon features an elaborate green-tiled stove, and the lady's salon is neo-Rococo in style. The first floor was reserved for the family's private rooms, with the upper floor used by the staff. Both are ranged around a wooden gallery carved and painted with East Asian motifs, above which is a glorious stained glass cupola.

The villa's extensive garden was laid out in the early 1890s by Swiss garden architect Evariste Mertens (1846–1907). Immediately to the rear of the villa, and covering a quarter of the total available area, Mertens established an English-style garden with formal flower beds, stands of ornamental trees, and a fountain fashioned from giant clam shells. A pavilion had been constructed at the same time as the house, and the two were connected by a tree-lined avenue. The rest of the garden was laid out in the style of an English park.

Almost from the beginning the idyllic surroundings of the Villa Patumbah were under threat. Although Grob purchased thirteen thousand square metres of land on which to build his home, it was not enough to keep the pressures of modernity at bay forever. During his tenure at the villa a new S-Bahn line was planned to pass right through his back garden, in response to which he contributed a hundred thousand Swiss Francs for the construction of a tunnel. After Grob's death from a tropical disease the villa passed through several hands before becoming an old people's home. In 1977 it became the property of the City of Zurich by which time the northern half of the garden had been sold off and subsequently built over. Fortunately the southern half was restored to its original condition during the late 1980s, and the recently-renovated villa is now home to the Swiss Heritage Society (Schweizer Heimatschutz).

Other places of interest nearby: 66, 68, 70, 71, 72, 73, 74

68　Dining in the Dark

District 8 (Mühlebach), the Restaurant blindekuh
at Mühlebachstrasse 148
Tram 2, 4 Höschgasse; Bus 33, 912, 913 Höschgasse
(Note: advance table reservation is recommended)

It is said that if a person is deprived of one of their senses, those remaining are often heightened. One way of testing this theory is to dine in a restaurant in total darkness, and to experience a meal using smell and taste alone. Such "dark restaurants" exist around the world from Beijing and Sydney to Paris and Istanbul, where far from being simply novelties they serve to remind the sighted of the everyday travails of the blind. The world's very first "dark restaurant", however, was established in Zurich, where it served as a blueprint for those that followed.

The seventy-seat Restaurant blindekuh at Mühlebachstrasse 148 (Mühlebach) opened in 1999, as part of an initiative mounted by the Blind-Liecht Foundation established a year earlier, which works to create employment opportunities for blind and visually impaired people. The venue chosen was a former Methodist chapel and the original proprietor was blind clergyman Jürg Spielmann, the first president of the foundation, ably assisted by a staff of three blind and visually impaired colleagues. The name of the restaurant (meaning 'Blind Cow') is the German equivalent of Blind Man's Bluff, a children's game with ancient origins in which a blindfolded child attempts to tag one of a group of sighted children, who in turn attempt to avoid the blindfolded one.

So popular was the blindekuh in Zurich that another restaurant of the same name opened in Basel in 2005. As with all "dark restaurants" the only light permitted in both restaurants is in the toilets and the entrance hall, where patrons are shown the weekly menu. All light-emitting gadgets, such as mobile telephones and even luminous watches, must be placed inside a locker for the duration of the visit. After making their selection diners are led into the pitch black dining room, placing their hands (and their trust) on the shoulders of the blind member of staff leading the way.

Once inside the dining room the customers can hear what's happening but see nothing whatsoever. The staff accompany diners throughout their meal, explaining what they are doing, where they are placing things, and when they are pouring drinks. This can be an enlightening experience, especially if one stays for about two hours as is recommended by the restaurant. Roles that the sighted consider normal are suddenly reversed: the sighted cannot see and are dependent on the blind, who are completely and comfortably in control of the proceedings (the cooks, incidentally, are sighted and renowned for their use of fresh produce). The experience can be unnerving at the beginning but with the friendly and highly professional staff always to hand no guest need feel fearful of the dark.

The Restaurant blindekuh on Mühlebachstrasse was the world's first "dark restaurant"

The blindekuh restaurants have won several awards for their innovative approach to social dining, and deservedly so. They also offer cultural events including readings and concerts in the dark. Inevitably their success has spawned a host of imitators around the world, with some novelty restaurants offering blindfolds to their diners only for them to be served by waiters wearing night vision goggles! The success of "dark restaurants" in China is even explained by the fact that they are popular with Internet daters, who find it easier to socialise in the dark. Compared with such relatively frivolous intentions, Zurich's blindekuh remains the first and the best "dark restaurant".

Zurich is also home to Hiltl, the world's oldest vegetarian restaurant. It was founded by Bavarian journeyman tailor Ambrosius Hiltl (1877–1969), who became interested in vegetarian diets after his doctor diagnosed rheumatoid arthritis and advised him not to eat meat. Accordingly he entered the city's Vegetarians' Home and Teetotallers' Café on Sihlstrasse (City), where he was cured. When the job of restaurant manager became vacant he applied for the job, and it has operated under his name ever since.

Other places of interest nearby: 66, 67, 69, 70, 71, 72, 73, 74

69 A Shrine to Coffee

District 8 (Mühlebach), the Johann Jacobs Museum
at Seefeldquai 17
Tram 2, 4 Feldeggstrasse; Bus 912, 916 Feldeggstrasse

Seefeldquai 17 (Mühlebach) has been a prestigious address since 1913, when an elegant neo-Baroque villa was built here for the wealthy Zurich engineer and politician Dr. Fritz Ernst. The grey-green sandstone walls and stately roofline still impart the impression of a country house in Bern, transposed to the lakeside of Zurich. Although Dr. Ernst is long gone, his marble-lined entrance hall, grand dining and music rooms, and cellar that once contained a bowling alley are still extant, only now they are home to the fascinating Johann Jacobs Museum.

The origin of the museum goes back to 1895, and the opening of a specialist coffee shop in Bremen by Johann Jacobs (1869–1958). By the time Klaus Johann Jacobs took control of his great uncle's company in 1970 the Jacobs coffee brand was well established, and in 1982 he merged the company with Swiss chocolate company Interfood, to form Jacobs Suchard. Two years later the Jacobs Suchard Museum was founded, and when the company was sold to Kraft Foods in 1990, the contents of the museum were passed to the Zurich-based Jacobs Foundation (a charitable organisation set up by Klaus Jacobs in 1988 to support the development of professional and social skills in young people around the world). Kraft, meanwhile, continue to market Jacobs coffee from the Baltic all the way to Iran.

The Johann Jacobs Museum illustrates the great socio-cultural im-

An ornate coffee service in the Johann Jacobs Museum on Seefeldquai

pact made by coffee following its introduction into Europe during the first half of the seventeenth century by way of the East India and Levantine trade routes, and the Ottoman Empire. Many people don't realise that not only is coffee today the second most important commodity in world trade after petroleum (and the most popular drink in Western Europe) but also that twenty five million people are employed in its cultivation and processing.

The museum's permanent collection consists of porcelain and silver coffee jugs, cups, and other accessories, and illustrates how artists responded to the growing popularity of what initially was an exotic beverage enjoyed only in aristocratic cir-

A splendid coffee pot in the Johann Jacobs Museum

cles. Typical are the porcelain sculptural groups of coffee drinkers, used to adorn well-to-do tables on special occasions, and the elegant English and French silver jugs with matching burners, their distinctive high spouts used to prevent the coffee grounds from falling into the cup. The permanent collection also includes numerous prints and paintings, including works by Henri de Toulouse-Lautrec, Edouard Manet, William Hogarth, and Roy Lichtenstein. The most interesting of them depict the habits not only of those drinking coffee but also of those preparing it.

Periodically the museum stages special exhibitions covering subjects as diverse as coffee culture in Japan, picture postcards of coffee houses, and the part played by coffee in the West's artistic representations of the Orient. Most enlightening was an exhibition entitled "The Dream of Happiness" telling the forgotten story of the two thousand impoverished Swiss men and women, who between 1852 and 1857 emigrated to the Brazilian province of Sao Paulo to work as coffee pickers. Publicity at the time made Brazil seem like an earthly paradise, whereas in reality the Swiss were treated like slaves, with little prospect of settling debts or becoming free farmers. After a revolt was staged against the bad working conditions the cause was taken up in Switzerland, and emigration rapidly dried up.

The extensive museum library, which is open by appointment only, contains some five thousand coffee-related items from around the world. Of particular interest are the early travelogues in which the coffee plant is depicted as an entirely new species, as well as historical works highlighting the part played by the humble coffee bean in shaping the colonial history of entire nations. Medical treatises contain debates over the pros and cons of imbibing the new coffee drink, whilst philosophical tracts ruminate over the cultural implications of coffee, and whether it should be banned. It's hard to imagine now that the growing popularity of coffee houses used by the middle classes was once seen in some quarters as providing a potential forum for revolution!

Since undergoing extensive refurbishment in 2013 the museum has broadened its scope considerably to illustrate the importance of global trade not only in coffee but also other important commodities such as oil, diamonds, cotton and tobacco.

To purchase fine coffees in Zurich try the old fashioned delicatessen Schwarzenbach at Münstergasse 19 (Rathaus), where beans are roasted in an open window, filling the street with wonderful aromas. Also recommended is the coffee specialist Kaffeepur at Glasmalerstrasse 5 (Langstrasse), where beans, blends, and coffee machines are available.

Other places of interest nearby: 68, 70, 71, 72

70 Le Corbusier's Last Stand

**District 8 (Seefeld), the Centre Le Corbusier
at Höschgasse 8
Tram 2, 4 Höschgasse; Bus 912, 916 Elektrowatt**

There are several distinctive structures in Zürichhorn Park on the eastern shore of Lake Zurich (Zürichsee), the most striking of which is undoubtedly the Centre Le Corbusier at Höschgasse 8 (Seefeld). Described as a *Gesamtkunstwerk*, that is a total work of art, it reflects the harmonic unity of the artist's views not only on architecture but also sculpture, art, writing, and interior design. As such it is perhaps the only structure of its kind in the world.

The origin of the structure goes back to the late 1950s, when the Swiss-born (naturalised French) architect Charles-Edouard Jeanneret-Gris – known to the world as Le Corbusier (1887–1965) – was befriended by Heidi Weber. A successful Zurich-based interior designer, Weber was impressed less by Le Corbusier's controversial modular concrete architecture, which had made him world famous, and more by his other artistic abilities, notably as a painter. Art was only a private passion for Le Corbusier but Weber believed it was every bit as important as his architecture, and that a way should be found for all his talents to be preserved for posterity.

Weber's friendship with Le Corbusier lasted for seven years during which time she visited him in Paris every couple of weeks. She staged regular exhibitions of his work in her gallery Mezzanin in Zurich, slowly winning his confidence and eventually the rights to represent his work

The colourful Centre
Le Corbusier in Seefeld

for a thirty year period. Little wonder that Le Corbusier described her as "a monster of perseverance, devotion and enthusiasm".

In 1960 Weber had the vision of creating a museum designed by Le Corbusier, where his ideas could be presented in an ideal environment. The result was a pavilion known variously as the Centre Le Corbusier or the Heidi-Weber-Haus, and it would be Le Corbusier's last commission. Begun in 1964 but only completed posthumously in 1967 the minimalist structure represents the culmination of Le Corbusier's studies in architecture, interior design, and the visual arts. Gone are the hulking concrete edifices he is so often remembered for and instead he has opted for a surprisingly light design formed by a pair of pre-fabricated glass-and-steel cubes.

It is interesting to note that Le Corbusier altered his original design from concrete to steel in 1962, suggesting that he was now moving in a new direction (only the floor is of concrete and the rest was put together using twenty thousand steel bolts). The exterior surfaces are enlivened by multi-coloured enamel plates, planned according to a specific rhythmic system, and over the entire structure are suspended a pair of umbrella-like grey steel roofs weighing forty tons. Some commentators have compared the building to a Mondrian painting set in parkland.

Inside the pavilion Le Corbusier's penchant for functionality is immediately apparent, bringing to mind his famous comment that "a house is a machine for living in". Undoubtedly Le Corbusier could have lived here and his spirit seems everywhere apparent. The items on display, which are spread across two storeys, were assembled by Weber herself and remind the onlooker that Le Corbusier was much more than just an architect.

A Zurich building inspired by the work of Le Corbusier is Kraftwerk 1, an apartment block at Hardturmstrasse 261–269 (Escher Wyss). It was completed in 2000 by a cooperative with the aim of experimenting with new types of living arrangements. The apartments range between two and thirteen rooms in size enabling up to fifteen people to share a single space. The main building's huge communal terrace is inspired by Corbusier's modernist residential housing design principle *Unité d'Habitation*.

Other places of interest nearby: 67, 68, 69, 71, 72, 73, 74

71   Inside an Artist's Studio

District 8 (Seefeld), Atelier Hermann Haller
at Höschgasse 6
Tram 2, 4 Höschgasse; Bus 912, 916 Elektrowatt

A must for anyone interested in applied arts is Zurich's Museum Bellerive at Höschgasse 3 (Seefeld), where since 1968 the city's holdings of furniture, jewellery, tapestry, ceramics, and stained glass have been displayed. The collection encompasses everything from fourth century Coptic textiles and ancient Peruvian weaving to Art Nouveau ceramics and Russian marionettes from the 1920s. And the imposing former villa housing the collection is of interest, too, having once been the home of textile manufacturer Julius Bloch.

Tucked between the museum and the adjacent Centre Le Corbusier is something altogether more intimate. The Atelier Hermann Haller at Höschgasse 6 is an idiosyncratic artist's studio with a unique atmosphere, and a visit during the summer months is highly recommended. The sculptor Hermann Haller (1880–1950) was born in Bern and was first inspired creatively aged fourteen after seeing a painting by the Swiss artist Ferdinand Hodler (1853–1918). Initially Haller studied architecture in Stuttgart but then relocated to Munich to take up art under Franz von Stuck (1863–1928). It was here that he became friends with fellow Bern artist Paul Klee (1879–1940). Another of Haller's acquaintances was author

Inside the Atelier Hermann Haller in Seefeld

Hermann Hesse (1877–1962), who borrowed the sculptor's name for Harry Haller, the protagonist of his novel *Der Steppen-wolf* (1927).

Patronage enabled Haller to travel to Rome, and it was during this time that he decided upon sculpture as his chosen discipline, and in which he now began to make a name for himself. Until 1914 he lived with his family in Paris but then returned to Switzerland and settled in Zurich. During the 1920s he became Switzerland's most renowned figurative sculptor, and his fame spread throughout the German-speaking world.

Haller designed his studio on Höschgasse in 1932 together with Hermann Herter, Zurich's chief municipal architect at the time and an advocate of the pared down Modernist style known as *Neue Sachlichkeit* (New Objectivity). Erected originally as a temporary structure because of planning regulations it is of light wooden construction with large windows and weatherproof *Eternit* tiles on the façade. As such the building is not only an important example of a purely functional artist's studio but also a rare example of *Neue Sachlichkeit* rendered in wood.

Haller was granted a doctorate in 1933 by Zurich University, and he remained based at the studio until his death in 1950. Afterwards it was preserved much as he left it by his wife and former student Hedwig Haller-Braus, and in 1982 she handed it over to the City of Zurich on the condition that it be opened to the public.

The studio today contains artefacts relating to all aspects of Haller's creative process, from spontaneous sketches, studies, and small-scale clay and cement models to full-sized plaster forms. The latter were used to create the moulds in which Haller cast his large scale bronzes using the lost wax technique. Also on display is a new casting of a portrait bust by Haller made by the Felix Lehner foundry in St. Gallen, using one of Haller's original plaster forms. Such busts recall the sculptor's extensive circle of acquaintances, which included key figures from the world of art, culture and science, who resided in Zurich during the 1920s and 30s.

Many other pieces on display speak eloquently of Haller's ongoing interest in representing the female form, whilst also creating a dialogue with the onlooker over the notion of beauty. Don't forget to climb the wooden staircase to peer inside the eaves of the studio, where row upon row of clay models are stored.

Two locations in Zurich give an impression of Haller's large-scale public works. One is his 1937 equestrian statue in front of the Fraumünster depicting former mayor of Zurich Hans Waldmann (1435–1489), and the other is his *Mäd-chen mit erhobenen Händen* (Woman with Raised Hands) on Mythenquai (see nos. 30 & 35). The original models for both of these works are displayed in the studio. Afterwards take time to relax on the studio's wooden veran-dah, where the lovely view can be enjoyed over coffee and cake.

A model for Hermann Haller's famous statue of Hans Waldmann

A striking new counterpart to the Museum Bellerive is the Museum für Gestaltung – Schaudepot in the Toni-Areal at Pfingstweidstrasse 96 (Escher Wyss). It contains the four permanent collections – Posters, Design, Applied Arts and Graphics – of the Zurich University of the Arts (Zürcher Hochschule der Künst) on the campus of which it stands. The museum is actively involved in education, teaching and research in the areas of design and visual communication, and together with the university's media and information centre it forms a globally-renowned visual archive of design history. The museum previously occupied a supremely functionalist building from 1933 at Aus-tellungsstrasse 60 (Gewerbeschuule), which now hosts temporary exhibitions.

Other places of interest nearby: 67, 68, 69, 72, 73, 74

72 In a Peaceful Chinese Garden

District 8 (Seefeld), the Chinese Garden Zurich
(Chinagarten Zürich) in Zürichhorn Park
on Bellerivestrasse
Tram 2, 4 Fröhlichstrasse; Bus 912, 916 Chinagarten

The Zürichhorn on the eastern shore of Lake Zurich (Zürichsee) is a river delta, formed after the retreat of the Linth glacier during the last Ice Age. It is difficult to imagine such elemental forces today since the river is now culverted and the area is the site of one of Zurich's most popular recreation areas. As the Zürichhorn Park it contains sculptures by modern artists such as Henry Moore and Jean Tinguely, several unusual buildings including the Centre Le Corbusier, and is the site of Switzerland's largest open-air cinema (see nos. 15, 70 & 71). Also located here is a traditional Chinese water garden and its high red-painted walls make it a welcome oasis of calm in what during the summer months is a very busy part of the city.

The Chinese Garden Zürich (Chinagarten Zürich) on Bellerivestrasse (Seefeld) was a gift from Zurich's twin town of Kunming, the capital and largest city of Yunnan Province in Southwestern China. The gift recalls Kunming's appreciation for help given by Zurich's Water Board during the development of its water supply and drainage system. Laid out in 1993 the garden represents a collaboration between gardeners in Zurich and Kunming, and was opened to visitors in Spring 1994. The mayor of Kunming attended the ceremony, as did the mayor of Zurich.

Before entering the garden look closer at the surrounding wall. It is topped with protective ceramic dragons and acts as a boundary between the profane world outside and the sacred one within. A trio of windows barred with bamboo staves permit no more than a tantalising glimpse from one world to the other. The visitor enters the garden through the main portal, over which the name "China Garden" is written on a golden nameplate. Notice the nine rows of nails attached to the door which were originally reserved exclusively for the emperor but are now commonplace in traditional Chinese gardens, especially in Kunming. An inner door bears carved panels depicting excerpts from Chinese legends.

Once inside the garden the visitor is confronted immediately by a miniaturised mountain. For the Chinese such rock formations give a garden stability, and are seen as representing bones in the human body, serving to fuse man and the landscape to the exclusion of the world outside. The rock is a synthesis of physical and mental landscapes, a geographical Yin and Yang.

To the left a traditional zigzag bridge connects the mainland with an island representing the land of immortality. The island's circular pavilion embodies the middle or fifth cardinal direction in Chinese culture. More prosaically the inscriptions on the pavilion remind the passer-by that water is the reason for the special friendship between the cities of Zurich and Kunming.

The mainland is regained on the other side of the island by means of a traditional humpbacked bridge. On the left is a rock garden and a six-sided pagoda, which provides the garden with geographical height. The carvings on the pagoda are heavy with allegory,

The Chinese Garden Zurich (Chinagarten Zürich) in Zürichhorn Park

for example the phoenix as a symbol of an empress, flowers representing female beauty, and on the inside of the pagoda, symbols of good luck. To the right the visitor reaches a square-shaped pavilion dedicated to Spring. It is adorned with a pair of golden phoenixes, a magpie, and plum blossoms, all motifs equated with the annual rebirth of nature. Beyond the pavilion are open galleries adorned with more than five hundred still life and landscape paintings; the carved arches of the galleries are a distinctive feature of traditional Yunnan garden design.

The pavilion also acts as an entrance to the water palace, the external decoration of which has been kept simple, so that visitors can focus entirely on the sumptuously-appointed interior. The palace terrace opens out almost level with the surface of the lake, whilst to the rear is a Moon Gate and bamboo grove.

Detail of a pagoda in the Chinese Garden Zurich (Chinagarten Zürich)

The planting in Zurich's Chinese Garden is an expression of an important theme in Chinese culture, namely the Three Friends of Winter. This refers to a trinity of plants that defy the cold season: pine, bamboo, and winter cherry. Each has a separate meaning, with pine representing longevity, bamboo symbolising the ever-abundant forest, and the cherry blossom a reminder that spring is on its way.

Other places of interest nearby: 67, 68, 69, 70, 71, 73, 74

73   A World Class Private
Art Gallery

District 8 (Mühlebach), the Sammlung E. G. Bührle
at Zollikerstrasse 172
Tram 2, 4 Wildbachstrasse; Bus 912, 916 Wildbachstrasse

Art lovers in Zurich usually keep one address in mind: Heimplatz 1 (Hochschule). This is where the Kunsthaus Zürich, Switzerland's greatest art gallery, can be found containing everything from medieval religious paintings and Dutch Old Masters to works by the Impressionists and the best Swiss artists (including Ferdinand Hodler, Johann Heinrich Füssli, and Arnold Böcklin). For a world-class art gallery the Kunsthaus is unusually serene. However, for real tranquillity one should make an appointment to visit the Sammlung E. G. Bührle at Zollikerstrasse 172 (Mühlebach), which has the atmosphere of a private home.

The art collection of Emil Georg Bührle (1890–1956), a German-born industrialist, is among the most important private collections of European art created during the twentieth century. The son of a civil servant Bührle enrolled to study philology at university but quickly became immersed in the world of art. Seeing the work of the French Impressionists at the National Gallery in Berlin in 1913 served to crystallise what henceforth became a lifelong obsession with the works of these painters.

After the First World War Bührle was posted to Magdeburg, where he met his wife and began work at the tool and machine factory of his future father-in-law. In 1924 he relocated to Zurich, where he acquired the patent for an artillery gun developed by a German engineer. Aided by the German Military Command he perfected the gun at a factory in the Zurich suburb of Oerlikon, as part of the covert German rearmament programme. The manufacture of arms within Germany had been forbidden by the Treaty of Versailles. When Germany began rearming openly, however, Bührle's firm met stiff competition and instead he began supplying Belgium, France and Britain. With the outbreak of war Bührle was instructed by the Swiss Federal Council to switch supplies back to Germany after which a complete export ban was imposed.

In 1937 Bührle acquired Swiss citizenship and moved his family into a large house on Zollikerstrasse. Immediately he began acquiring pictures for the walls, including works by classic French Impression-

A world class gallery is contained in this mansion on Zollikerstrasse

ists such as Monet, Pissarro, Renoir, Manet, Cézanne, and van Gogh, as well as lesser known artists of the Barbizon School. When the collection outgrew the premises he purchased the nineteenth century villa next door at Zollikerstrasse 172, which he used as a store.

From the safety of a neutral country Bührle was able to amass a great fortune based on the worldwide export of his guns. Perhaps not surprisingly some of the paintings Bührle purchased during the war were found later to have been stolen from their Jewish owners by crooked German officials. Others were smuggled out by Jewish owners and sold under stress at a fraction of their market value. Many have subsequently been subject to high profile law suits although it was always ruled that Bührle could not have known that any of his pictures might have been sold to him illegally.

In the immediate post-war period there were not many Europeans who could write a hundred thousand pound cheque for a painting – but E.G. Bührle was one of them. As an art collector his greatest period of acquisition came in the last decade of his life between the end of the war and 1956. Blacklisted briefly by the Western Allies, Bührle's Oerlikon factory was soon back in business after the Swiss Federal Council relaxed the export ban on military exports to the West, in order to position Switzerland favourably in the impending Cold War. As the company supplied more anti-aircraft hardware so Bührle acquired more paintings, broadening his interests to include the work of the post-1900 French *avant-garde*.

A couple of years before his death Bührle financed an extension to the Kunsthaus Zürich, in which some of his own collection was temporarily displayed. After his death his family placed a representative collection of works in a foundation and in 1960 opened it to the public in the former storage villa at Zollikerstrasse 172, where they can still be seen today. The collection can be viewed on the first Sunday of each month by appointment only, tel. 0041 (0)44 422 00 86, www.buehrle.ch.

Other places of interest nearby: 64, 66, 67, 68, 74, 75

74 Food in Old Factories

District 8 (Mühlebach), a tour of restaurants in former
industrial premises beginning with the Restaurant Blaue Ente
at Seefeldstrasse 223
Tram 2, 4 Wildbachstrasse; Bus 912, 916
Wildbachstrasse

In common with other European cities that underwent industrialisation during the nineteenth century, Zurich today contains many former factories and warehouses. It is fascinating to see how these buildings have been adapted for a range of new usages, including shops, leisure centres, cultural complexes, and even a brewery (see nos. 37, 48, 78, & 83). One area in which Zürchers have excelled themselves is the conversion of former industrial premises into eateries, and what follows is a selection of the best of them.

The precursor to all Zurich's industrial-era eateries is the Restaurant Blaue Ente at Seefeldstrasse 223 (Mühlebach) on the eastern shore of Lake Zurich (Zürichsee). Opened in the early 1990s this upmarket French restaurant is part of a cultural centre housed inside the Mühle Tiefenbrunnen, a former late nineteenth century flour mill and brewery (see no. 62). The elegantly-laid dining tables are ranged around an impressive steam engine built in Winterthur in 1918, which is comple-

Restaurant Blaue Ente in Mühlebach occupies a former steam-powered flour mill

The Restaurant Rosso is located inside a converted warehouse in Escher Wyss

mented by the modern ceiling ducts, enhancing the overall post-industrial feel.

Much of Zurich's industrialisation occurred in the north and west suburbs of the city. A former paper factory at Giesshübelstrasse 15 (Alt-Wiedikon), for example, has been converted into the Sihlcity shopping and leisure complex, and a part of it is today the high-end Restaurant Rüsterei at Kalanderplatz 6. Its lofty ceilings, huge windows, and graffiti-covered concrete pillars sit surprisingly well with the elegant dining furniture, chandeliers, and ceiling-to-floor curtains (Sihlcity also contains a modern church (Sihlcity-Kirche) with striking stained glass windows by Hans Erni (b. 1909)). More modest is the Restaurant Giesserei opened inside a former foundry at Birchstrasse 108 (Oerlikon) after its closure in 1996. Used initially as an artists' squat the new occupants began cooking, which lead eventually to the building's transformation into a *bona fide* and very successful restaurant.

Not surprisingly the greatest concentration of converted factories and warehouses is in Zurich's so-called Industrie-Quartier (District 5), which is in throes of being reinvented as the fashionable Zürich-West. This was Zurich's industrial heartland, and it today offers several unusual dining possibilities. The Restaurant LaSalle is located together with a theatre, bar and jazz club inside the cavernous shell of the Schiffbau, a former foundry at Schiffbaustrasse 4 (Escher Wyss) in which lake steamers were once constructed (see no. 83). The restaurant itself is located inside a huge glass cube on the old factory floor. Less exclusive and definitely more affordable is the Restaurant les Halles inside a former food distribution warehouse reinvented as the Markthalle les Halles at Pfingstweidstrasse 6 (Escher Wyss). Together with a small bar and organic health food shop this busy restaurant is renowned for its *Moules mit Frites* (mussels and chips), which are served at communal wooden tables. The atmosphere in the restaurant is pleasantly relaxed and its design features include retro décor, Francophone wall adverts, and table football.

More modest is the Restaurant Rosso inside a converted warehouse at Geroldstrasse 31 (Escher Wyss). Regarded as one of Zurich's best places for pizza, the restaurant backs onto the railway line, and the former loading bay serves as a sun terrace. Only a pile of timber for the pizza oven stacked outside gives any clue that a restaurant is here.

Adaptive reuse in Zurich applies not only to industrial-era buildings. In the Lindenhof district, for example, there are two much older buildings that have been converted into very popular restaurants. The boisterous Restaurant Reithalle at Gessnerallee 8 (Lindenhof) is a former military riding school, where diners sit amongst the wooden stalls and drinking troughs or else in the spacious cobblestoned courtyard. The equally lively Restaurant Zeughauskeller at Bahnhofstrasse 28a (Lindenhof) occupies a converted fifteenth century arsenal, and is famous for its *Steins* of local beer and metre-long sausages! The arsenal was commissioned by Zurich's mayor Hans Waldmann (1435–1489), as a repository for weapons seized during the Burgundy Wars (see no. 30).

Other places of interest nearby: 64, 66, 67, 68, 72, 74, 75

75 A Stuffed Bison and a Caribou Coat

District 8 (Mühlenbach), the North America Native Museum
(Nordamerika Native Museum) (NONAM) at Seefeldstrasse 317
S-Bahn 6, 7, 16 Bahnhof Tiefenbrunnen; Tram 2, 4 Bahnhof
Tiefenbrunnen

Of the more than fifty museums and galleries in Zurich there are many specialist collections, covering subjects as diverse as coffee, toys, *moulage*, and civil defence. Perhaps the most surprising of all is the North America Native Museum (Nordamerika Native Museum) at Seefeldstrasse 317 (Mühlenbach). It's certainly the only place in the city where one can find a stuffed bison!

At the heart of the North America Native Museum is the private collection of Gottfried Hotz, which was purchased by the City of Zurich in 1961. In 1963 the collection was made available to the public for the first time as the Zurich Indian Museum, inside a school building in District 4 (Aussersihl). Hotz continued as curator of the

A totem pole stands outside the North America Native Museum (Nordamerika Native Museum) (NONAM) on Seefeldstrasse

museum until 1977, and then in 2003 the museum moved to its current address and took a new name.

As the North America Native Museum – or NONAM for short – the museum has been able to place more of its collection on permanent display. NONAM's aim is to create a better understanding of the cultural diversity of North America's indigenous peoples. To only use the blanket term "Indian" to describe the many different tribes and groups living between the Arctic North and the deserts of the Southwest would be like describing the Swiss and the Spaniards merely as "European", without delving further into their idiosyncracies.

In North America there are three distinct groups of indigenous people: the Arctic Inuit, the First Nations people living in what is now

Canada, and the Métis, who are people of mixed European and First Nations ancestry. The groups, and the many sub-groups they contain, live under completely different climatic and topographical conditions, which in turn impact greatly on their way of life and cultural habits. It is the enlightening and enjoyable way in which these differences both past and present are conveyed that makes NONAM such a worthwhile museum.

The first floor of the museum is reserved for annual temporary exhibitions: the second floor is where the permanent collection is displayed. Using around seven hundred artefacts the visitor is taken on an atmospheric journey of many thousands of miles across six distinct regions. Commencing with the Great Plains and Prairies, and the Northeastern Woodlands, the exhibition moves up to the Sub-Arctic, and the Arctic, before returning southwards down the Northwest Coast, and then concluding in the Southwestern Desert. Along the way many fascinating themes are highlighted, including Native American myths (the creation of the world by the raven and coyote), rituals associated with hunting (the ceremony of the first salmon), the adoption of the domesticated horse from the Spanish, and the importance of the bison, which provided not only food and clothing for Plains Indians but also skin for *Tipis*, bone for tools and jewellery, and horn for vessels. The stuffed bison on display was donated by Zurich Zoo, and reminds the visitor of the millions of animals shot for their hides by the white man during the nineteenth century.

Amongst the canoes, moccasins, pipes, and snow shoes can be found the museum's oldest and most precious object. It is a coat made of painted caribou hide and is one of only four known examples in the world. Thought to date from around 1700 the coat was probably made by the nomadic Innu people of the Quebec/Labrador region.

Upon leaving the museum don't forget to take a peek at the premises next door, which are home to the City of Zurich's Departments of Underwater Archaeology and Dendrochronology. Although not open to the public there are usually a few interesting artefacts and photographs displayed in the window.

Other places of interest nearby: 64, 73, 74

76   The Old Villages of Zurich

District 9 (Albisrieden), the old village of Albisrieden
Tram 3 Albisrieden

Until the late nineteenth century the boundaries of the City of Zurich were more or less synonymous with those of the former medieval walls of the Old Town (Altstadt) (see no. 22). Two large expansions of the city limits occurred in 1893 and 1934, when numerous outlying villages, which had merged gradually as a result of urbanisation, were incorporated into the city. Despite this it is still possible to make out the centres of these former self-governing municipalities, some of which retain a distinctly rural feel.

Timber-framed houses
in the old village of
Albisrieden

A detail of the so-called Studerhaus in Altstetten

One of the best preserved examples is Albisrieden, which can be reached in just twenty minutes by tram from Bahnhofplatz. The contrast between the busy city centre and peaceful Albisrieden could not be more stark. Lying at the foot of the Uetliberg the place has clung on to much of its original village character.

Roman coins provide the earliest evidence for a settlement at Albisrieden, although it was abandoned suddenly and destroyed by fire. By 1270 a chapel was standing here, and the first documentary evidence for the village (given simply as Rieden) dates from the early 1500s, when it is listed as part of the manor of a Zurich collegiate church. This settlement withstood the subsequent ebb and flow of the region's history, including the famines of the 1770s and the formation of the Helvetic Republic under the French in 1798, when Zurich lost control of its lands.

Rapid industrialisation prompted the incorporation of Albisrieden into District 9 of the City of Zurich, together with the former village of Altstetten to the north. Like other villages incorporated into Zurich at the same time, Albisrieden and Altstetten received a new guild *(Zunft)* to engender civic pride. Despite this, many inhabitants of Albisrieden still speak of their community as something quite distinct from the City.

Until the 1950s the area was subject to much building activity, and in recent times the population has increased as industrial-era construction has given way to that of modern housing. It is the old timber-framed buildings *(Riegelhäuser)* of Albisrieden, however, which remain the most interesting, and a cluster of them stand on Im Kratz, a few steps from the tram terminus. The largest of them at Triemli Strasse 2 is called the Haus zum obren Haller, which dates back to the seventeenth century and today contains the village museum (Ortsmuseum Albisrieden). Others which originated as sixteenth century farm buildings are more difficult to discern, their wooden elements long since obscured by layers of plaster.

A little farther uphill at Albisrieder Strasse 404 there is a former rapeseed oil mill, which until the mid-eighteenth century was the property of Zurich's Grossmünster (the grinding machinery has long since been removed). In front of the mill stands a fountain and trough dated 1778. Beyond at Albisriederstrasse 418 stands a two-storey former wood dye mill (Farbholzmühle). Established in 1861 it bears witness to the industrialisation of Albisrieden. The mill owner's balconied, three-storey house was installed alongside the mill in 1888, and is constructed in the yellow brick used to build factories of the same period. Meanwhile, at the bottom end of the village, there can be found another mill, the Mühle Albisrieden, at Wydlerweg 19, identified by the old millstones lined up outside it.

Albisrieden's original chapel of 1270 was replaced in 1818 by the church now standing on the main road. Burials were made here until 1839, at which time the cemetery was expanded along Triemlistrasse. A rise in population necessitated the opening in 1902 of a second cemetery on Untermoosstrasse. The Jews of Albisrieden, meanwhile, are buried in two distinct cemeteries. The oldest on Goldackerweg (1913) is for members of the orthodox Agudas Achim community (Jüdische Orthodoxe Gemeinde Agudas Achim), whilst the other on Schützenrain (1982) is reserved for the liberal Or Chadasch community (Jüdische Liberale Gemeinde Or Chadasch) (see no. 41).

Bus 80 runs northwards from Albisrieden to Lindenplatz in Altstetten, where the old village church sits on top of a Roman villa, and the village museum occupies the superbly-preserved, timber-framed Studerhaus at Dachslernstrasse 22.

77 Pinball Paradise

District 9 (Altstetten), the Outlane private pinball machine
collection and games bar at Badenerstrasse 571a
Tram 2 Kappeli (Note: the collection is open by appointment
only on the last Thursday and Friday of each month
www.outlane.ch)

Located behind the Turbinenbräu, a small independent brewery in the
Zurich quarter of Altstetten, something unexpected awaits the city explorer. Outlane at Badenerstrasse 571a is a private shrine to the pinball
machine. A twenty five year labour of love on the part of its proprietor,
Ivo Vasella, this is the place to go for an exciting reminder of what it
was like to visit a 1980s-era games arcade, in the days before digital
technology changed gaming forever.

Outlane is open to the public on the last Thursday and Friday of
each month from 8pm onwards – and it's like entering another world!
Hidden in a basement is a large room containing more than sixty working pinball machines on which players score points by manipulating a
ball on a playfield inside a glass-covered cabinet. The feeling one has
of taking a step back in time is enhanced by the classic rock and pop
music pumping out of the *Rockola* jukebox, and the cold beers and hot
dogs available at the bar. The bar itself is made from illuminated recycled pinball playfields.

Pinball has ancient origins being derived from outdoor games such
as bowls, *boules*, *bocce*, and *pétanque*, which themselves find a common
ancestry in the games of ancient Rome. These in turn led to variants
that could be played inside, such as billiards, and eventually table top
versions (notably *bagatelle* in the 1770s) in which moveable wickets
were replaced by fixed pins.

French soldiers carried *bagatelle* boards with them when they went
to America to help fight the British during the American Revolutionary War, and the game quickly caught on from there. Ironically, it was
a British settler, Montague Redgrave, who saw the commercial potential in *bagatelle* and in 1869 he patented a board with a spring-loaded
ball cue. Such pinball games were especially popular during the 1930s
American depression, when people were eager for affordable entertain-
ment.

The golden age of pinball followed the Second World War, especially after player-controlled flippers were pioneered in 1947 by pinball
manufacturer David Gottlieb. The classic American pinball machine

The Outlane private pinball machine collection in Altstetten

had been born. By the 1960s most machines offered a host of other features, too, including rubberised bumpers, slingshots, targets, and a nudge facility. By the 1970s the introduction of solid-state technology brought sound effects and elaborate light displays, too.

The arrival of the video game in the 1980s, however, signalled the end of the pinball boom, and the familiar rows of pinball machines were soon ousted by new table top video games such as *Space Invaders*, *Pac-Man*, and *Asteroids*. But somehow the simple mechanical pleasures of the traditional pinball machine endured, and during the 1990s pinball enjoyed a renaissance on the back of feature film tie-ins such as *Star Trek* and *Indiana Jones*. Full use was made of the machine's vertical back glass, on which eye-catching graphics were employed to lure punters away from their video screens.

All this can be experienced at Outlane, from vintage pinballs such as *New Star Jiggers* (1932), *A-B-C Bowler* (1941), and *Turf Champ* (1958) to high-tech models such as *Eight Ball Deluxe* (1981), *Creature from the Black Lagoon* (1992), and the very latest, *Iron Man* (2010). And there are more than a dozen table top video games, too. The machines are arranged chronologically giving the appearance of a museum on one side of the room and a modern pinball arcade on the other. In this way each machine presents a graphic reflection of the time in which it was made.

As a private collection Outlane relies entirely on admission fees for

Outlane also contains modern pinball machines

its income, which is why the premises can be rented for private events by those looking for a party with a difference.

For the technical details of each of Outlane's various machines visit the International Pinball Database at www.ipdb.org. The world's largest searchable database of pinball machines it encompasses a hundred years of manufacturing and includes over thirty thousand images.

Pinball machines can be found elsewhere in Zurich if one knows where to look. A *Rolling Stones* machine from 2011, for example, adorns the Les Halles Restaurant at Pfingstweidstrasse 6 (Escher Wyss).

Other places of interest nearby: 78

78 The Freshest Beer in Town

District 9 (Altstetten), the TurbinenBräu at Badenerstrasse 571
Tram 2 Kappeli (Note: tours of the brewery are not currently
available)

1996 was a bad year for Zurich's beer drinkers. The city's last large brewery, the Hürlimann Brewery (Brauerei Hürlimann) at Brand-schenkestrasse 110 (Enge), closed its doors after more than a century, taking its famously potent *Samichlaus* Bock with it (it is now produced in Austria). The brewery had been founded by Albert Hürlimann, who made his name in the scientific study of yeast (necessary to produce the fermentation of malted barley as stipulated in the *Reinheitsgebot* brewing law of 1516). The site of the brewery has subsequently been transformed into an office, shopping, and bathing complex called the Hürlimann Areal, with the former brewery mash house now the lobby of the smart B2 Boutique Hotel + Spa.

All was not lost, however, since in 1997 three entrepreneurs stepped forward with the idea of creating a new, albeit smaller brewing con-cern in Zurich. As their base of operations they selected a disused part of the Sulzer-Escher Wyss turbine factory on Pfingstweidstrasse (Escher Wyss). This innovative reuse of a former industrial-era build-ing typifies the recent transformation of the former Industrie-Quartier (District 5) into the fashionable Zürich-West (see no. 83). By way of a tribute to the old factory, where turbines for ships and aircraft had once been produced, the new brewery was named TurbinenBräu.

The TurbinenBräu produces beer for the local Zurich market only, and as such avoids the need for pasteurisation and preservatives neces-sary in larger breweries, whose beers need to be stored for longer and shipped greater distances. Instead, the TurbinenBräu fills its barrels and bottles on a weekly basis, confident in the knowledge that the pH value of the beer and the alcohol it contains will preserve the beer in perfect condition for at least two months.

The customer base for the TurbinenBräu has expanded rapidly – and deservedly so. Capacity was doubled after the first year, and in 2001 the company relocated to a disused machine hall at Badener-strasse 571 (Altstetten). Now the largest brewery in the Canton of Zurich, the TurbinenBräu supplies bottled and draft beers to more than a hundred outlets across the city. The three main brands are *Goldsprint* (Swiss-style regularly fermented beer, 5.2%), *Start* (German-style unfiltered top-fermented wheat beer, 5%), and *Rekord* (malted

A selection of
beers brewed
at the TurbinenBräu
on Badenerstrasse

Munich-style cloudy beer, 5.2%). The brewery also produces seasonal specials such as the enormously refreshing *Taifun*, made from rice and ginger.

It is a pity that tours of the TurbinenBräu are not yet available. Instead visit one of the breweries characterful Zurich outlets, such as Bar 63 at Rolandstrasse (Langstrasse), Hafenkneipe at Militärstrasse 12 (Langstrasse), or Rio Bar at Gessnerallee 17 (City). For those who prefer to drink in the comfort of their own home there is always the possibility to collect their beer directly from the brewery's dispatch ramp, from where the brewery's clanking bottle-filling plant can be seen. The ramp is open Monday to Friday 8.30am to 6.30pm, and on Saturday from midday until 4pm. And no beer comes fresher than that!

It can be an experience to visit the bars at the northern end of Niederhofstrasse (Rathaus), including the refreshingly downbeat Kontikibar at number 24. The Rheinfelder Bierhalle at number 76 is the oldest, although it doesn't serve TurbinenBräu beers. Opened in 1870 it is rough and ready, with wooden benches and little in the way of decoration. A cheap and cheerful menu is on offer to accompany the liquid refreshment.

Other places of interest nearby: 77

79 Keeping Zurich Clean

District 9 (Altstetten), a tour of the Werdhölzli Wastewater
Treatment Plant (Kläranlage Werdhölzli) at Bändlistrasse 108
Tram 17 Werdhölzli

Zurich's reputation for being a clean and efficient city is not only based
on its longstanding Protestant work ethic. Since the late nineteenth
century the city has also boasted a waste water system run every bit as
efficiently as one of its banks. Few guidebooks mention that Switzerland's largest waste water treatment plant is in Werdhölzli in Zurich,
and that it can be visited on a tour which provides a rarely seen facet of
Zurich's urban scene.

The first modern European sewage systems were built in London
and Paris during the 1850s. The story of Zurich's modern waste water
treatment begins in the 1860s with the passing of the so-called Kloakenreform (Sewage Reform). City engineer Arnold Bürkli (1833–1894) was
tasked with installing closed drainage culverts, where since medieval
times open gulleys *(Ehgräben)* had transferred raw sewage directly into
the River Limmat. Domestic toilet bowls were connected to the new
culverts by pipes *(Abtrittkübelsystem)*, and sieves were installed in the
pipes to separate the solids; these were removed manually by sewage
workers from within the culverts, whilst the liquid drained away naturally into the river (flushing toilet bowls were not introduced until after
the First World War). One of the narrow and gloomy culverts can be
explored beyond an unassuming door between Schifflände 30 and 32
(Rathaus), where a series of information boards explain how the system worked (a key for the culvert
can be obtained on production of
a passport from the Building History Archive (Baugeschichtliches
Archiv) at Neumarkt 4).

Zurich's first waste water
treatment plant opened in 1926
at Bändlistrasse 108 in Werdhölzli (Altstetten). As the Werdhölzli Wastewater Treatment Plant
(Kläranlage Werdhölzli) it was
supplemented in 1949 by a second
plant in Opfikon (to handle waste
from Districts 11 and 12) but this

Green technology at the Werdhölzli Wastewater
Treatment Plant (Kläranlage Werdhölzli) on
Bändlistrasse

was closed in 2001, when these districts were connected to Werdhölzli by a 5.3 kilometre-long pipeline. Today, all of Zurich's waste water – as well as that of six surrounding municipalities (Adliswil, Kilchberg, Opfikon, Rümlang, Wallisellen, and Zollikon) – makes its way to Werdhölzli by means of a four thousand kilometre-long network of pipes, punctuated by more than fifty pumping stations, as well as storm reservoirs and flood discharge channels to handle heavy rain and melting snow.

To witness the treatment process at Werdhölzli first-hand an appointment should be made with ERZ (Entsorgung + Recycling Zürich) (tel. 0041 (0)44 645 77 77). During the two-hour tour it is explained how the plant processes between seventy and eighty million cubic metres of waste water a year by means of a four-stage treatment process. First the water is cleaned mechanically with rakes to remove non-soluble pollutants such as paper, textiles and wood; gravel and mud naturally sink to the bottom, whilst oil and fat are blown to the surface with air jets. It is incredible to think that thirty three thousand tons of non-soluble pollutants are extracted at the plant each year! Next the water is cleaned biologically using micro-organisms to convert dissolved organic pollutants into less problematic materials (for example, ammonium is converted into gaseous nitrogen). The third stage is to clean the water chemically using iron salt, so as to remove the phosphates contained in cleaning agents. In the final stage any remaining solids are filtered through sand and the resulting clean water is then fed safely into the Limmat.

It is admirable that almost all of the electricity requirements of the Werdhölzli plant are generated by the plant itself using the sludge generated by the treatment process. Together with other non-soluble pollutants the sludge is drained and transported to one of the city's two incineration plants *(Kehrichtheizkraftwerk)*, where it is converted into carbon-neutral energy used to generate power and heat (see no. 84). Werdhölzli also has its own composting department (Kompostierwerk Werdhölzli) in which green waste is converted to compost and supplied to gardeners.

80 A Suburban Vineyard

District 10 (Höngg), the Rebberg Chillesteig
vineyard on Winzerstrasse
Tram 13 Zwielplatz; Bus 80 Zwielpatz

Swiss wines ranks amongst the best in Europe but as little over two percent is ever exported (mainly to Germany) they remain an unknown delight to most. First introduced by the Romans the country's best vineyards are located in the Cantons of Valais and Vaud, particularly on the sheltered hillsides around Lake Geneva; it is here that the white *Chasselas* grape is grown, the full-bodied dry and fruity wine which partners *fondue* so well (see no. 45). One should not forget, however, that good red grape varieties (notably Pinot Noir) come from the Canton of Zurich, to where they were brought from Italy by Swiss mercenaries in the early sixteenth century.

To see a vineyard within Zurich's city boundaries take Tram 13 from Bahnhofstrasse and travel out along the Limmat River to the suburb of Höngg. It's a fascinating journey in itself as the tram passes from the city centre, through the former industrial area of District 5, and out into the leafy suburbs of District 10, in the lee of the Hönggberg and Käferberg.

Alight the tram at Zwielplatz, where a few steps away at Am Wet-

The Rebberg Chillesteig vineyard in Höngg

tingertobel 38 stands the small Church of Höngg (Kirche Höngg). The present structure with its distinctive red spire was erected in 1703, although the foundations date back to at least the ninth century. The history of Höngg is much older than that though. In the woods on Heizenholz north-west of the church archaeologists have discovered grave mounds erected around 700 BC by people of the Iron Age Hallstatt Culture.

From the graveyard at the rear of the church there is a lovely view over the Rebberg Chillesteig vineyard, with the Limmat and the city beyond. That viticulture has been important here since the seventeenth century is reflected by the coat of arms of Höngg, which depicts a vine bearing three bunches of blue grapes. To one side of the churchyard a track leads down past the vineyard towards the suitably-named Winzer Strasse, or Winemaker's Street.

Elsewhere in the city other street names also recall the wine trade. The area running eastwards of Weinbergstrasse (Oberstrass), for example, was once occupied by vineyards, where the almost forgotten Räuschling variety of white grape was grown. Restricted almost entirely to the German-speaking parts of Switzerland it can still be seen together with Blauburgunder, Gewürztraminer, and Riesling varieties at the Weinberg Riesbachs, a vineyard on the slopes of the BurghölzliHügel (Weinegg) (see no. 64).

The charming Vintners' Fountain (Winzerbrunnen) (1908) on Weinplatz (Lindenhof) recalls that this square was used by local wine sellers during the seventeenth century. The well takes the form of a wrought iron baldachin beneath which is the bronze figure of a vintner carrying a basket of grapes on his back. The figure was cast by a man called Prasser, who must have been something of a joker, as he adorned the well with the following pun: "Ich, Hans Prasser, trink lieber Wein als Wasser. Tränk ich das Wasser so gern wie den Wein, könnt ich ein reicher Prasser sein" (I, Hans Prasser, drink dear wine like water. If I could drink water as gladly as wine, I could a richer Prasser be); the name Prasser also being the German word for an idler or good-for-nothing.

And Prasser wasn't alone in this. There is documentary evidence from the seventeenth century that in the Canton of Zurich approximately one hundred litres of wine were produced annually for every man, woman, and child! This is because until the nineteenth century the most common beverages in Zurich were water and wine, as well as non-alcoholic sweet and sour *Most* derived from pressed apples and pears. Milk was hardly ever drunk at this time and nor was beer.

The Vintners' Fountain (Winzerbrunnen) on Weinplatz

To purchase Swiss wines visit Baur au Lac Wein at Börsenstrasse 27 (Lindenhof) and HoferWeine at Zeltweg 26 (Hottingen). To drink Swiss wine there are many possibilities. Why not try the two hundred year-old Restaurant Oepfelchammer at Rindermarkt 12 (Rathaus)? With its creaking timbers and uneven ceilings it is renowned for its association with Zurich's literary hero, Gottfried Keller (1819–1890). In the upstairs front room tradition states that if a customer can clamber over two ceiling beams and drink a glass of wine hanging upside down they can inscribe their name on one of the wooden benches.

Ojo de Agua at Oetenbachgasse 13 (Lindenhof) is a tiny, wood-floored bar and restaurant with just six tables. It serves Argentinian wines and beef produced by Dieter Meier, the singer of Swiss electronica band Yello. Equally distinctive but in a very different way is Edi's Weinstube at Stüssihofstatt 14 (City). The walls of this small bar are adorned with pornographic art, a glass of decent wine costs only three Swiss Francs, and a flight of stairs at the end of a red-painted corridor leads up to the legendary Stüssihof sex cinema.

81 An Air Raid Shelter in Wipkingen

District 10 (Wipkingen), the Civil Defence Museum
(Zivilschutz-Museum) opposite Habsburgstrasse 17
S24 Bahnhof Wipkingen; Bus 33, 46 Bahnhof
Wipkingen

During both world wars, Switzerland managed to maintain a stance of armed neutrality, and was not involved militarily. However, precisely because of its neutral status, the country was of considerable interest to all parties involved, as a place for diplomacy, espionage, commerce, and as a safe haven for refugees (see no. 26). A usually hidden aspect of Switzerland's "armed neutrality" is the provision of air raid shelters to protect civilians and strengthened bunkers to house military personnel. Most impressive of these was the so-called *Réduit suisse*, a fortress hollowed out of the Alps by Swiss General Henri Guisan (1874–1960) to deter a possible German invasion.

More prosaic were the reinforced cellars with blast proof doors constructed beneath many apartment blocks. Now commonly used to store wine and personal valuables, Switzerland's old air raid shelters have been kept intact ever since, indeed even the idea of an alpine *Réduit* was maintained until the late 1980s, as a deterrent against Soviet invasion.

Although domestic air raid shelters are rarely seen by the visitor, an intact civilian shelter dating from the Second World War can be visited on the first Saturday of each month in the suburban quarter of Wipkingen. Constructed in 1941 opposite Habsburgstrasse 17 it is reached by means of a sloping passageway, leading from pavement level down to a bombproof door. Beyond is the shelter itself, cylindrical in plan and constructed of steel-reinforced concrete, reaching down three storeys into the ground. As well as a place to escape air raids, the shelter also functioned as a field hospital, where eighty or more victims of fire and gas attack could be treated simultaneously. The operating theatre is located in the upper storey, with accommodation areas in the storeys beneath consisting of simple, plank-built beds for around three hundred people.

Scarcely altered since the 1940s the Wipkingen shelter still contains most of its original features, including a ventilation system, diesel generator, sanitary fittings, and sirens. Fittingly it is today home

The entrance to the Second World War air raid shelter in Wipkingen

to the Zurich Police Department's Civil Defence Museum (Zivilschutz-Museum), which illustrates Switzerland's Second World War air defence organisation, as well as its Cold War-era civil defence preparations dating from the 1950s onwards. The museum includes many associated artefacts such as blackout lamps, gas masks, food ration coupons, rescue equipment, and surgical instruments.

A similar shelter located beneath Marktplatz in the suburb of Oerlikon is identified only by a steel cover in the middle of the bustling market square. Constructed in 1939 and consisting of two subterranean storeys it too contained a hospital and is the oldest civilian shelter of its type in Zurich. It is not open to the public but an impression of its size can be gained from the fact that it occupies at least half the square above. Plans to convert the shelter into an unusual hotel, similar to the recently-opened Null Stern hotel inside a Cold War-era shelter in Teufen, have so far come to nothing.

With the onset of the Cold War the older shelters became outmoded and were replaced by nuclear radiation-proof shelters (an example is the one beneath Lindenhofstrasse (Lindenhof), which now serves as the Urania car park). As the threat of nuclear attack receded, so the emphasis was placed once again on domestic shelters. So much so that articles 45 and 46 of the Swiss Federal Law on Civil Protection (1963) stipulate that "Every inhabitant must have a protected place that can be reached quickly from his place of residence" and "apartment block owners are required to construct and fit out shelters in all new dwellings". Consequently, Switzerland now has radiation-proof shelters for everyone residing within its borders, and with room to spare. In 2006, for example, there were 300 000 private shelters in Swiss dwellings, in-

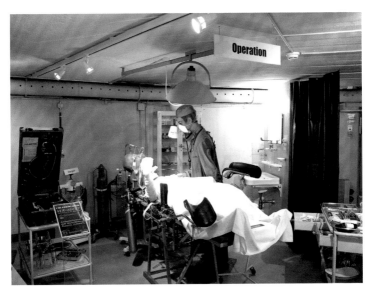

A scene inside the Civil Defence Museum (Zivilschutz-Museum)

stitutions, and hospitals, with a further 5100 public shelters, providing protection for a total of 8.6 million people, the highest ratio of shelter space to population anywhere in the world.

Other relics of the Second World War in Zurich include a series of concrete machine gun posts built in 1940 to guard the city's river approaches. Examples can be found at General-Guisan-Quai 21 and 31, Mythenquai 3 and 11, and Seestrasse 41 and 104.

Other places of interest nearby: 82

82 An Urban Lido Culture

District 10 (Wipkingen), the Flussbad Unterer Letten
at Wasserwerkstrasse 141
Tram 4, 13, 17 Limmatplatz; Bus 32 Limmatplatz

Named after a popular bathing beach on an island near Venice, the word *lido* has been used since the twentieth century to describe any fashionable open-air public bathing area. Despite the fact that Zurich lies over fifteen hundred kilometres from the Mediterranean, the city has developed its own unique urban lido culture, taking full advantage of the pristine waters of Lake Zurich (Zürichsee) and the waterways it feeds.

The origins of Zurich's lido culture go back to the 1830s, when a craze for therapeutic and leisurely outdoor bathing swept across Europe. To protect the modesty of the bathers, wooden changing rooms were constructed at the water's edge. Known in the German-speaking world as *Kastenbäder* they enabled bathers to change and enter the water both easily and discreetly. Although covered pools appeared in Zurich a decade later, river bathing has remained popular ever since.

Zurich's first bathing cabins appeared in 1837 at Stadthausquai 12 (Lindenhof) on the west bank of the Limmat. In 1888 these were replaced by the graceful wooden pavilion seen today, known officially as the Flussbad Stadthausquai. Its local name of *Frauenbadi*, however, reflects the fact that bathing here is reserved for women only. Like Zurich's eighteen other lidos it is open daily (9am–8pm) from the middle of May until the middle of September depending on the weather. Since the 1990s some of Zurich's lidos have doubled up after hours as lounge bars and the *Frauenbadi* is no exception: from 8pm onwards on Wednesdays, Thursdays and Sundays it is transformed into the popular Barfussbar ('barefoot bar') and open to both sexes.

Zurich's oldest extant river lido is the Flussbad Schanzengraben at Badweg 10 (City). A men-only bath it is known as the *Männerbadi*, and was constructed in 1864. The Schanzengraben, however, is not a natural river but rather an artificial moat, dug to protect Zurich's former city wall (see no. 22). One of the old bastions still looms above the lido, whilst on the opposite bank at Badweg 21 (City) stands an early eighteenth century water tower once used to distribute spring water to wells in this part of the city (see no. 27). On summer evenings the lido is transformed into the Rimini Bar, and at this time women are admitted.

Away from the city centre there is a pair of lidos in the district of Wipkingen. The Flussbad Unterer Letten – "de underi Lätte" in Swiss German – was built in 1910 at Wasserwerkstrasse 141. It consists of a row of red-tiled wooden cabins, with walkways running out across the Limmat. Upstream from here at Lettensteg 10 is the corresponding Flussbad Oberer Letten, built in concrete in 1952. Crossing the river at this point is a disused nineteenth century railway viaduct, the arches of which are now used by over thirty independent fashion and furniture designers, as well as small galleries, restaurants, and a market hall. The former Sultana cigarette factory on Sihlquai recalls the area's industrial past.

Further still down the Limmat is the Badeplatz Au-Höngg on Werdinsel (Höngg). The relatively modest bathing facilities here are located on the upstream part of the island, whilst downstream is a popular nudist area (legalised in 1983), the larger part of which is popular with Zurich's gay community. There is also a historic hydroelectric installation – the Flusskraftwerk Höngg – inserted into the northern arm of the river in the late nineteenth century (tours by appointment only on Wed, Fri and the first Sat in the month 1–4pm, tel. 0041 (0) 58 319 4960, www.ewz.ch).

On the shores of Lake Zurich itself there are also lidos, including the Seebad Enge (1960) at Mythenquai 9 (Enge), which caters for

The Flussbad Stadthausquai is known locally as the *Frauenbadi*

The Flussbad Unterer Letten in Wipkingen

well-groomed thirtysomethings, and the Seebad Utoquai (1890) and Strandbad Tiefenbrunnen (1954) on Bellerivestrasse (Seefeld).

Away from the rivers and the lake, Zurich also has several open air swimming pools, of which the largest is the Freibad Allenmoos at Ringstrasse 79 (Unterstrass) (constructed in 1939 the main pool is fifty metres long). The most interesting historically is the Freibad Letzigraben at Edelweissstrasse 5 (Albisrieden), opened in 1949 to a design by the Swiss architect and author Max Frisch (1911–1991), as part of a larger project to develop this part of Altstetten. Fellow author Bertolt Brecht (1898–1956) visited him on site during construction. Archaeological excavations at the pool have thrown further light on the area's history, which was once the site of a Roman villa, and latterly the site of the city's gallows, last used in 1810. Skeletons of three of those hung here have been unearthed.

Other places of interest nearby: 81

**District 11 (Oerlikon), a tour of converted factories finishing
with the MFO-park on James-Joyce-Strasse
Tram 10, 11, 14 Sternen Oerlikon**

Zurich has an exemplary record when it comes to adapting disused industrial buildings for modern reuse. Most date back to the nineteenth and early twentieth centuries, when the city underwent rapid industrialisation. Former foundries, breweries, factories, and machine halls have all been transformed into a wide range of exciting leisure and cultural facilities (see nos. 48, 74 & 78).

Of particular interest are those structures adapted to serve as arts centres. The most controversial is a former silk mill at Seestrasse 395 (Wollishofen), which has been converted into the Rote Fabrik, a publically-funded arts centre. To avoid being seen as elitist the building still looks much as it did a century ago, albeit with the addition of some modern graffiti (see no. 37). In most cases, however, only the outer brick shell of the old structure is retained, and new glass, steel, and concrete elements inserted as required. This is the case with the Schiffbau, a cavernous former foundry *(Giessereihalle)* at Schiffbaustrasse 4 (Escher Wyss) in which lake steamers were once constructed; the enormous shell today contains a stage for Zurich's Schauspielhaus, as well as a bar, a jazz club, and a stylish restaurant (see no. 74). Behind the Schiffbau on Giessereihallestrasse is Puls 5, another converted former foundry, which now serves as a shopping and leisure centre.

A few roads away to the east can be found another large-scale industrial conversion. The Löwenbräuareal at Limmatstrasse 270 (Escher Wyss) is, as its name suggests, a converted brewery. The light and lofty rooms on the first floor lend themselves perfectly to the display of modern and conceptual art, which explains the presence here of the Migros Museum for Contemporary Art (Migros Museum für Gegenwartskunst) and the Kunsthalle Zürich, as well as art galleries such as Hauser & Wirth. Another converted brewery at Brandschenkestrasse 110 (Enge) is now home to the Hürlimann Areal, containing shops, offices, and a sleek public baths fed by one of Zurich's two thermal springs. Called the Thermalbad & Spa Zürich the vaulted stone arches of the former brewery are cleverly incorporated into several of the pools.

This tour finishes with a pair of unique industrial conversions. The first is that of a former electric power station built in the 1930s at

The MFO-park on James-Joyce-Strasse was once a factory

Selnaustrasse 25 (City) on the banks of the River Sihl. In 2001 it was transformed into the Haus Konstruktiv, where exhibitions by the Foundation of Concrete and Constructivist Art are displayed. Zurich has been a centre for such art since the founding of the Zürcher Schule der Konkreten in the 1930s by the Abstractivist artist Max Bill (1908–1984). Other members included Richard Paul Lohse (1902–1988), Camille Graeser (1892–1980), and Verena Loewensberg (1912–1986).

The other conversion couldn't be more different. Rather than preserving an old structure and reusing its interior, the MFO-park on James-Joyce-Strasse (Oerlikon) is an entirely new structure. The site was originally occupied by the Maschinenfabrik Oerlikon, a large machine hall established in 1876. Its final owner was the industrial group ABB, who in 2001 cleared the site and handed it over to the City of Zurich. Over the next two years the old machine hall rose once again, only this time it took the form of a four-storey skeleton of steel. Entirely open to the elements the structure has subsequently been adorned with climbing plants such as ivy, clematis, roses, wisteria, hops, and jasmine. The plants are kept alive by rainwater gathered in an underground reservoir. Beneath this green canopy are benches where people can relax in a green oasis where formerly there was a noisy factory. The MFO-park is a triumph of industrial conversion that rightly deserves the design awards it has so far garnered.

Other places of interest nearby: 49

84 A Pile of Old Rubbish!

District 12 (Saatlen), the Hagenholz Municipal
Waste Incinerator (Kehrichtheizkraftwerk
Hagenholz) at Hagenholzstrasse 110
Tram 10, 11, 14 Bahnhof Oerlikon Ost, then Bus 781
Kehrichtverbrennung

Twice in the past it seemed Zurich might disappear under the rubbish and waste generated by its inhabitants! Firstly during the late nineteenth century, when the city and its population expanded with industrialisation, and secondly during the 1970s and 80s, with the advent of the throw-away society. On both occasions Zurich rose admirably to the challenge, making it today a Swiss model for the management and disposal of urban waste.

Until 1867 it was still normal in Zurich for household latrines to empty into open gulleys, which transferred raw sewage directly into the River Limmat (see no. 79). As the population increased so did the likelihood of the spread of disease. The so-called Kloakenreform (Sewage Reform) changed all this, and the old gulleys were culverted.

During the 1920s Zurich continued to make breakthroughs in the management of waste. In 1927, for example, the Zurich firm J. Ochsner invented the *Ochsner-Kübel*, a sturdy metal refuse bin with a hinged lid; it remained a common site in the city until the introduction of the ubiquitous plastic *Züri-Sack*, which because it must be purchased by the user has gone a long way towards managing waste levels in Zurich (eleven million are collected annually!). A year earlier in 1926 Zurich's first waste water treatment plant opened on in Werdhölzli (Altstetten). Still in operation today it is powered by the burning of gas emanating from sewer sludge. The sludge, which is a combination of non-soluble pollutants such as paper, textiles, wood, oil, fat, faeces, and other screenings, is drained and transported to one of the citys' two waste incineration plants *(Kehrichtheizkraftwerk)*, where up to ninety eight percent of it is burned and the carbon-neutral energy used to generate power and heat.

Zurich's first waste incineration plant opened on Josefstrasse (Escher Wyss) in 1904, and from the start the energy it generated was harnessed to provide heating. Today it supplies heat to approximately eight thousand premises in the revitalised Zürich-West area, and power to around thirteen thousand of them. To understand the workings of such a plant an appointment should be made with ERZ (Entsorgung +

An aerial view of the Hagenholz Municipal Waste Incinerator (Kehrichtheizkraftwerk Hagenholz)

Recycling Zürich) to visit the Hagenholz Municipal Waste Incinerator (Kehrichtheizkraftwerk Hagenholz) at Hagenholzstrasse 110 (Schwamendingen-Mitte) (tel. 0041 (0)44 645 77 77). One of the most modern municipal waste incinerators in Switzerland the plant was constructed in 1969 in response to a significant increase in Zurich's waste. Greater efficiency in waste management came in 1993 with the introduction of household recycling, and within a few years more than fifty thousand tons of recyclable waste were being processed annually at Hagenholz. Today, the plant handles over 330 000 tons of waste each year, 35 000 tons of which is sewer sludge sent from the Werdhölzli Waste Water Treatment Plant.

A cargo tram at the Hagenholz Municipal Waste Incinerator (Kehrichtheizkraftwerk Hagenholz)

Alongside the Hagenholz Municipal Waste Incinerator is the Aubrugg Distance Heating Plant (Heizkraftwerk Aubrugg). It is here that water heated by the burning of refuse is circulated in well-insulated pipes around the city, where in turn it provides eighty percent carbon-neutral heating to around one hundred and seventy thousand homes, hotels, offices, laundries, and public buildings, including Zurich's Main Station (Hauptbahnhof Zürich). It is impressive to think that in the hospital of Zurich University (UniversitätsSpital Zürich) at Rämistrasse 100 (Hochschule) alone, Distance Heating *(Fernwärme)* is used to cook 4500 meals a day, as well as for sterilizing surgical instruments. That's really not bad for a pile of old rubbish!

***

Standing outside the Hagenholz Municipal Waste Incinerator is perhaps the ideal place to finish this odyssey during which some of the more unusual and unsung corners of Zurich have been explored. Looking back across the city, towards the river and the lake which accounted for the founding of the city two thousand years ago, gives the satisfied explorer the chance to reflect on the many cultures and characters that have helped shape this financial powerhouse in the alpine heart of Europe.

Opening times

for museums and other places of interest (after each name is the district, followed by the quarter in brackets) Correct at time of going to press but may be subject to change.

Adler's Swiss Chuchi, District 1 (Rathaus), Rosengasse 10, daily 11.30am–11.15pm

Aelpli-Bar, District 1 (Rathaus), Ankengasse 5, daily 5–12pm

Alprausch, District 1 (Lindenhof), Werdmühleplatz 1, Tue–Fri 10am–7pm, Sat 10am–5pm

Altstadt-Antiquariat Rita H. Schnellmann, District 1 (Rathaus), Oberdorfstrasse 10, Tue–Fri 11am–6pm, Sat 10am–4pm

Amok, District 4 (Langstrasse), Ankerstrasse 61, Mon–Fri 1–6.30pm, Sat 12am–4pm

Anthropological Institute and Museum of the University of Zurich (Anthropologisches Institut und Museum der Universität Zürich), District 6 (Oberstrass), Üniversität Zürich-Irchel, Winterthurerstrasse 190, Tue–Sun 12am–6pm

Antik Marangoni, District 1 (Rathaus), Rindermarkt 26, Tue 12am–6.30pm, Wed–Fri 10am–6.30pm, Sat 10am–4pm

Archaeological Collection of the University of Zurich (Archaeologische Sammlung der Universität Zürich), District 1 (Hochschulen), Rämistrasse 73, Tue–Fri 1–6pm, Sat & Sun 11am–5pm

Atelier Hermann Haller, District 8 (Seefeld), Höschgasse 6, Jul–Sep Fri–Sun 12am–6pm

Bäckerei Vohdin, District 1 (Rathaus), Oberdorfstrasse 12, Tue–Fri 7am–6.30pm, Sat 9am–4pm

Badeplatz Au-Höngg, District 10 (Höngg), Werdinsel, mid May–mid Sep daily 9am–8pm

Barth Bücher, District 1 (Lindenhof), Bahnhofstrasse 94, Mon–Fri 8am–6pm, Sat 8am–6pm

Baur au Lac Wein, District 1 (Lindenhof), Börsenstrasse 27, Mon–Fri 9am–6.30pm, Sat 9am–6.30pm

Beatrice Wetli, District 1 (Rathaus), Froschaugasse 22, Tue & Thu 9–12am, 1.30–6pm, Wed & Fri 9–12am, 1.30–6pm, Sat 9am–2pm

Biblion Antiquariat Leonidas Sakellaridis, District 1 (Rathaus), Kirchgasse 40, Mon–Fri 10am–6.30pm, Sat 10am–4pm

Bogen33, District 5 (Escher Wyss), Geroldstrasse 33, Mon–Fri 12am–7pm, Sat 10am–6pm

Bord, District 4 (Wird), Badenerstrasse 123a, Mon–Fri 2–7pm, Sat 10am–4pm

Bovet, District 1 (Lindenhof), Talacker 42, Mon–Fri 8.30am–6.30pm, Sat 8.30am–4pm

Brocki-Land, District 3 (Alt-Wiedikon), Steinstrasse 68, Tue–Fri 10am–5pm, Sat 9am–4pm; Antik-Shop Tue–Thu 1–5pm; Bücher-Land, Steinstrasse 68a, Sat 9am–1pm; Musik-Land, Steinstrasse 70, Tue–Fri 1–6pm, Sat 11am–4pm

Bücher-Brocki, District 2 (Enge) Bederstrasse 4, Mon–Fri 10.30am–6.30pm, Sat 9am–4pm

Buchhandlung Beer, District 1 (Lindenhof), Peterhofstatt 10, Tue–Fri 9am–6.30pm, Sat 9am–4pm

Buchhandlung im Licht, District 1 (Rathaus), Oberdorfstrasse 28, Tue–Fri 11am–6.30pm, Sat 9am–5pm

Buchhandlung Medieval Art & Vie, District 1 (Rathaus), Spiegelgasse 29, Tue–Fri 11am–6pm, Sat 11am–4pm

Buddhist Centre Zurich (Buddhistisches Zentrum Zürich), District 7 (Hirslanden), Hammerstrasse 9 (Hirslanden), daily meditation 7.30pm

Building History Archive (Baugeschichtliches Archiv), District 1 (Rathaus), Haus zum Rech, Neumarkt 4, Mon–Fri 1–5pm, Tue–Fri 8am–5pm, first Sat in the month 10am–4pm; City Model (Stadtmodell) Mon–Fri 8am–6pm, Sat 10am–4pm

Cabaret Voltaire, District 1 (Rathaus), Spiegelgasse 1, Mon 8am–12pm, Tue–Thu 12.30am–12pm, Fri & Sat 12.30am–2pm, Sun 12.30am–7pm

Café Odeon, District 1 (Rathaus), Limmatquai 2, Mon 7am–1am, Tue–Thu 7am–2pm, Fri & Sat 7am–4am, Sun 9am–1am

Café Schober, District 1 (Rathaus), Napfgasse 4, Mon–Wed 8am–7pm, Thu–Sat 8am–11pm, Sun 9am–7pm

Café Terrasse, District 1 (Rathaus), Limmatquai 3, Mon & Tue 10am–1pm, Wed–Sat 10am–2pm, Sun 10am–12pm

Caligramme, District 1 (Rathaus), Häringstrasse 4, Tue–Fri 10am–6.30pm, Sat 10am–4pm

Centre Le Corbusier/Heidi-Weber-Haus, District 8 (Seefeld), Zürichhorn Park, Höschgasse 8, Jul-Sep Wed –Sun 12am–6pm

Chäs Vreneli, District 1 (Lindenhof), Münsterhof 7, Mon–Fri 7am–6.30pm, Sat 7am–4pm

Chinese Garden Zurich (Chinagarten Zürich), District 8 (Seefeld), Zürichhorn Park, Bellerivestrasse, Apr-Oct daily 11am–7pm

Church of St. Peter (St.-Peters-Kirche), District 1 (Lindenhof), St-Peter-Hofstatt 1, Mon–Fri 8am–6pm, Sat 10am–4pm, Sun 11am–5pm

Church of St. Augustine (Augustinerkirche), District 1 (Lindenhof), Münzplatz, Mon–Fri 10am–5pm, Sat 12am–5pm, Sun 10am Mass

Civil Defence Museum (Zivilschutz-Museum), District 10 (Wipkingen), opposite Habsburgstrasse 17, guided tours first Sat in the month at 2 and 4pm

Clock and Watch Museum Beyer (Uhrenmuseum Beyer), District 1 (City), Beyer Chronometrie, Bahnhofstrasse 31, Mon–Fri 2–6pm (guided tours by appointment); shop Mon–Fri 9.30am–6.30pm, Sat 9.30am–4pm; electronic clock collection at Sihlfeldstrasse 10 (Sihlfeld), tours by appointment only first Wed of the month 2–5pm, tel. 0041 (0)43 344 63 63

Collection of Prints and Drawings of the Swiss Federal Institute of Technology (Graphische Sammlung der Eidgenössisches Technisches Hochschule), District 6 (Oberstrass), Rämistrasse 101, daily 10am–4.45pm during exhibitions

Comic Shop, District 1 (Rathaus), Froschaugasse 7, Mon–Wed 10am–6.30pm, Thu & Fri 10am–8pm, Sat 10am–5pm

Confiserie Sprüngli, District 1 (City), Bahnhofstrasse 21, Mon–Fri 7.30am–5.30pm, Sat 8am–5pm

Des Balances, District 1 (Rathaus), Kruggasse 12, Tue–Fri 11am–6.30pm, Sat 11am–4pm

Dolderbahn, District 7 (Hottingen), Römerhofplatz, daily 6.20am–11.30pm every ten minutes

Dolmetsch, District 1 (Rathaus), Limmatquai 126, Mon–Thu 9am–9pm, Fri 9am–10pm, Sat 11am–7pm

Edi's Weinstube, District 1 (City), Stuessihofstatt 14, Mon–Thu 11am–12pm, Fri & Sat 11am–2am, Sun 2–10pm

Edo Popken, District 1 (City), Bärengasse 10, Mon–Fri 9am–6.30pm (Thu until 8pm), Sat 9am–5pm

EOS Buchantiquariat Benz, District 1 (Rathaus), Kirchgasse 17, Tue–Fri 10am–6pm, Sat 10am–4pm

Ethnographic Museum of the University of Zurich (Völkerkundemuseum der Universität Zürich), District 1 (City), Pelikanstrasse 40, Tue, Wed & Fri 10am–5pm, Thu 10am–7pm, Sat 2–5pm, Sun 11am–5pm

Fabric Frontline, District 4 (Langstrasse), Ankerstrasse 118, Mon–Fri 10am–12.30am, 1.30–6pm, Sat 10am–4pm

Flohmarkt am Bürkliplatz, District 1 (Lindenhof), Bürkliplatz, May–Oct, Sat 6am–4pm

Flohmarkt Kanzlei, District 4 (Langstrasse), Kanzleistrasse 56, Sat 8am–4pm

Fluntern Cemetery, District 7 (Fluntern), Zürichbergstrasse 189, Mar–Apr & Sep-Oct 7am–7pm, May–Aug 7am–8pm, Nov–Feb 8am–5pm

Flussbad Oberer Letten, District 10 (Wipkingen), Lettensteg 10, mid May–mid Sep daily 9am–8pm

Flussbad Schanzengraben (Männerbadi), District 1 (City), Badweg 10, Jun–mid Sep daily 11am–7pm; Rimini Bar Mon–Sat from 5.30pm

Flussbad Stadthausquai (Frauenbadi), District 1 (Lindenhof), Stadthausquai 12, mid May–mid Sep daily 9am–7.30pm; Barfussbar Wed, Thur & Sun 8–12pm

Flussbad Unterer Letten, District 10 (Wipkingen), Wasserwerkstrasse 141, mid May–mid Sep daily 9am–8pm

Flusskraftwerk Höngg, District 10 (Höngg), Winzerhalde, tours by appointment only Wed, Fri and first Sat in the month 1–4pm, tel. 0041 (0)58 319 4700, www.ewz.ch

FocusTERRA, District 6 (Oberstrass), Swiss Federal Institute of Technology (Eidgenössische Technische Hochschule (ETH), Department of Natural Sciences (Departement Erdwissenschaften), Sonegggstrasse 5, Mon–Fri 10am–5pm, Sun 10am–4pm; guided tours Sunday 2pm, earthquake simulator Sun 11am, 1pm 3pm

Fraumünster, District 1 (Lindenhof), Münsterhofplatz, Nov–Mar daily 10am–4pm, Apr–Oct 10am–6pm; cloister Mon–Fri 7.30am–6.30pm, Sat 8am–6pm

Freibad Allenmoos, District 6 (Unterstrass), Ringstrasse 79, mid May–mid Sep daily 9am–8pm

Freibad Letzigraben, District 9 (Albisrieden), Edelweissstrasse 5, mid May–mid Sep daily 7am–8pm

Freitag Zürich, District 5 (Escher Wyss), Geroldstrasse 17, Mon–Fri 11am–7.30pm, Sat 10am–6pm

Fribourger Fondue-Stübli, District 4 (Langstrasse), Rotwandstrasse 38, Mon–Fri 11.30am–2pm, 6–12pm, Sat & Sun 6–12pm; closed Jun–Aug

Fundbüro der Stadt Zürich, District 1 (Lindenhof), Werdmühlestrasse 10, Mon–Fri 7.30am–6.30pm

Gerhard Zähringer Antiquariat und Galerie, District 1 (Rathaus), Froschaugasse 5, Tue–Fri 10am–1pm, 2–6pm, Sat 10am–4pm

Ghost Walk of Zurich, District 1 (City), Paradeplatz, Feb-May, Aug-Nov, Thu & Fri 8pm (also Halloween Oct 31)

Giacometti-Halle, District 1 (Lindenhof), Amtshaus 1, Bahnhofquai 3, daily 9–11am, 2–4pm; identification must be shown on entry

Globus-City, District 1 (City), Schweizergasse 11, Mon–Sat 9am–8pm

Greenwich, District 1 (Hochschulen), Rämistrasse 2, Tue–Fri 2–5.30pm, Sat 11.30am–3.30pm

Grossmünster, District 1 (Rathaus), Grossmünsterplatz, March–Oct Mon–Sat 10am–6pm, Nov–Feb Mon–Sat 12.30am–4.30pm; South Tower (Karlsturm) Mar–Oct Mon–Sat 10am–6pm, Nov–Feb Mon–Sat 12.30am–4.30pm; cloister Mon–Fri 10am–6pm

Hagenholz Municipal Waste Incinerator (Kehrichtheizkraftwerk Hagenholz), District 12 (Saatlen), Hagenholzstrasse 110, tours by appointment only tel. 0041 (0)44 645 77 77

Handbuchbinderei, District 1 (Lindenhof), Wohllebgasse 10, Mon 1–5pm, Wed 10-12am, Thu & Fri 10am–5pm

Hare Krishna Temple Zurich (Hare-Krishna-Tempel Zürich), District 7 (Hottingen), Bergstrasse 54, Sunday celebration 3pm; shoes must be removed before entering the building

Haus Konstruktiv, District 1 (City), Selnaustrasse 25 (City), Tue & Thu–Sun 11am–5pm, Wed 11am–8pm

Helsinkiklub (Helsinki Hütte), District 5 (Escher Wyss), Geroldstrasse 35, opening times dependent on live programme, www.helsinkiklub.ch

Helvti Bar, District 4 (Werd), Stauffacherquai 1, Mon–Thu 8am–12pm, Fri 8am–2am, Sat 10am–2am, Sun 10am–11pm

HoferWeine, District 7 (Hottingen), Zeltweg 26, Mon–Fri 9–12am, 1.30–6pm, Sat 11am–4pm

Honold La Confiserie, District 1 (Lindenhof), Rennweg 53, Mon–Fri 8am–6.30pm, Sat 8am–6pm

Hotel Rothaus, District 4 (Langstrasse), Sihlhallenstrasse 1, café and restaurant Mon–Fri 6.30am–11pm, Sat & Sun 7.30am–11pm

James Joyce Pub, District 1 (City), Pelikanstrasse 8, Mon–Fri 11.30am–12.30am, Sat 11.30am–6pm

James Joyce Foundation, District 1 (Lindenhof), Augustinergasse 9, Mon–Fri 10am–5pm; public readings of *Ulysses* Tue 5.30–7pm & Thu 4.30–6pm, *Finnegans Wake* Mon 3-4.30pm & Thu 4.30–6.30pm & 7–8.30pm

Jelmoli, District 1 (City), Seidengasse 1, Mon–Sat 9am–8pm

Johann Jacobs Museum, District 8 (Mühlebach), Seefeldquai 17, Tue 6–11pm, Sat & Sun 11am–5pm

Jules Verne Panorama Bar, District 1 (Lindenhof), entrance through Brasserie Lipp, Uraniastrasse 9, Mon–Thu & Sun 11am–12pm, Fri & Sat 11am–1am, Sun 11.45am–11pm

Jürg Bosshart, District 1 (Rathaus), Froschaugasse 30, Mon–Fri 9–12am, 1–6pm

Kaffeepur, District 4 (Langstrasse), Glasmalerstrasse 5, Tue–Fri 11am–6.30pm, Sat 10am–4pm

Kinderbuchladen Zürich, District 1 (Rathaus), Oberdorfstrasse 32, Mon–Fri 9am–6.30pm, Sat 9am–5pm

Kafischnaps, District 10 (Wipkingen), Kornhausstrasse 57, Mon–Wed 8am–12pm, Thu & Fri 8am–1am, Sat 9am–1am, Sun 9am–12pm

KLIO, District 1 (Rathaus), Zähringerstrasse 41–45, Mon–Fri 8.30am–6.30pm, Sat 8.30am–4pm

Kontikibar, District 1 (Rathaus), Niederhofstrasse 24, Sun–Thu 5–12pm, Fri & Sat 12am–2am

Kunsthalle Zürich, District 5 (Escher Wyss), Limmatstrasse 270, Tue, Wed & Fri 11am–6pm, Thu 11am–8pm, Sat & Sun 10am–6pm

Kunsthaus, District 1 (Hochschule), Heimplatz 1, Tue & Fri–Sun 10am–6pm, Wed & Thu 10am–8pm

Kuriositätenmarkt Rosenhofmarkt, District 1 (Rathaus), Rosenhof, Mar-Dec Thu 10am–8pm, Sat 10am–5pm

Landesmuseum Zürich, District 1 (City), Museumstrasse 2, Tue–Sun 10am–5pm (Thu until 7pm)

Law Institute Library of the University of Zurich (Rechtswissenschaftliches Institut Bibliothek Universität Zürich), District 7 (Fluntern), Rämistrasse 74, Mon–Fri 8am–9pm, Sat 8am–5pm

Liebfrauenkirche, District 6 (Unterstrass), Zehnderweg 9, Mon–Fri 8am–6pm, Sat 9am–4pm, Sun 11am–5pm

Mahmud Mosque (Mahmud-Moschee), District 8 (Weinegg), Forchstrasse 323, Friday prayers 1pm–5pm

Medical History Museum of the University of Zurich (Medizinhistorisches Museum der Universität Zürich), District 1 (Hochschulen), Rämistrasse 69, Tue–Fri 1–6pm, Sat & Sun 11am–5pm

Metzgermuseum, District 1 (Lindenhof), Hotel Widder, Rennweg 7, tours by appointment only tel. 0041 (0)44 224 25 26, www.zunft-widder.ch

Migros Museum for Contemporary Art (Migros Museum für Gegenwartskunst), District 5 (Escher Wyss), Limmatstrasse 270, Tue, Wed & Fri 11am–6pm, Thu 11am–8pm, Sat & Sun 10am–5pm

MoneyMuseum, District 6 (Oberstrass), Hadlaubstrasse 106, first Fri each month 10am–5pm

Moulage Museum (Moulagenmuseum), District 6 (Oberstrass), Haldenbachstrasse 14, Wed 2–6pm, Sat 1–5pm

Mühlerama, District 8 (Mühlebach), Mühle Tiefenbrunnen, Seefeldstrasse 231, Tue–Sat 2–5pm, Sun 10am–5pm

Museum Bellerive, District 8 (Seefeld), Höschgasse 3, Tue–Sun 10am–5pm (Thu 8pm)

Museum für Gestaltung – Schaudepot, District 5 (Escher Wyss), Toni-Areal, Pfingstweidstrasse 96, Tue–Sun 10am–5pm (Wed 8pm)

Museum Rietberg (including Villa Wesendonck, Smaragd, and Park-Villa Rieter), District 2 (Enge), Gablerstrasse 15, Tue–Sun 10am–5pm (Wed 8pm)

Musikhaus Thurnheer, District 1 (Rathaus), Froschaugasse 28, Tue–Sat 2–6pm

My Place, District 7 (Fluntern), Hottingerstrasse 4, Mon–Fri 8am–12pm, Sat 10am–12pm

Nepomuk-Kinderladen, District 5 (Gewerbeschule), Klingenstrasse 23, Tue–Fri 10.30am–6.30pm, Sat 10am–4pm

Neumarkt 17, District 1 (Rathaus), Neumarkt 17, Tue–Fri 9am–6.30pm, Sat 10am–5pm

New Botanical Garden of Zurich University (Neuer Botanischer Garten der Universität Zürich), District 8 (Mühlebach), Zollikerstrasse 107, Mar-Sep Mon–Fri 7am–7pm, Sat & Sun 8am–6pm, Oct-Feb Mon–Fri 8am–6pm, Sat & Sun 8am–5pm; Glasshouses Mar-Sep Mon–Fri 9.30am–4pm, Sat & Sun 9.30am–5pm, Oct-Feb daily 9.30am–4pm

Nordbrücke, District 10 (Wipkingen), Dammstrasse 58, Mon 4pm–1am, Tue–Thu 7.30am–1am, Fri 7.30am–2am, Sat 9am–2am, Sun 9am–12pm

Nordheim Cemetery (Friedhof Nordheim), District 6 (Unterstrass), Nordheimstrasse 28, Mar-Apr & Sep-Oct 7am–7pm, May-Aug 7am–8pm, Nov-Feb 8am–5pm

North America Native Museum (Nordamerika Native Museum) (NONAM), District 8 (Mühlenbach), Seefeldstrasse 317, Tue–Fri 1–5pm, Sat & Sun 10–5pm

Oberer Friesenberg Jewish Cemetery (Israelitischer Friedhof Oberer Friesenberg), District 3 (Friesenberg), Friesenbergstrasse 330, Sun–Thu 8am–5pm, Fri 8am–4pm, closed Sat; men must cover their heads when visiting the cemetery

Ojo de Agua restaurant and bar, District 1 (Lindenhof), Oetenbachgasse 13, Mon–Wed 10am–10pm, Thu–Sat 10am–11pm

Old Botanical Garden (Alter Botanischer Garten), District 1 (City), Park zur Katz, Schanzengraben, Apr-Sep daily 7am–7pm, Oct-Mar 8am–6pm

Orell Füssli, District 1 (Lindenhof), Bahnhofstrasse 70, Mon–Fri 9am–8pm, Sat 9am–6pm

Orell Füssli, District 1 (City), Füsslistrasse 4, Mon–Fri 9am–8pm, Sat 9am–6pm

Outlane, District 9 (Altstetten), Badenerstrasse 571a, last Thu & Fri in the month from 8pm or by appointment, www.outlane.ch

Palaeontology Museum of the University of Zurich (Paläontologisches Museum der Universität Zürich), District 1 (Hochschulen), Karl-Schmid-Strasse 4, Tue–Fri 9am–5pm, Sat & Sun 10am–5pm

Paranoia City, District 4 (Langstrasse), Ankerstrasse 12, Tue–Fri 10am–6.30pm, Sat 10am–5pm

Pastorini Spielzeug, District 1 (Lindenhof), Weinplatz 3, Mon 1.30–6.30pm, Tue–Fri 9.30am–6.30pm, Sat 9.30am–5pm

Piz Buch & Berg, District 4 (Langstrasse), Müllerstrasse 25, Tue–Fri 10am–1pm, 2–6.30pm, Sat 10am–4pm

Platzspitz-Park, District 1 (City), Museumstrasse, daily 6am–9pm

Polybahn, District 1 (Rathaus), Central, Mon–Fri 6.45am–7.15pm, Sat 7.30am–2pm every 2–5 minutes

Predigerkirche, District 1 (Rathaus), Predigerplatz, Mon 1–6pm, Tue–Fri 10am–6pm, Sat & Sun 12am–5pm (Apr–Oct Sat & Sun 6pm)

Pretôt Delikatessen, District 1 (Lindenhof), Kuttelgasse 3, Mon 10am–6pm, Tue–Fri 9am–6.30pm, Sat 9am–4pm

Raclette Stube, District 1 (Rathaus), Zähringerstrasse 16, Mon–Sun 6pm onwards

Rena Kaufmann, District 1 (Lindenhof), Fraumünsterstrasse 9, Mon–Fri 9am–6.30pm, Sat 9am–5pm

Restaurant Blaue Ente, District 8 (Mühlebach), Seefeldstrasse 223, Mon–Fri 11.30am–2pm, 6–12pm, Sat 6–12pm

Restaurant blindekuh, District 8 (Mühlebach), Mühlebachstrasse 148, Mon–Wed 6.30–11pm, Thu 11.30am–2pm, 6.30–11pm, Fri 11.30–2pm, 6–11pm, Sat & Sun 6–11pm

Restaurant Café Zähringer, District 1 (Rathaus), Zähringerplatz 11, Mon 6–12pm, Tue–Sun 9am–12pm

Restaurant Cantinetta Antinori, District 1 (Lindenhof), Augustinergasse 25, Mon–Sat 11.30am–11.30pm, Sun 11.30am–10.30pm

Restaurant Degenried, District 7 (Hottingen), Degenriedstrasse 135, Mon–Sat 9am–11pm, Sun 10am–10pm

Restaurant Eight 25, District 3 (Enge), Lavaterstrasse 33, Sun–Thu 12am–2.30pm, 6–10pm, Fri 12am–2.30pm

Restaurant Giesserei, District 11 (Oerlikon), Birchstrasse 108, Mon–Fri 11.30am–2pm, 5.30–12pm, Sat 6–11pm, Sun 10am–2.30pm

Restaurant Kaiser's Reblaube, District 1 (Lindenhof), Glockengasse 7, Mon–Fri 11.30am–2.30pm, 6–11.30pm

Restaurant Kronenhalle, District 1 (Hochschulen), Rämistrasse 4, daily 12am 12pm

Restaurant LaSalle, District 5 (Escher Wyss), Schiffbau, Schiffbaustrasse 4, Mon & Tue 11am–12pm, Wed & Thu 11am–1pm, Fri 11am–2am, Sat 5pm–2am Sun 5–12pm

Restaurant Le Dézaley, District 1 (Rathaus), Römergasse 7, Mon–Sat 11.30am–2.30pm, 6–12pm

Restaurant Les Halles, District 5 (Escher Wyss), Markthalle les Halles, Pfingstweidstrasse 6, Mon–Wed 11am–12pm, Thu 11am–1am, Fri & Sat 11am–2am

Restaurant Oepfelchammer, District 1 (Rathaus), Rindermarkt 12, Tue–Fri 10am–12pm, Sat 4–12pm

Restaurant Reithalle, District 1 (Lindenhof), Gessnerallee 8, Mon–Wed 11am–11pm, Thu & Fri 11am–12pm, Sat 6pm–12pm, Sun 6–11pm

Restaurant Rosso, District 5 (Escher Wyss), Geroldstrasse 31, Mon–Fri 11.30am–12.30pm, Sat & Sun 5–12.30pm

Restaurant Rüsterei, District 3 (Alt-Wiedikon), Sihlcity, Kalanderplatz 6, Mon–Fri 12am–2pm, 6–12pm, Sat 6–21pm, Sun 10am–2.30pm

Restaurant Schipfe 16, District 1 (Lindenhof), Schipfe 16, Mon–Fri 11.30am–4pm

Restaurant Santa Lucia, District 1 (Hochschulen), Rämistrasse 32, daily 11.30am–11.30pm

Restaurant Trichtenhausermühle, District 7 (Witikon), Trichtenhauserstrasse 60, Tue–Sat11am–2.30pm, 5–11.30pm, Sun 11am–10pm

Restaurant Zeughauskeller, District 1 (Lindenhof), Bahnhofstrasse 28a, daily 11.30am–11pm

Restaurant zum Kropf, District 1 (Lindenhof), In Gassen 16, Mon–Sat 11.30am–11.30pm

Rote Fabrik, District 2 (Wollishofen), Seestrasse 395, Tue–Thu & Sun 11am–12pm, Fri & Sat 11am–1am

Sammlung E. G. Bührle, District 8 (Mühlebach), Zollikerstrasse 172, tours first Sun in the month by appointment only, tel. 0041 (0)44 422 00 86, www.buehrle.ch

Schwarzenbach, District 1 (Rathaus), Münstergasse 19, Mon–Fri 9am–6.30pm, Sat 9am–5pm

Schweizer Heimatwerk, District 1 (Lindenhof), Bahnhofstrasse 2 and Uraniastrasse 1, Mon–Fri 9am–8pm, Sat 9am–6pm

Seebad Enge, District 2 (Enge), Mythenquai 9, mid May–mid Sep daily 9am–8pm

Seebad Utoquai, District 8 (Seefeld), Utoquai, mid May–mid Sep daily 7am–8pm

Seilbahn Rigiblick, District 6 (Oberstrass), Rigiplatz, daily 5.20am–12.40pm every 6 minutes

ShopVille RailCity, District 1 (City), Zürich Hauptbahnhof, Bahnhofplatz, Mon–Fri 9am–9pm, Sat & Sun 9am–8pm; Bahnhofkirche Mon–Fri 7am–7pm, Sat & Sun 10am–4pm

Sihlcity, District 3 (Alt-Wiedikon), Giesshübelstrasse 15, Mon–Sat 9am–8pm; Sihlcity-Kirche daily 9am–8pm

Sihlfeld Cemetery (Friedhof Sihlfeld), District 3 (Sihlfeld), Aemtlerstrasse 151, Mar–Apr & Sep–Oct 7am–7pm, May–Aug 7am–8pm, Nov–Feb 8am–5pm; office inside Gate A Mon–Fri 8.30–11.30am, 1.30–4.30pm

Sonja Rieser, District 1 (Rathaus), Neumarkt 1, Tue–Fri 11am–2pm, 3–6.30pm, Sat 10am–4pm

Sphères, District 5 (Escher Wyss), Hardturmstrasse 66, Mon–Fri 8am–12pm, Sat & Sun 9.30am–7.30pm

Spitzenhaus Degiacomi, District 1 (Lindenhof), Börsenstrasse 14, Tue–Fri 9.30–12.30am, Sat 9.30–12.30am, 1.30–5pm

Sportantiquariat, District 1 (Rathaus), Frankengasse 6, Tue, Thu & Fri 12am–6.30pm, Sat 11am–4pm

Stadtgärtnerei, District 3 (Sihlfeld), Sackzelgasse 25–27, daily 9am–4.30pm

Strauhof Museum, District 1 (Lindenhof), Augustinergasse 9, Tue–Fri 12am–6pm, Sat & Sun 10am–6pm

Strandbad Tiefenbrunnen, District 8 (Seefeld), Bellerivestrasse, mid May–mid Sep daily 9am–8pm

Succulent Collection (Sukkulentensammlung), District 2 (Enge), Mythenquai 88, daily 9am–4.30pm

Thermalbad & Spa Zürich, District 2 (Enge), Brandschenkestrasse 150, daily 9am–10pm

Thomas Mann Archive (Thomas-Mann-Archiv), District 1 (Hochschulen), Schönberggasse 15, Wed & Sat 2–4pm

Travel Bookshop, District 1 (Rathaus), Rindermarkt 20, Mon 12am–6.30pm, Tue–Fri 9am–6.30pm (Thu 8pm), Sat 9am–5pm

Triibhuus, District 9 (Altstetten), Salzweg 50, Mon–Sat 11.30am–12pm, Sun 10am–7pm

Türler Uhren & Juwelen, District 1 (City), Bahnhofstrasse 28/Paradeplatz, Mon–Fri 9.30am–6.30pm, Sat 9.30am–5pm

TurbinenBräu, District 9 (Altstetten), Badenerstrasse 571, dispatch ramp open for sales Mon–Fri 8.30am–6.30pm, Sat 12am–4pm

Urania Observatory (Urania Sternwarte), District 1 (Lindenhof), Uraniastrasse 9, guided tours Thu, Fri & Sat 9pm

Villa Patumbah, District 8 (Mühlebach), Zollikerstrasse 128, Wed, Fri & Sat 2–5pm, Thu & Sun 12am–5pm; the Patumbah-Garden can be accessed from Mühlebach-Platz Apr–Sep 5am–10pm, Sep–Mar 5am–6.30pm

Villa Tobler, District 1 (Rathaus), Winkelwiese 4, garden daily 6am–7.30pm

Volkshaus, District 4 (Langstrasse), Stauffacherstrasse 60, Mon–Thu 8am–12pm, Fri 8am–2am, Sat 9am–2am, Sun 10am–12pm

Wasserkirche, District 1 (Rathaus), Limmatquai 31, Tue 9–12am, Wed–Fri 2–5pm, Sat 12am–5pm

Werdhölzli Wastewater Treatment Plant (Kläranlage Werdhölzli), District 9 (Altstetten), Bändlistrasse 108, tours by appointment only tel. 0041 (0)44 645 77 77

Wings Airline Bar & Lounge, District 1 (Rathaus), Limmat-Quai 54, Mon–Thu 6–12pm, Fri 4pm–2am, Sat 2pm–2am

Xenix-Bar, District 5 (Langstrasse), Kanzleistrasse 52, May–Aug Mon–Wed 4–12.30pm, Thu–Sat 4pm–1.30am, Sun 11.30am–12.30pm, Sep-Apr Mon–Thu 4–12.30pm, Fri 4pm–1.30am, Sat 11.30am–1.30am, Sun 11.30am–12.30pm

Zoo Zürich, District 7 (Fluntern), Zürichbergstrasse 221, Mar–Oct daily 9am–6pm (Masoala Rainforest 10am–5pm), Nov–Feb daily 9am–5pm (Masoala Rainforest 10am–5pm); Penguin Parade Oct–Mar 1.30pm when temperature less that 10 °C

Zoological Museum of the University of Zurich (Zoologisches Museum der Universität Zürich), District 1 (Hochschulen), Karl-Schmid-Strasse 4, Tue–Fri 9am–5pm, Sat & Sun 10am–5pm

Zürcher Brockenhaus, District 5 (Gewerbeschule), Neugasse 11, Mon–Fri 10am–6.30pm, Sat 10am–4pm

Zunfthaus zur Meisen, District 1 (Lindenhof), Münsterhof 20, Thu–Sun 11am–4pm

Zurich Central Library (Zentralbibliothek Zürich), District 1 (Rathaus), Zähringerplatz 6, Mon–Fri 8am–8pm, Sat 9am–5pm

Zurich Central Library Predigerchor (Zentralbibliothek Zürich Predigerchor), Predigerplatz 33, Mon–Fri 1–5pm, Sat 1–4pm

Zurich Toy Museum (Zürcher Spielzeugmuseum), District 1 (Lindenhof), Fortunagasse 15, Mon–Fri 2–5pm, Sat 1–4pm

Zurich Tram Museum (Tram-Museum Zürich), District 7 (Hirslanden), Forchstrasse 260, Wed, Sat & Sun 2–5pm; Museumslinie 21 trams taking visitors to the museum run Apr–Oct every half hour on the last weekend of the month, stopping at Hauptbahnhof, Paradeplatz, Bellevue, and other city-centre stops

Bibliography

GUIDEBOOKS

Zürich: Ein Führer durch die Stadt (Walter Baumann), Verlag Zürich, 2003

Eyewitness Switzerland (Adriana Czupryn, Malgorzata Omilanowska & Ulrich Schwendimann), Dorling Kindersley, 2010

Von Baum zu Baum: Ein Führer zu besonderen Bäumen Zürichs (Walburga Liebst), Haupt Verlag, 2009

Überleben in Zürich – 365 Dinge, die man über diese Stadt wissen sollte (Susann Sitzler), Ch. Links Verlag, 2010

Zürich: Stadtführer für Zürcher und Nichtzürcher (Wilfried Spinner & Gladys Weigner), Pendo Verlag, 1998

Rough Guide Switzerland (Matthew Teller), Rough Guides, 2010

City Spots Zurich (Various), Thomas Cook Publishing, 2009

Wallpaper City Guide Zürich (Various), Phaidon Press, 2008

Tankstellenführer Zürich (Sabrina Volkart), Walkwerk, 2011

Lonely Planet Switzerland (Nicola Williams & Kerry Walker), Lonely Planet Publications, 2009

James Joyce in Zürich (Zurich James Joyce Foundation), Zurich James Joyce Foundation, 2002

HIDDEN ZURICH

Stille Winkel in Zürich (Dagmar & Richard Bhend and Bernd Zocher), Ellert & Richter Verlag, 2008

Die Geheimen Gärten von Zürich: Traumhafte Refugien in der Stadt und am See (Andreas Honegger), Deutsche Verlags-Anstalt, 2011

Magisches Zürich: Wanderungen zu Orten der Kraft (Barbara Hutzl-Ronge), AT Verlag, 2006

Zürich zum Nulltarif: Skurriles, Merkwürdiges, Unbekanntes (Hannes Maurer), NZZ-Verlag, 2011

ILLUSTRATED BOOKS

Zürich City Panoramas 360° (Helga Neubauer, Hartmut Röder & Wolfgang Vorbeck), NZVP Books, 2009

Tausendundeine Stadt Zürich (Toni Luisa Villiger), Orell Fuessli, 2009

Zürich Bewegt: Eine Stadtgeschichte in Bildern (Willi Wottreng), Elster Verlag, 2011

ARCHITECTURE AND MONUMENTS

Berühmte und vergessene Tote auf Zürichs Friedhöfen (Daniel Foppa), Limmat Verlag, 2000

Die Kunst im öffentlichen Raum der Stadt Zürich: 1300 Werke – Eine Bestandesaufnahme (Bernadette Fülscher), Chronos, 2011

Achtung: Archäologie! – Fenster in Zürichs Vergangenheit (Hochbauamt der Stadt Zürich, Baugeschichtliches Archiv/Büro für Archäologie Gestaltung), Atelier für wissenschaftliche Zeichnungen, undated

Zürich wird gebaut: Ein Führer zur zeitgenössischen Architektur 1990–2010 (Roderick Hönig), Scheidegger & Spiess, 2010

Der Friedhof Sihlfeld in Zürich-Wiedikon (Regula Michel), Gesellschaft für Schweizerische Kunstgeschichte GSK, 2002

Zürich: Ein Begleiter zu neuer Landschaftsarchitektur (Claudia Moll), Callwey, 2006

Die Giacometti-Halle im Amtshaus I in Zürich (Dieter Nievergelt & Pietro Maggi), Gesellschaft für Schweizerische Kunstgeschichte, 2000

Architektur neues Zürich (Various), Braun Publishing, 2007

HISTORY

Das neue Bild des Alten Zürich (Jürg Hanser, Armin Mathis, Ulrich Ruoff & Jürg E. Schneider), Juris Druck + Verlag AG, 1983

Literaturszene Zürich – Menschen, Geschichten und Bilder 1914 bis 1945 (Gustav Huonker), Unionsverlag, 2002

Zürich 1933–1945 (Stefan Ineichen), Limmat Verlag, 2009

Literarisches Zürich: 150 Autoren – Wohnorte, Wirken und Werke (Arlette Kosch), Verlag Jena, 2002

Zürich von der Urzeit zum Mittelalter (Ernst Meyer, Conrad Peyer & Emil Vogt), Berichthaus Verlag, 1971

Dada Zürich: Texte, Manifeste, Dokumente (Karl Riha & Waltraut Wende-Hohenberger), Reclam, 1992

WEBSITES

www.stadt-zuerich.ch
(Home page of the City of Zurich)

www.zuerich.com
(Official website of Zurich tourism)

www.alt-zueri.ch/turicum/
(Zurich history old and new)

www.stattreisen.ch
(Walks through the real Zurich)

www.frauenstadtrundgangzuerich. ch
(Idiosyncratic city walks off the beaten track)

www.ghostwalk.ch
(Ghost walk of Zurich)

www.spottedbylocals.com/zurich
(Useful and entertaining city Blog)

www.zuercher-maerkte.ch
(All Zurich's different types of markets)

www.zvv.ch
(Zurich Public Transport)

www.myswitzerland.com
(Swiss Tourist Board)

Carpet detail at the Beyer Clock and Watch Museum (Uhrenmuseum Beyer) (see no. 7)

Acknowledgements

First and foremost I would like to thank my Viennese publisher, Christian Brandstätter Verlag, for realising the first edition of this book, especially Elisabeth Stein (commissioning editor), Else Rieger (editor), Ekke Wolf (design), Walter Goidinger (German translation), and Helmut Maurer (maps).

For kind permission to take photographs, as well as for arranging access and the provision of information, the following people are most gratefully acknowledged:

Dominik Bachmann (Stiftung Patumbah); Fady Barcha; Karsten Blum (Zoo Zürich); Chris Bohr (Edi's Weinstube); Andreas Bommer & Riccarda Rohner (Mühlerama); Susana Braillard & Karin Strübin (ERZ Entsorgung + Recycling Zürich); Edith Burkhard (Zürcher Spielzeugmuseum); Café Odeon; Manuela Consenti (Chäs Vreneli AG); Alessia Contin (Museum für Gestaltung); Krishna Premarupa das (Hare Krishna-Tempel Zürich); Prof. Dr. Mareile Flitsch, Dr. Peter Gerber, Martina Wernsdörfer, & Kathrin Leuenberger (Völkerkundemuseum der Universität Zürich); Mariella Frei & Linda Isenschmid (Schweizerisches Nationalmuseum/Landesmuseum Zürich); Esther Fuchs & Mara Miljkovic (Baugeschichtliches Archiv); Nicky Gardner (www.hiddeneurope.co.uk); Michael Geiges & Corina Roffler (Moulagenmuseum); Gregory Germond (Sportantiquariat); Corina Gloor & Elisabeth Ott (Nordamerika Native Museum/NONAM); Cordelia Graber (Thieme:Klima); Samuel Haettenschweiler (Gemeinschaftszentrum Wollishofen); Holly Hayes (www.sacred-destinations.com); Paul Herman & Angela Stricker (Widder Hotel/Metzgermuseum); Gabi Hollender (Thomas-Mann-Archiv der ETH Zürich); Sven Hollmann & Viki Kiss; Beat Hübscher (BlueWaterCom GmbH); Jürg Peter Hug (Zivilschutz-Museum); Kurt Hunziker & Robert Knöpfel (Dampferzeitung); Natalia Huser (Johann Jacobs Museum); James Joyce Foundation; Jack Joyce (ITMB Publishing Ltd.); Zsuzsanna & Tivadar Kiss; Christoph Laszlo, Lisa Laurenti (Gesellschaft für Schweizerische Kunstgeschichte GSK); Monika Leonhardt (Beyer Uhrenmuseum); Sylvie Leu (Friedhof Sihlfeld); James Linkogle & Kristin Teuchtmann; Andreas Mäder & Christine Michel (Amt für Städtebau – Unterwasserarchäologie Zürich); Doris Mechner (Israelitische Cultusgemeinde Zürich); Esther Merki (Brocki-Land); Ruth Nagel (Stiftung Sammlung E.G. Bührle); Helena Nejedlá; Adrian Notz (Cabaret Voltaire); Basha O'Reilly; Franco Gargiulo, Corinne Dittes & Warner Pearson (Grossmünster); Nieves Pérez; Marek Pryjomko; Restaurant Ziegel au Lac (Rote Fabrik); Marie-Alix Roesle (MoneyMuseum); Christina Rüeger (Städtische Sukkulentensammlung); V. Ryser (Friedhof Nordheim); Adrian Schafner (Restaurant blindekuh); Margriet Schnaibel (Restaurant Blaue Ente); Rita H. Schnellmann (Altstadt-Antiquariat); Simon Schwendimann (Uto-Kino); Silvio Severino; Maryam Soliman (Rechtswissenschaftliches Institut Bibliothek Universität Zürich); Sandra Stamm (www.sandrastamm.ch); Jürg Stauffer (Zoologisches Museum der Universität Zürich); Verena Steinmann (Handbuchbinderei); Alfred Strotz (Privatfriedhof Hohe Promenade); Diego Tarantino (Bovet AG); Ulrike Toth; Tram-Museum Zürich; Gisela Treichler (Travel Book Shop); Peter Trösch; Franz Türler (Türler Uhren & Juwelen); Ivo Vasella (Outlane); Adrien Weber (TurbinenBräu AG); Pascal Wehrle (Buchhandlung Medieval Art & Vie); Olivia Weiss; Urs Wenzel (Aktion pro Raddampfer); Stephan Wyss.

For accommodation, the staff at Apartments Marc Aurel and Olympia Hotel Zürich.

For assistance in selecting the photographs, Bob Barber, Andreas Eberhart, Simon Laffoley, and Ekke Wolf, and for invaluable website support, Richard Tinkler.

Particular thanks go to Roswitha Reisinger for her assistance with translations, Dan Dent for his fascinating ghost tour of Zurich (www.ghostwalk.ch), Jan Leiser for welcoming me into his studio (www.janleiser.ch), Priska Held Schweri (Atelier Hermann Haller) for providing invaluable information regarding Zurich's less well known sculptures, and to Jürgen Rüsch and Heinz Wirth for kindly buying me a beer.

Thanks also to my great cousin James Dickinson for support, newspaper cuttings and bringing my work to a wider audience.

Finally, special thanks to my late father Trevor for inspiring me to track down unusual locations in the first place.

2nd Revised Edition published by The Urban Explorer, 2015
A division of Duncan J. D. Smith
contact@duncanjdsmith.com
www.onlyinguides.com
www.duncanjdsmith.com

First published by Christian Brandstätter Verlag, 2012

Graphic design: Stefan Fuhrer
Typesetting and picture editing: Ekke Wolf
Revision typesetting and picture editing: Franz Hanns
Maps: APA, Vienna
Printed and bound by GraphyCems, Spain

ISBN 978-3-9503662-8-0

Door knocker in the old village of Altstetten
(see no. 76)